Paying Less Tax
2005/2006 For Dummies®

Cheat Sheet

Income Tax

Personal Allowances	2005–2006	
Under 65	£4,895	
65 to 74	£7,090	£6,830
75 upwards	£7,220	£6,950
Age allowance limits *		
	£19,500	£18,900

* The higher personal allowance paid to those aged 65 and over is reduced for incomes at this level by £1 for every £2 of income until the extra age allowance rates come down to the personal allowance for under 65s.

Income bands of taxable income for tax calculations

Band	2005–2006	2004–2005
10%	£0 – £2,090	£0 – £2,020
22% (20% savings rate)	£2,091 – £32,400	£2,021 – £31,400
40%	£32,401 or more	£31,401 or more

How tax is layered

In general terms, you take your total income in the following order for tax computations:

- ✓ Personal allowance
- ✓ Income from employment or self-employment
- ✓ Savings income
- ✓ Dividends
- ✓ Capital gains

National Insurance

Employees 2005–2006

Weekly earnings

Up to £94	0%
£94.01 to £630	11%**
£630.01 or more	1% on earnings over this level

Self employed 2005–2006

Pay 8% of profits between £4,895 and £32,760 with 1% on sums above the upper limit.

**9.4% if employee is contracted out of the state second pension.

For Dummies: Bestselling Book Series for Beginners

Paying Less Tax
2005/2006 For Dummies®

Inheritance Tax

	2005–2006	2004–2005
Nil rate band	£0 – £275,000	£0 – £263,000
40% rate band	£275,001 or more	£263,001 or more

Capital Gains Tax

Annual exemption	2005–2006	2004–2005
	£8,500	£8,200

Stamp Duty

Property purchase price	Rate
Up to £120,000	0%
£120,001 to £250,000	1%
£250,001 to £500,000	3%
£500,001 plus	4%

You pay the rate applicable to the purchase price on the whole amount.

Value Added Tax

Rates

0%	newspapers, books, children's clothes, most food items
5%	domestic gas and electricity/energy-saving materials
17.5%	standard rate

Traders must register if their annual sales exceed £60,000 for the previous 12 months or expect to pass this level within the next 30 days.

Traders whose sales fall below £58,000 may (but are not obliged to) deregister.

Paying Less Tax 2005/2006
FOR
DUMMIES®

by Tony Levene

JOHN WILEY & SONS, LTD

Paying Less Tax 2005/2006 For Dummies®
Published by
John Wiley & Sons, Ltd
The Atrium
Southern Gate
Chichester
West Sussex
PO19 8SQ
England

E-mail (for orders and customer service enquiries): cs-books@wiley.co.uk

Visit our Home Page on www.wileyeurope.com

Copyright © 2005 John Wiley & Sons, Ltd, Chichester, West Sussex, England

Published by John Wiley & Sons, Ltd, Chichester, West Sussex

Wiley also publishes its books in a variety of electronic formats. Some content that appears in print may not be available in electronic books.

British Library Cataloguing in Publication Data: A catalogue record for this book is available from the British Library.

ISBN-10: 0-7645-7053-6 (PB)

ISBN-13: 978-0-7645-7053-7 (PB)

Printed and bound in Great Britain by TJ International, Padstow, Cornwall

10 9 8 7 6 5 4 3 2

WILEY

About the Author

Tony Levene is a member of *The Guardian* Jobs & Money team, writing on issues including investment and consumer rights as well as on taxation. He has been a financial journalist for nearly thirty years after a brief foray into teaching French to school children. Over his journalistic career, Tony has worked for newspapers including *The Sunday Times*, *Sunday Express*, *The Sun*, *Daily Star*, *Sunday Mirror*, and *Daily Express*. He has written seven previous books on money matters including *Investing For Dummies*. Tony lives in London with his wife Claudia, 'virtually grown up' children Zoe and Oliver, and cats Plato, Pandora, and Pascal.

Dedication

This book is dedicated to Claudia, who has shouldered many of the household tasks I should have done during the writing of this book – her unfailing good humour was 101 per cent necessary; to Zoe for her invaluable help in suggesting ideas; and to Oliver for making sure I kept to my deadlines. I'd also like to thank my brother Stuart for keeping my computer working and for letting me use the peace and quiet of his home, where no one knew the phone number, for writing some of the chapters.

Author's Acknowledgements

I would like to thank everyone at Wiley for their help and patience. In particular, Jason Dunne, who had the idea for this book and faith in me to ask me to write it; to Alison Yates, who guided me during the early stages; and to Daniel Mersey, my main editor, who has unfailingly responded to my blacker moments with light. And an especial thank you to Kathleen, whose behind the scenes labouring turned my manuscript from a book about taxation into *Paying Less Tax For Dummies*. I would also like to thank my colleagues at *The Guardian* for their patience and forebearance every time I mentioned 'the tax book'.

Most of all, however, I would like to thank all those who have helped me over the years in understanding the complications and convolutions of our tax system. They have to remain anonymous but besides accountants, they also include those in the Inland Revenue that I have encountered both as a journalist and as a tax-payer.

Publisher's Acknowledgements

We're proud of this book; please send us your comments through our Dummies online registration form located at www.dummies.com/register/.

Some of the people who helped bring this book to market include the following:

Acquisitions, Editorial, and Media Development

Project Editor: Daniel Mersey

Commissioning Editor: Alison Yates

Copy Editor: Martin Key

Proofreader: Kate O'Leary

Technical Editor: Andy Lymer

Executive Editor: Jason Dunne

Executive Project Editor: Amie Jackowski Tibble

Cover Photo: © EJ Images / Alamy

Cartoons: Ed McLachlan

Composition Services

Project Coordinator: Maridee Ennis

Layout and Graphics: Denny Hager, Heather Ryan, Julie Trippetti

Proofreaders: Susan Moritz, Brian Walls

Indexer: Steve Rath

Publishing and Editorial for Consumer Dummies

> **Diane Graves Steele,** Vice President and Publisher, Consumer Dummies
>
> **Joyce Pepple,** Acquisitions Director, Consumer Dummies
>
> **Kristin A. Cocks,** Product Development Director, Consumer Dummies
>
> **Michael Spring,** Vice President and Publisher, Travel
>
> **Kelly Regan,** Editorial Director, Travel

Publishing for Technology Dummies

> **Andy Cummings,** Vice President and Publisher, Dummies Technology/General User

Composition Services

> **Gerry Fahey,** Vice President of Production Services
>
> **Debbie Stailey,** Director of Composition Services

Contents at a Glance

Table of Contents

Introduction

*H*ow many times do you see the word *tax* in a day? Well,
I admit to not knowing how often it appears, but I'd bet
adding up all the mentions of this three-letter word in newspapers, on television, and on radio (and ignoring Internet hits),
must come to hundreds or more every day.

There's another three-letter word ending in 'x' that's also
widely used in the media. But whereas you can choose to
ignore sex, you have no option when it comes to tax. Paying
tax when it is due is compulsory. Failing to do so brings a
range of penalties from a simple fine to a long spell in prison.

Paying Less Tax For Dummies is the only book in the Dummies
series that focuses on a legal obligation. So it's different.
There are no ifs or buts. Instead, there are plenty of must-dos.

It is very difficult to avoid dealing with the Inland Revenue.
When your grandparents or great-grandparents were young,
only a minority paid tax. Most people earned their weekly
cash wage packet and that was that.

Now practically no one escapes the tax inspector's net. You
start paying income tax and national insurance at just over half
the national minimum wage when you work full-time. And if you
are lower paid, or out of work, many state benefits are now part
of the tax collector's job as well. You can be a customer of the
tax system as an employee, employer, self-employed worker,
a student with outstanding student loans, a parent, a parent
wanting help with childcare, and as a consumer – because VAT
is now part of the Inland Revenue remit. About the only tax
not included is Council Tax. One way or another, around one-
third of the average pay packet ends up in taxation with the
Chancellor of the Exchequer and the Treasury.

I've been writing about the tax system and how it impacts on
everyone from the richest to the least well off for over 20
years. During that time, much has changed in the tax world.
One factor remains unaltered: We all need what the taxes pay
for such as hospitals, schools, roads, and the police. Yet, we

would all rather have more money to spend on our families and ourselves.

I hope reading this book helps you square this circle by using the many legitimate ways available to reduce your tax bill while paying what you owe on time.

About This Book

Paying Less Tax For Dummies is designed to help you pay the right amount for your situation. It contains tax-saving tips and then more tax-saving tips. These are the carrots.

But paying less tax is not just about considering ways to reduce your tax bill. This book has two other strands to save you money. In this book, I show you how the tax system works. I tell you where you can find more information at no cost. I give you hints and tips on how to deal with the Inland Revenue. All this saves you hiring expensive professionals who, in any case, take no responsibility for the tax form you sign.

And *Paying Less Tax For Dummies* can help you avoid the sticks – the penalties, fines, and interest payments that the Inland Revenue uses to enforce the rules. So more carrots, and, it is to be hoped, no sticks.

You can read this book in several ways. Obviously, one way is to start at the front cover and end up with the index pages. Reading it like a novel will give you a good idea of the wide range of tax-saving possibilities. Or you can pick a topic that interests you and go there straight away.

But my preferred way is to first read Part I on tax basics, and then move on to the sections that interest you in your current lifestyle. Perhaps, after Part I, you decide to move straight on to Part IV because savings and investments are really important to you. Then in Part IV, you might want to skip Chapter 16 on life insurance as you've decided that, as a single person, you have no dependants and so you don't need any.

Irrespective of how you approach reading this book, note that it is designed to dip in as a reference. So there will be some repetition. Doesn't matter. Some things cannot be repeated often enough. And as long as you end up paying less tax, why worry?

Conventions Used in This Book

The taxation world revolves around jargon. Initials, numbers, and combinations of initials and numbers are rife. I've tried to avoid this as much as I can. But you can't dodge tax language completely, and it does no harm to learn a few of the most common terms. Whenever I use tax-insider language, the first mention in a chapter is *italicised* and I define the basics in an easy to understand fashion.

You'll notice text in grey boxes throughout the book. The information in these sidebars is deemed interesting but not essential. So, you can choose to read a sidebar if the topic appeals to you, but if you skip it, you won't miss out on anything you need to know.

Foolish Assumptions

While writing this book I made some assumptions about you:

- ✔ You are not a tax professional. If you are, you have plenty of manuals to choose from you, some taking up a full bookshelf.

- ✔ You don't need hand-holding through every dot and comma of the annual income tax return. I don't go through the self assessment form step-by-step. Instead I offer tips you can put to use beforehand to make filling in the form easier.

- ✔ You don't want tax to dominate your life. You want to know just enough to make sure that you are paying the right amount and claiming what is due to you.

- ✔ You want to know the disadvantages as well as the plus-points where you have an option. This applies particularly to investment choices, and to lifestyle preferences such as being married or not, or whether to give assets away to your children and grandchildren.

How This Book is Organised

This book has six major parts, or themes. Each part is divided into chapters relating to the theme, and each chapter is subdivided into individual sections relating to the chapter's topic. Additionally, to help you pinpoint a specific area of interest, there's a Table of Contents at the start of this book and a detailed Index at the end.

Part 1: Tax Basics

This part is essential for understanding the tax system in general. I take you through the Inland Revenue's inner workings; give you a general understanding of how taxes impact on your life; scrutinise the process; and, most importantly for a subject which relies on paperwork (and which can penalise you if you don't have it), show how to get organised and keep records.

Part 11: Tax, You, and Your Family

In this part, I look at how tax affects each household. I start with some problematic personal issues including marriage and divorce. I then continue with how tax can work both for the very young and for those old enough to have retired. And I include what the tax inspector will do to what you leave to your family and others after your death.

Part 111: You Work Therefore You're Taxed

This part concentrates on work. It looks at what your boss can legitimately deduct from your salary packet. And it tells you how to check if the amount is correct.

But it's not all one way. There's a variety of perks you can have. This part will guide you through which are taxable and which are tax-free. And this part will also tell you what happens to you tax-wise if you decide to become your own boss either through self-employment or setting up your own limited company.

Part IV: Save on Your Savings and Investments

In this part, I show you the wide variety of savings that can be tax-free; and how to cut tax costs if you are prepared to take risks, or prepared to take none. Then, I look at what is probably your biggest investment – your home. And from there, it's a short step to the increasingly popular buy-to-let market.

This part also tells you about the tax nightmare life insurance can be; and how you can retire more profitably by using all the tax help on pensions that the Inland Revenue offers.

Part V: Self Assessment and Getting Help

If this book were a piece of music, this part would be the crescendo. These chapters deal with the essentials of form filling which everyone has to at least think about once a year even if they don't have to file a return. It also looks at whether you should pay for additional help and what happens if you are unlucky enough to have to undergo a tax investigation into your affairs.

Part VI: The Part of Tens

This part is an essential ingredient in any *For Dummies* book. Each of the two chapters contains ten succinct, must-know points. The first is a vital résumé of tax savings including how to help a good cause with tax relief on any charitable donation you make; the second Part of Tens is a rapid revision course on how to deal with the Inland Revenue.

Icons Used in This Book

The little graphics in the margins point out bits of text to pay special attention to for one reason or another.

This icon points out instances where I put names and amounts to explanatory text. These examples can give you a better understanding of how to put theory into practice, but if you have a grasp of the topic, you don't need to read them.

Keeping in mind the tips that this icon highlights can make your tax life easier.

Tax ins-and-outs are highlighted with this icon. You can gain from reading the information, but if you skip it, you won't miss out on anything crucial.

The advice marked by this bull's eye is right on target for every tax situation. If you read nothing but these tips, you'll be well on your way to paying less tax.

This icon marks things you absolutely shouldn't do if you want to stay on the good side of the Inland Revenue – or in a good tax position generally.

Where to Go from Here

This book is set up so you read what concerns you in self-contained sections. But of course, you can read in any way you wish. It's your call.

Wherever you go from here, whenever you find a piece of advice or a warning that applies to you, copy it and then fix it to the fridge with a magnet or pin it up on your notice board.

And as you read through this book, don't forget to make pencil notes on your tax form when necessary. Pencils sound very low-tech. But you'd be surprised how often tax professionals really do use them. You can always rub your markings out and start again before you present a definitive, signed version!

Part I
Tax Basics

"Ah – Mr Pinocchio, come in."

In this part . . .

This is where you start from scratch. If that's what you need, then this is where you'll find it.

Here I tell you how the tax system really works; what you must do to keep on the right side of the Inland Revenue; and how to make your life easier (as well as avoiding hassles) by keeping records properly. I also give you some background facts that may not be essential but which may help you understand better where the tax inspector's coming from. There's a lot of info here. Consider this part the foundation of paying less tax, and a solid foundation on which to build later on.

Chapter 1

Understanding the Process and Your Role in It

The truth about taxes is that they pay for the services the government provides such as education, the National Health Service, and the police. Lower taxes mean either the government provides fewer services so you get less, or it has to borrow money in order to provide the same services. If it borrows, interest rates go up so your mortgage, credit card, and any other loans cost you more. Simple, isn't it!

The UK has one of the world's most complex tax systems. But that bold statement only holds true for some people some of the time. Provided you earn around the average amount and don't get income from a second home, investments overseas, a spare job, an at-home business – or any of a number of other sources – and aren't concerned with what happens to your money and assets after you die, you need never come into direct contact with the Inland Revenue. Your employer, banks, or investment companies will often pay tax liabilities on your behalf.

However, if you're better-off than average, worse-off than average, have much in the way of savings, have children, are retired, are saving up for a pension, run a business, make profits buying and selling things, have spare-time work, or hope to leave reasonable amounts to your family after you die, then you have to interact with the Inland Revenue.

Even if you don't currently need to have direct dealings with the Inland Revenue, the UK's all-powerful tax organisation, you'll need to understand the tax system sooner or later. If you buy one investment, or have a child, or get a workplace perk such as free or subsidised private medical insurance cover, you have a reason to interact with the Inland Revenue.

And you may have to work out how various taxes interact with each other. This chapter gives an overview of how the tax system works.

Filing Facts

Every January, the personal money pages of newspapers are full of advice on getting your self assessment tax return in on time. It's wise advice even if, as I know personally only too well, it's because a lot of the people who write these pages have failed to give any serious thought to their own tax returns and are feeling panicky and guilty and are fearful of a fine for late filing (and wondering where they will find the money for such a fine).

Only one in three tax-payers has to fill in a self assessment form. That's around nine million people. But millions more can save tax or get a refund if only they bothered. There are scores of perfectly legal tax-saving loopholes that anyone can easily access without paying big accountancy fees. The Inland Revenue will tell you about them if you ask. But in most cases it will not volunteer the information or send you letters begging you to claim a refund.

The Inland Revenue only wants what it is correctly owed. It gets on well with 99 per cent of tax-payers! It's up to you to save tax. This book shows how you can get the best out of the system and pay the least, legally, into it.

Distinguishing between avoidance and evasion

Every year, lawyers and accountants argue out thousands of tax cases for their usually well-off clients. Whatever the decisions in these cases, one tax law judgement is never far from the thoughts of the legal teams representing the Inland Revenue and the tax-payer. And that's an old case from nearly 70 years ago known as *Inland Revenue Commissioners vs. Duke of Westminster.*

The judge in this 1936 vintage tax law case concluded: 'Every man (women rarely paid taxes in those days) is entitled if he can, to order his affairs so the tax attaching under the appropriate act is less than it otherwise would be.'

Translating out of legalese, this means you can take advantage of every tax-break going. You do not have to pay as much as the government would like if you don't have to, whether you're as rich as the Duke of Westminster was or just an average person.

Following the rules laid down in this judgement is called *avoiding tax*. Avoidance is totally legal. What's illegal, and what can cause you to end up in one of Her Majesty's less choice establishments as an enforced guest of the tax-payer, is *evading tax*. Evasion is strictly illegal.

The differences are:

- ✔ **Avoidance is legal:** Arranging your savings in such a way that you do not draw interest or dividends until some future date when your tax rate falls is legal. So too is claiming the cost of a computer for use in your business if you run your own company.

- ✔ **Evasion is illegal:** Putting your money into an offshore tax haven and then denying you've stashed this cash or claiming the cost of a computer that you use only to play games or watch DVDs is certainly not legal.

You can't invent things to take advantage of legal tax-avoidance methods.

Putting the brakes on avoidance schemes

Accountants made fortunes out of inventing legal but very complex tax-avoidance schemes that they then sold to rich clients. By the mid-1970s, this had got out of hand – or so the Inland Revenue reckoned.

So back to the courts, and, in a 1981 judgement called *Ramsey vs. Inland Revenue Commissioners*, the law said the Inland Revenue can clamp down on artificial schemes designed to save tax. And it also held that tax dodges already in place, or already used, can be ruled offside. It meant the Inland Revenue can look at what was really behind the tax-avoidance schemes and not just at the legal issues on the surface.

Two decades and more on, the Inland Revenue is still using this principle to look at the reality of tax returns. The basic test is would someone carry out a particular practice if there were no tax considerations. If the answer is yes, then everything is fine. But if the scheme exists only to try to save on tax, then tax inspectors can challenge it (and they usually win).

Moving to One-Stop Tax and Benefits Shopping

All taxes including national insurance, Stamp Duty, and Value Added Tax are administered by one of the very many departments of the Inland Revenue. Since 1997, Inland Revenue has taken over the running of most benefits such as child tax credit (but not all at once).

This bringing together of all the taxes and benefits under one roof is still in its early days. There have been plenty of teething troubles. But the effect will be to abolish some of the more ridiculous parts of the system where one government department was taking money from individuals that they had been given by another part of the government. Sometimes, this was even more than they had been given in the first place so for every extra £1 they received, they paid more than £1 back to the government.

It should also make form filling less onerous as you should be able to glide effortlessly from one tax to a benefit and back to a tax as your personal or family situation changes.

This isn't a New-Age tax guide. But if it was, it would use the word 'holistic' to describe the new Inland Revenue approach to taxes and benefits. It's only an approach, though. There's a lot of time and lot of work that will be needed before the UK has anything approaching a rational tax system with fully joined-up thinking.

Laying Out the Basics of the Tax System

I bet you thought tax was tax! But there's a huge variety of ways the state takes what it needs from the tax-payers who provide the wealth that pays for all those hospitals, schools, and roads. So here's a list of the taxes that can involve you as an individual:

- **Income tax** is levied on what you earn at work or the profit you make if you are self-employed. You also have to pay it on the returns you make on savings. Surprise: State benefits such as the basic retirement pension are counted. Income tax levels are currently at 0 per cent, 10 per cent, 20 per cent, 22 per cent, 32.5 per cent, and 40 per cent.

- **National insurance** is a tax on those who work and the people they work for. Both employee and employer have to pay. There are special rules for the self-employed. Surprise: You can pay national insurance even if you don't earn enough to pay income tax. The rates are very complicated but most people pay 11 per cent across most of their earnings from work. (Chapter 8 explains national insurance in more detail.)

- **Capital Gains Tax** is payable on the profit you make when you sell certain assets such as shares and proper- ties. Surprise: There's no tax to pay if you sell something with an expected useful life of 50 or fewer years. So you'd have to pay on selling an Old Master but not on a piece of Britart that probably won't last so long (try thinking dead sheep pickled in formaldehyde). You could lose up to 40 per cent of your profits to Capital Gains Tax (which is addressed in more detail in Chapter 14).

✔ **Inheritance Tax** is paid on what you leave behind when you die. Surprise: One great way of reducing the tax is to spend, spend, spend, while you are living. There's just one rate – 40 per cent – but Chapter 7 points out ways to reduce or avoid paying any.

✔ **Corporation tax** is a tax on company profits. Surprise: There is a zero per cent rate. (See Chapter 12 for more on this.)

✔ **Value Added Tax (VAT)** is added by most businesses every time goods change hands or they go through another process. The end result is a sales tax on many items and services you buy. Surprise: Millions of pounds were spent on a legal case to decide whether a Jaffa Cake is a cake or a biscuit. Cakes are tax-free, biscuits are taxed. The current VAT rate is 17.5 per cent and Chapter 12 has more on VAT.

✔ **Council Tax** is paid on your residence whether you own it, are buying it, or are renting it. Surprise: Two can't live as cheaply as one as there are rebates if a property has only one adult occupant rather than two or more. What you pay depends on where you live and the value of your property. (Chapter 15 explains more.)

✔ **Stamp Duty** is paid on most property transactions and on most stock market deals. Stamp duty ranges from one per cent to five per cent depending on the value of the property. Surprise: The tax does not go up evenly. Sell a house for £499,999 and you pay £14,999.97. But if you get £500,001 for the same property, the tax goes up to £20,000.03. Turn to Chapter 15 for more information on Stamp Duty.

Considering Tax and Your Family

Single people without dependants or partners have an easier tax life than most. The rest of the population has to juggle roles as parents, grandparents, or children. Many may have to deal with their own parents and their own children at the same time.

Family tax-saving pointers to consider include:

✔ **Deciding whether to marry:** Thanks to independent taxation, women's tax lives are no longer subordinate to their husband's tax concerns. Crazy as it sounds, there are still lots of occasions when married people can do better out of the tax system. Try Chapter 4 for information on whether to tie the financial knot or not.

✔ **Passing assets between spouses:** Swapping savings accounts between the two of you can save a lot in tax. But do you trust each other that much? And what happens if you divorce? Chapter 4 is better than a visit to a matrimonial guidance agency.

✔ **Working out the best way for children to pay less tax on savings accounts:** It should be easy. But it all depends on where the money came from. Turn to Chapter 5 for childhood tax issues.

✔ **Looking at employing partners and children in family businesses:** This is fine as long as the work's real and the rates you pay are sensible. Chapters 11 and 12 have more details.

✔ **Arranging the best way to take advantage of Capital Gains Tax exemptions:** Two can sell more cheaply than one if you follow some simple rules. Take a look at Chapter 14.

✔ **Taking advice on how to deal with the tax benefits of pension payments:** Simplification is on the way. But for the moment, you can be paying into five different pension tax types. See Chapter 17 for much more.

✔ **Knowing how to deal with your pension when you take it:** There's a basic choice for many which can mean paying more or less tax for the same income. It all comes down to how you invest retirement cash, as Chapter 6 shows.

✔ **Calculating tax bills in retirement:** Just because you stop work doesn't mean your relationship with the Inland Revenue changes. It can get more complicated. Chapter 6 can help simplify matters.

✔ **Realising that the old saying about the inevitability of taxes and death is correct:** Items such as your home and certain savings and investments that escape tax while you are alive will be caught for possibly even more tax after you die. Turn to Chapter 7 for tips.

Looking at How You Pay

Most people pay income tax through the Pay As You Earn (PAYE) scheme through their employer. This system makes tax and national insurance deductions as painless as possible. The money goes straight out of your pay packet to the Inland Revenue without you ever seeing or touching it.

If life was that simple, this book would be half the size. Millions of people on PAYE have to fill in self assessment forms as well. They might have perks from work such as company cars or healthcare schemes, or they might have bigger than average savings or a spare-time job or even a profitable hobby. They face an annual January and July tax bill as well.

If you work for yourself, you have to fill in an annual self assessment tax form. You then pay the income tax and national insurance due in two annual installments. So you have to be sure to keep some cash around in a bank account to meet these bills.

Failing to pay your tax on time brings automatic penalties. And, you're fined the same £100 automatic penalty if you are a day late filing a return on which you owe £1,000, or a week late owing £1 million!

Saving Smartly

You can put £1,000 in a bank paying five per cent interest and pay no tax on the interest. Or you can save the same amount at the same rate with 40 per cent of the interest going in tax. It's your choice as to the type of saving scheme you opt for.

Think you earn too little for the tax authorities to be bothered with you? Then think again. The all-encompassing Inland Revenue wants to give you back tax on savings interest taken automatically by the bank or building society. And they want to help you claim tax credits. Tax inspectors can really be quite generous! But you have to know what to ask for to get the best out of the system. There's plenty in Chapter 13 on how to save more of your savings.

Investing for tax savings

Almost every different type of investment has its own tax rules. Non-tax-payers can reclaim some tax deductions but not others. High-earning top-rate tax-payers can do well with the taxation of some investments but others are a waste of space. So it's no wonder there's a whole section of *Paying Less Tax For Dummies* devoted to savings and investments (Part IV).

Some investments that save tax are really very risky. Always ask yourself if you would want to buy into these if there was no tax savings. Unless you are sure, avoid them. Tax deals on investments are not government guarantees of success!

Treating your home as your tax castle

Your home, if you are buying or have bought it, is probably your biggest single financial asset. There are ways of using your own home to save tax and to give you a tax-free income. But there are also ways to invest in property that can save you tax. Chapter 15 gives you more details.

Chapter 2

Looking at the Players and the Process

*G*etting to grips with the Inland Revenue's powers and how it works will not reduce your tax bill. Sorry. And this chapter does not have any tips you can put into immediate action. Sorry, again.

But this chapter can help keep more money in your pocket. How? By letting you know about the tax collection process, which can help you make fewer mistakes. Errors can be costly, especially if you lose out on rebates, benefits, or credits, and certain errors can be potentially ruinous if you are hit by penalties, fines, and bankruptcy as a result of mismanaging your tax affairs.

And discovering more about what makes the Inland Revenue tick gives you more clout in dealing with your accountant, if you use one. The accountant will realise that you're not a novice or a complete clot and treat you better. The accountant may even realise you might query your accountancy bill if it's outrageous.

This chapter gives you the information you need to understand the tax process and your place in it.

Understanding the Inland Revenue's Role

When income tax was first introduced in the UK in 1799, it was as a temporary measure to pay for one of Britain's seemingly eternal wars against France. In 1802, income tax was repealed but it didn't disappear for long. In 1803, income tax was re-introduced after a sadly brief period of abolition. In those days, it was thought wrong for any government department or civil servant to have complete details of anyone's financial affairs. All that has changed. These days the Inland Revenue is a cradle-to-after-the-grave service.

If you think the Inland Revenue is just about collecting income tax from the nation's better-off folk, you're a bit behind the times. The Inland Revenue absorbed the management of the grandly named Her Majesty's Customs and Excise, and now goes well beyond traditional taxes, embracing just about every financial dealing you may have with the government or any government agency. The Inland Revenue collects every tax around and is increasingly responsible for handing out benefits.

Virtually all your dealings with the Inland Revenue revolve around your national insurance number. You get this number when you turn 16 whether or not you are in work or pay any tax. This number never changes throughout your life no matter how often you change your address or your name. It is your unique identifier as a UK citizen and only a few very elderly people who did not work after 1948 don't have one. But you don't have to be a citizen to have a number. Those working here with work permits have to have one as well.

Administering and collecting

The Inland Revenue's responsibilities include:

- ✔ Collecting taxes, including income, capital gains, and inheritance tax as well as stamp duty, Value Added Tax, and corporation tax on companies.

- ✔ Administering national insurance. The Inland Revenue collects the money in, although the main benefit, the state retirement pension, is paid out by the Department for Work and Pensions.

- ✔ Collecting customs duties.

- ✔ Dispensing benefits and credits, including the child benefit and child tax credit and the Working Tax Credit.

- ✔ Policing the National Minimum Wage and investigating employers who try to pay below the level.

- ✔ Collecting the interest and repayments on loans to students from the government's Student Loans Company.

- ✔ Overseeing the work and spending of *business support teams* – local organisations set up to encourage new and small businesses.

- ✔ Valuing land for council tax and other purposes.

Imposing penalties

Around one million people each year have to pay extra money to the Inland Revenue for making mistakes or not getting forms in on time. Only a tiny proportion of these are deliberate tax cheats. The rest either can't be bothered with their tax returns or have their affairs in a total mess or cut corners.

One-stop shopping or total intrusion?

Depending on your point-of-view, the way the Inland Revenue has emerged at the top of the pile in collecting all the various amounts we have to pay to the government (and in returning some of that money in the shape of benefits and tax credits) is either a move towards convenient one-stop shopping or a further incursion by an all-powerful state into our personal affairs.

In fact, it's neither so far. You still have to shop at various outlets to pay all the taxation you owe. For the moment, the takeover by the Inland Revenue of Customs and Excise has had little visible effect on those who ask you whether you have anything to declare on a return from a visit abroad. Nor will your income tax inspector know if you have been fined for illegally importing tobacco or alcohol. But eventually their computers will interlink at the front-line level. There's a surprisingly large amount of correlation between those who cheat the customs and those who cheat the taxman.

The Inland Revenue doesn't take you to task for mistakes in your arithmetic or other unintentional errors, but they take a serious view of failing to file a self assessment form and failing to meet other deadlines. And it's even worse if they catch you out cheating.

The Inland Revenue has the power to make your life quite miserable and the ability to impose stiff fines. My advice is to do all you can to avoid finding out the scope of their powers. (If you do become the object of a tax inspection, Chapter 20 offers some advice.)

Penalties and late fees can be very expensive. They start out at £100 for being even a day late after the 31 January deadline with filing your self assessment form. They can hit £3,000 in penalties with interest mounting up daily. In the worst cases of tax evasion, you'll end up in prison (something often celebrated by the taxman in a press release!).

It is not generally an excuse to say you did not receive the proper documents from your employer in time. It is your duty to nag your boss. But the Inland Revenue does accept there are difficulties when employers go bust or, in a small firm, where the person responsible falls ill.

Respecting the Inland Revenue

The Inland Revenue is very serious about collecting its due, as one of my friends found out to his cost. A succession of missed dates for returning the self assessment form, plus some very poor accountancy advice resulted in what would have been manageable payments on a year-by-year basis mounting up to well over £100,000.

My friend didn't fill out his forms, so he didn't know how much tax he owed. He spent all the money he had, including what he owed to the taxman. On top of that, he borrowed more money to pay for a messy divorce and some very expensive school fees.

The result was that the Inland Revenue took out a bankruptcy order against him. Now he's lost his very valuable home. All the costs involved in his bankruptcy and selling his home added tens of thousands of pounds onto the bill which had, anyway, more than doubled over the years by penalties and interest.

Coping as a Ratepayer

The Inland Revenue is increasingly run as a business with budgets and costs and production targets. It wants, believe it or not, to make life as easy as it can for the great majority of people who want to pay the tax they owe in full and on time. By making things easy for the average tax-payer, the Inland Revenue can control its own expenditure on sorting out tax-payers' money and concentrate its resources on the small minority of deliberate cheats or those who have exceptionally complicated affairs.

The Inland Revenue even has service standards its representatives are bound to follow:

- Representatives should get responses to you right the first time.
- It aims to answer 90 per cent of calls to local offices within 20 seconds (which is down from the 30 seconds it used to take). So, you shouldn't have to hang on the phone too long.
- Eighty per cent of written enquiries must be fully answered within 15 days.
- Eighty-five per cent of callers who walk into an Enquiry Centre (a local tax office) without an appointment should be able to see an agent within 30 minutes of their arrival.
- Repayments of tax taken off bank and building society interest should be returned to qualified individuals within 15 days.

These service standards change year by year. Some get better, such as the phone answer time, but not all standards improve. The target at Enquiry Centres used to be seeing 95 per cent of callers without an appointment within 15 minutes.

Getting help from the Inland Revenue

An important tax-payer's right is access to information. This includes information on the basics of the tax system, the way that the Inland Revenue deals with the public, service standards, and ways to complain. The Inland Revenue publishes the following aids and explanations, all of which are available at no cost through the Inland Revenue Web site at www.inlandrevenue.gov.uk. Or you can phone 0845 9000 404 for printed versions of their publications. These include

- ✔ Explanatory leaflets, booklets, and information sheets on various aspects of the tax and the benefits system.

- ✔ Details of extra statutory concessions. These are tax reliefs and rebates which are not available under strict interpretations of tax law but which result from common sense or where the amounts involved are so small that pushing the law to its utmost makes no sense for the Inland Revenue. The current list is 108 pages long and covers everything from tax rules for monks and nuns living in contemplative communities, via ignoring small luncheon voucher benefits, to tax relief on sums paid in compensation to victims of slavery.

- ✔ Statements of practice explain how the Inland Revenue interprets the law and helps you to see the law from their point of view. Tax-payers can mount legal challenges to the Inland Revenue's interpretations, if they can afford it, or find a friendly tax lawyer willing to work on a no win, no fee basis, or find a money advice organisation to help them.

- ✔ Press releases, which explain the Inland Revenue's plans as well as clarifying current thinking. But you cannot access the Inland Revenue press office directly unless you are a journalist.

- ✔ The *Tax Bulletin* is published once every two months and is a round-up of Inland Revenue plans, philosophy, and interpretations of tax rules. It is aimed at tax professionals but if you've got this far, you're well on your way to rivalling them.

Additionally, and this is getting really advanced, you can access Internal Guidance Manuals, which tell tax inspectors how to interpret various legal points. Not all of these are available on the Web site, but you can get them through your local tax office.

The Inland Revenue does not give tax advice to individuals. And the leaflets and other information they provide offer general advice which may not answer your specific query.

But if you write a letter, make a phone call, or visit an Enquiry Centre in person, you can get a reply to questions about the general workings of the system and how that affects a specific tax-payer – namely, you! The Inland Revenue does provide help with completing self assessment and other tax or tax credit returns.

The Inland Revenue will also tell you the legal mechanics of how to appeal against a decision. But don't expect help with the details of actually doing so – you have to consult a tax lawyer for help with that.

Under Open Government legislation, the Inland Revenue provides information on its general policy in areas such as services to tax-payers, and on how it interprets tax law provided that this information is not in contention in the courts. This service can be charged for at around £20 an hour, although most requests cost a flat £15.

But the Inland Revenue has a public interest let-out on revealing information, so don't waste your time asking it to tell you how it combats tax dodging!

Tracking down your tax inspector

My tax office and my tax inspector used to be around ten minutes' walk from my home in London. Okay, the building was ugly and the lift to the fifth floor (where the tax inspector and his staff worked) was a filthy nightmare, but at least it was close. Now my file has been removed to sunny Devon. My wife also works in London. Her file is held in Edinburgh. It's all part of the long-standing Inland Revenue move to decentralise staff.

But you don't have to take a day or more off work or spend a fortune to travel hundreds of miles to find your tax office. You can deal with your tax office by post, telephone, or over the Internet.

If you want or need face-to-face contact, you can arrange to sort things out at a more convenient location provided sufficient notice is given.

Your employer can normally tell you your tax office. Otherwise, any local tax office can look it up for you. Should your office be changed, the Inland Revenue will write to tell you. You can give in self assessment and other forms at any convenient tax office.

Tax Enquiry Centres, which are listed in your local phone book, can deal with general enquiries as well as a number of simple items including changes of address, marriage, separation or divorce, new employment details, and claims for professional subscriptions up to £100. More complicated matters have still to be put in writing. Remember to bring your driving license or passport because they do check your identity.

Playing Your Part

Your role in the tax game mostly involves meeting deadlines and telling the truth. Sounds pretty simple – and it is really.

You must be truthful on your forms and in your dealings with the Inland Revenue, replying promptly and truthfully to any questions you're asked. If you have reason to believe that you might have a tax bill to pay but have not received a tax return form from the Inland Revenue, it is your responsibility to request one.

It's not a valid excuse to say you didn't know you had to pay a tax bill or make a return. Nor can you blame your accountant, bank manager, or financial adviser for not telling you. You're responsible for your own tax affairs, and you're the one the Inland Revenue will come to with questions and penalties.

If you're questioned by the Inland Revenue, they can check your answers for accuracy in order to prevent or detect crime, or to protect public funds – jargon for stopping people cheating. This is a pretty broad brush, and if the Inland Revenue decides to take a closer look at your fiscal (that's a posh French-style word for tax) affairs, even the dimmest tax official can find something. My advice is not to give them a reason to look further into your affairs than they have to: Being honest upfront can save you time and trouble.

Chapter 20 has details of what can happen if you fail to follow the tax rules.

Filing forms

If you do not have to fill in a self assessment form, you can skip this section. For complete information on filling out the self assessment form, turn to Chapter 18.

Much of the tax-gathering vocabulary remains unchanged over two hundred years. The basis of income tax remains schedules and cases (complete with Roman numerals). A *schedule* is a major body of tax law affecting a large group, such as the self-employed or property investors. A *case* is a sub-division of a schedule.

Tax officials still use this vocabulary. It is precise, and they know what it means. But it can be frightening to the uninitiated. Needless to say, accountants use tax terms all the time to impress clients that they are worth the huge fees they charge. You could pay their fees or you could follow the tax advice in this book. I know which I would prefer!

So here's a quick run down of all the confusing schedules and cases and how they apply to you.

- ✔ **Schedule A** applies to income from property situated in the UK. You file this if you have income from letting out furnished rooms in your house or a holiday home. This schedule doesn't take in buy-to-let properties – they go under schedule D, as does property you own overseas.

- ✔ **Schedule D** applies to self-employment and to many interest payments. It is divided into cases, the first two of which are rooted in the Inland Revenue snobbery of the past. Case I is for profits arising from professions such as the law or architecture; Case II is for self-employment for more mainstream professions such as interior designers, plumbers, and publishers; Case III covers interest payments from banks and building societies; Case IV and Case V are concerned with overseas earnings; while Case VI is a ragbag to pick up anything not covered elsewhere!

- ✔ **Schedule E** is now called Employment Income. But it still has cases. Most people are taxed under Case I, which is for earnings received by UK residents. But in case you really want to know, Case II is for various people in the

UK who usually live outside the UK, and Case III covers earnings for work carried out abroad.

✔ **Schedule F** is all about dividends and other payments you earn from shares.

You may have noticed that Schedules B and C aren't in the list. I didn't forget about them: They were abolished in 1988 and 1996, respectively. And the other cases and schedules are due for the scrapheap, with new simpler laws expected to come into force for the 2006–07 tax year.

Exercising your rights

The Inland Revenue wants you to get your tax affairs right. And that can even include persuading you to apply for a *rebate* – that's the technical word for getting money back from the taxman!

But once you sign your tax return as correct, you have no legal right to ask the Inland Revenue if you can change your mind.

You do, however, have the right to know the legal basis of any move the Inland Revenue makes towards you as an individual. You can challenge the legality of decisions.

The Inland Revenue has a legal duty under data protection law to ensure that any information that they receive from you remains confidential. The taxman can't sell your files and your personal information can't be sold on to other organisations for commercial purposes.

Running through the Tax Year

A number of key dates and deadlines run through each year. Some involve your employer sending various forms that you will need to incorporate on your tax return; others involve deadlines for claiming credits.

The tax year starts on 6 April each year. Whatever the reason for that date (the nearby 'What a silly date!' sidebar shares some theories), the Inland Revenue realises that most people are paid monthly, so it works on the basis that 31 March is the end of the year for many employees. But 5 April as a year-end still applies to many investment-related matters such as individual savings accounts or Capital Gains Tax. However, more up-to-date tax systems such as Value Added Tax (VAT) use the standard calendar.

When 5 April is a weekend or a Bank Holiday (such as Good Friday or Easter Monday), fund management firms publicise any special arrangements on last-minute individual savings accounts (ISAs) because if you don't use your ISA in the tax year, you lose it for ever. Some investment firms bring the staff in on a weekend or Bank Holiday. But whatever day of the week 5 April falls on, it is the date on the paperwork that determines which year counts for tax-free benefits or taxable transactions.

What a silly date!

No other nation has such a daft tax-year date. No one is too sure why this date was chosen. But here are some possibilities.

✔ Some think it was because the Christian calendar features Easter as a starting time. This also reflects pre-Christian Europe, when the end of the winter snows and the start of plants growing marked the beginning of the year.

✔ Another theory is related to the historical use of the Feast of Annunciation of the Virgin Mary on 25 March – nine months before Christmas. The feast day, called Lady Day, was the start of the religious year, and when the church was paramount, the start of the secular year as well. When Britain moved to the Gregorian calendar in 1752, 11 days were added to 25 March (making 6 April) as the tax authorities wanted to maintain a full 365-day tax year.

✔ Some say 6 April came about because of the largely rural nature of the UK when income tax was introduced during the Napoleonic wars. April gave farmers a chance to work out how much they had earned over the whole year. It also gave landlords a fortnight or so after they collected quarterly rents on March 25.

✔ In pre-railway Britain, the April date gave tax-payers the chance to send in details of their income in the summer when the roads were easily passable by stage coaches.

Each tax year follows a set pattern:

- ✔ **6 April:** The self assessment return form for the tax year which has just ended is sent out to those who previously received a return, to those who have declared they should in future have one, and to anyone else the Inland Revenue thinks should get one. The form is also available online for downloading and printing. You can electronically file a return via the Internet from this date should you wish. See Chapter 18 for information on the form itself.

- ✔ **31 May:** The deadline for receiving form P60 showing your previous year's earnings from your employer. This is the latest date you can get this.

- ✔ **5 July:** The deadline for tax credit applications backdated to the start of the tax year. This is a use-it-or-lose-it benefit – you cannot go back further than three months. Chapter 5 has more information.

- ✔ **6 July:** The deadline for receiving form P11D or form P9D from your employer. These forms give financial details of the value of any fringe benefits such as a company car or a medical insurance scheme your employer provided over the previous tax year. Chapter 9 explains benefits-in-kind.

- ✔ **31 July:** The final date for sending in the second interim installment of tax due for the tax year which ended in the preceding April. This only applies to some who file self assessment returns, usually the self-employed or those with large investment incomes.

- ✔ **30 September:** The filing deadline if you want the Inland Revenue to calculate your tax due under self assessment. It is also the last date if you want the Inland Revenue to collect any tax due out of your future Pay As You Earn (PAYE) deductions via a tax code change (but see 30 December as well).

- ✔ **5 October:** The deadline for informing the Inland Revenue that you had new sources of income such as self-employment earnings during the previous tax year. You risk having to pay a penalty if you don't notify the Inland Revenue of changes in your tax status by this date. This is also the deadline to report new sources of capital gains over the preceding tax year.

✔ **30 December:** The notification deadline for employees who file tax returns over the Internet (known as e-filing) to opt for tax due up to £2,000 to come out of their regular income via a PAYE tax code change.

✔ **31 January:** The big date! It's the final day for filing the self assessment return. And it is the day for the first interim payment on the current tax year as well as the final, balancing payment, for the tax year that ended the previous April. In the past, the Inland Revenue has stretched January 31 by one or two days when it falls on a weekend.

✔ **1 March:** The automatic surcharge starts for those who failed to comply with the January 31 deadline. This is in addition to the automatic fine levied on February 1.

✔ **5 April:** End of the tax year.

To qualify for tax savings, you have to take care of a number of financial and investment transactions *before* the end of the tax year. These are use-them-or-lose-them allowances.

New forms are sent out again on April 6 and the whole cycle starts all over again.

Chapter 3

Organising Your Records

● ●

In This Chapter

▶ Understanding the system

▶ Living up to your record-keeping duties, both business and personal

▶ Keeping track of your records

● ●

*W*hen you get one of those pieces of paper from an investment company or bank headed *Keep This,* it means what it says.

One of the best ways to ensure that your tax affairs are up-to-date and incur no penalties or fines is to keep all the paperwork that forms the basis of your self assessment return. Conversely, if there's a tax probe into your affairs and you do not have any evidence to back up all those sections in which you are asking for tax relief, you are likely to end up empty-handed and may even find yourself at the end of a big fine!

The difficulty is not every piece of paper that should be kept has *Keep This* inscribed on it. In this chapter, I tell you the who, the what, the how, and the how long of record-keeping.

Looking at How the System Works

The UK self assessment tax filing scheme works on a 'process now, check later' routine. The Inland Revenue would go into a tail spin if everyone sent in every piece of paper to back their tax return. If it had to check every piece of paper, it would need a far larger staff. It does not operate like tax systems in many other countries where you have to send written proof of everything along with your return for every potential taxable item and for everything you are claiming for. However, just because you don't have to send your paperwork in at the time of filing, don't think that means that you can chuck it away. The sections later in this chapter let you know what you have to save and for how long.

You can, in theory, send in whatever numbers you want and let the processing take over. Printed returns get fed into an optical character recognition machine for reading. And the increasing number of forms filed online are also automatically read and digested.

It's only once the form has been processed that any checking takes place. And it's only then that mistakes, omissions, and possibly deliberate errors come to light.

The Inland Revenue usually rectifies accidental mistakes – the mostly minor arithmetic errors or putting items under the wrong heading – that have little or no effect on the final bill without bothering to contact you. (Around half of these tax form repairs work out in the tax-payer's favour, so check your maths!) If there are more serious problems or queries, the tax inspector will contact you and may ask for the paperwork to back up what you put down on the form.

In most cases, however, the Inland Revenue never looks at or even asks for the paperwork you have gathered to fill out your tax form. But you can never be certain – a small number of totally innocent tax-payers each year have to submit to random checking.

Keeping Good Personal Records

Keeping good records can help you save on tax. It is often only when the tax year is finished that you realise you could have claimed for something or that tax deducted at source should not have been. Having the paperwork to hand simplifies everything. Additionally, you should only make a claim for tax relief on an item such as a personal pension purchase if you have the paperwork as a back-up.

Failing to keep records; paying fines

You can be fined up to £3,000 for each year when you fail to keep the required records. This amount is intended as a deterrent. It is only used sparingly. You will usually receive a written caution for a first offence unless you have deliberately destroyed records you are known to have had. In this latter case, you can expect the full fine and some more for other offences that may be uncovered.

Your failure to show records is more likely to result in the tax inspector refusing to allow you to claim tax relief. Small or spare-time businesses may be barred from deducting legitimate expenses, for example.

Don't forget, the Inland Revenue can uncover bank interest payments as well as details of payments in and out of your bank accounts if it has to.

But the Inland Revenue is aware that it can sometimes be difficult for an individual to approach an employer for paperwork, especially if the employee has left. In some circumstances, it can approach your employer, or former employer, for records on your behalf.

Keeping only some of the required records can be almost as bad as keeping none at all. It won't take a genius at the Inland Revenue to spot suspicion-raising gaps. This may sound really, really basic, but it is far easier to have a regular day once a month to get on top of the paperwork than let it all pile up over a year. If there's not a *Keep Your Home Tidy For Dummies,* then the For Dummies publishers should get around to commissioning it! (But I'm not putting myself forward to write it.)

Identifying who needs to keep records

Everyone should keep financial records. Even if you don't have to fill in a self assessment form, you should still maintain good record-keeping.

If your earnings are low enough, you may be able to claim a rebate of the tax taken from the interest on your bank accounts. And look on the bright side: You may be a basic rate tax-payer at the start of the tax year, but who knows? Your mediocre share portfolio might soar in value so you sell out at a huge profit leading to a Capital Gains Tax liability. Or you might get a big pay rise that takes you into the top-rate zone when you'll need to fill out a form and declare all your savings and investment returns. Or you might scoop the lottery!

People who use an accountant to file their tax forms still need to keep records themselves. Many accountants and tax professionals limit their help to processing the figures you give them. You need records for that.

But even if your tax form filler is willing to take a big pile of paper and create some order out of your chaos, make sure you take photocopies of everything as well as insisting on the return of the originals. And expect to pay an awful lot for this.

Sorting out what to keep

Record-keeping should start from the viewpoint that you only recycle paperwork that you know you won't need. Keep everything else, starting with anything that says *Keep This*. Bank statements, wages slips, and paperwork from investment firms are all vital.

Pension information is important to keep, including records showing how much you paid in to personal pension plans. If you are retired, keep details of pension payments you receive whether from company schemes or insurance companies.

Save statements from the Benefits Agency about your State Pension or any other taxable Social Security benefit.

Keep records of payments you make under the Gift Aid scheme for charitable giving.

Keeping records goes beyond tax

Obviously, proper record-keeping makes it easier to fill in your tax form or less costly if you employ an accountant on your behalf. But record-keeping goes beyond keeping straight with the Inland Revenue.

The discipline can help you see when you are spending too much or getting too little from your investments and savings. You may also find it easier to get loans if you can show full proof of earnings and other income.

When you give money or assets away to reduce the impact of Inheritance Tax, receipts or similar proof can come in handy if the Inland Revenue decide to query the reduction in your capital.

Holding onto work-related paper

Keep forms your employer gives you such as the P60 form showing end-of-year earnings. If you are out of work, or you have changed jobs, the P45 you were given when you left your last workplace becomes a vital document to show your earnings up to that date. Likewise, keep information on redundancy or other termination payments.

Some other employment-related records to keep include:

- ✔ The P11D (or P9D) which shows your payments-in-kind from your employer. *Payments-in-kind* are perks such as a company car, gym membership, and private medical insurance.

- ✔ Details of any bonuses you earned. These can include 'prizes' for achievements such as visits to 'conferences' in exotic locations.

- ✔ Records of any share incentive schemes operated by your employer to which you subscribed.

- ✔ Evidence of expenses paid by your employer for use of your own car. In addition, if you use your own vehicle or pedal cycle for work travel you can claim for the cost of fuel, and something towards other expenses such as maintenance and vehicle depreciation, but you cannot claim for commuting. So keep records. Chapter 9 has more details.

Keep evidence of payments made to professional bodies if you claim membership fees.

If you are lucky enough to get benefits such as expensive gifts or foreign travel (a supplier-sponsored golfing weekend at St. Andrews, for example) from an organisation other than your employer as part of your work, keep those records because there is a chance you may be taxed on them as a perk of your employment even if your own boss did not pay for them. (Don't worry, you can ignore low cost items such as diaries or pens or calculators or paperweights with a negligible value of less than £25. And non-monetary gifts costing no more than £250 in total over a year are also outside the tax net whether given to you or your family provided they are not linked to any specific services you have supplied.)

Certain professions have specific record-keeping duties:

- ✔ If you're a sub-contractor in the construction industry, save certificates of tax deducted under the special scheme for people like you.

- ✔ If you receive tips, keep records of any amounts you receive that are not entered elsewhere.

Securing interest and investment information

You may want to save bank records for your own uses, but you do not need to keep records of personal bank accounts where no interest is paid to you unless you are also running a spare-time business. Records you do need to keep include:

- ✔ Interest statements from banks and building societies. You can keep your bank statements and building society passbooks as additional back up.

- ✔ Contract notes that show how much you paid for shares or investment trusts or unit trusts. These will be needed for Capital Gains Tax calculations if you decide to sell them.

- ✔ Details of dividends on any foreign shares from which tax has been deducted.

- ✔ Dividend statements from shares. You must also include those where you receive extra shares instead of a cash dividend.

- ✔ Interest statements from bonds and bond funds.

Deciding how long to keep tax records

You must retain personal investment and savings-related items for one year after the final 31 January date for filing a self assessment form. So the records for the 2005–06 tax year that you use to fill out the self assessment form due by 31 January 2007, must be kept until 31 January 2008.

Travelling for work

Most employers pay your expenses when you have out-of-pocket costs such as travelling on behalf of your firm or organisation.

But there may be cases where your employer does not refund expenses which you have had to incur as part of your work. In that case, keep a record of mileage details if you drive (including dates, destinations, parking fees and tolls); foreign travel itineraries including tickets, hotel receipts, credit card statements, and cheque stubs.

Your employer will probably require you to keep these proofs anyway to show the money is a refund of expenses and not an attempt to pay you without an income tax or a national insurance deduction.

The Inland Revenue cannot challenge your records or ask you to produce them after that date unless it alleges fraud or other criminality and opens a formal investigation into your affairs. The Inland Revenue can open an investigation whenever they suspect wrongdoing – there's no time limit on this. But you need only worry if you are seriously concerned about facing tax evasion charges.

Keeping some records for far longer

Records of items you purchase which can incur a Capital Gains Tax if you sell them later on at a profit should be retained until you dispose of them, unless, of course, the entire Capital Gains system is replaced – which is very unlikely! These items include shares, unit trusts, investment trusts, other investments such as hedge funds, works-of-art, stamp collections, and antiques.

Saving some records your whole life

Documentary evidence of trusts should be kept for as long as the trust is in force. With some trusts set up for Inheritance Tax purposes working to a seven- or ten-year timetable, the paperwork has to be retained for that time period even if there are no assets left in the trust.

Records of disposals and gifts that can eventually reduce your estate for Inheritance Tax on your death are important to your heirs. So keep records of the amounts and the recipients for seven years after they are made. After seven years, the gifts drop out of tax contention, provided you are still alive.

Retaining Business Records

Running a business involves noting every transaction from the very first day. You record transactions under two basic headings:

- ✔ **Income** is for money that you take in for your goods or services.

- ✔ **Outgoings** are what you spend on acquiring stock, materials, or items required to run the business such as a telephone, stationery, or a computer.

Retain utility and other bills for your home if you operate the business from your family property so you can claim the proportion of the total you use in your business. The same 'proportionality' of costs applies if you use the same vehicle for private and for business use.

The simplest way of establishing how much you use your car for business is to keep a note of business-related mileage and work this out as a proportion of the annual mileage. The tax authorities appreciate it is not possible to get this precisely right as urban and motorway driving tend to have different costs, so no one expects figures down to several decimal points. But you can keep accurate records of parking fees or toll road costs.

You must file away any statements for bank accounts you use in your business even if they are personal accounts as well. Here the Inland Revenue may want to check transactions, not just any interest received. You must, of course, be able to show which entries on your statement are for your business and which for your personal use if you have one account for these two purposes.

Asking for receipts

Keep as many receipts and other items of proof of purchase as you can.

Obviously, you can't ask for a receipt if you put coins in the slot for a phonecall related to your self-employment. And the same applies to other small cash items such as the local evening paper that you might buy for the small ads, particularly if your business is buying old bikes, doing them up, and selling them on.

The Inland Revenue accepts that you cannot always get written proof of expenditure. But they still expect you to make a note of all such expenditure as soon as possible. List the amount, where you spent it, and why.

To save yourself hassle, use these tips:

- ✔ If you cannot or don't want to use a mobile, buy a phone card and get a receipt rather than put coins into public call boxes. Call boxes can be cheaper for many calls than mobile phones, while credit calls involve paying more in most situations.

- ✔ Use a regular newsagent who can hand out a monthly receipt for the newspapers you buy.

- ✔ Get receipts for taxi fares and train tickets, and keep your bus tickets.

- ✔ Photocopy receipts from shops. Many use thermal printers and the ink fades rapidly. Even if you copy them, retain the originals, even if they become virtually illegible.

Remember that the Inland Revenue is run on increasingly commercial lines. It does not wish to enter protracted correspondence or arguments over a 90p bus fare. (And nor should you!)

Keeping business records for a long, long time

You have to keep personal financial records for one year past the final 31 January filing date. With business records, including spare-time earnings, you need a much larger filing system. Businesses have to keep records not for just one year past the final filing date but for five years.

Your records for the 2005–06 tax year form the basis for the self-employment section on the self assessment form due to be filed by 31 January 2007. You must then keep this paperwork a further five full years after the final filing date so you only get to send the documents to the recycling bin after 31 January 2012. That's four years after you're allowed to throw personal stuff away.

When you dispose of an item such as machinery, a car, or a computer that you use in your business, you need to show how much you paid for it so that you can finalise your accounting, irrespective of whether you make a profit or a loss. Keep records of these capital items as long as you own them and then for the statutory five years after you don't own them anymore.

The same rules apply to assets such as a work-of-art your business might buy in the eventual hope of selling it on at a profit. Your paperwork will help establish a capital gain or loss.

Ensuring a part-time business follows the rules

When the tax folk are not busy checking your tax returns, they are out and about reading classified ads in local papers, noting down details from newsagents' notice boards, and having a good look at who's trading what on Internet auction sites.

They're not interested when you sell the bicycle your child has grown out of. Or when you get rid of your student books online. Or when you get on the Internet and try to auction that stuffed donkey your aunt brought you back from Spain. But if they see you offering to buy unwanted two-wheelers from local families and then selling them on at a profit, or regularly dealing in books which you acquire to sell for gain, or advertising for unwanted souvenirs to sell them to someone else's favourite aunts at prices less than they would pay in souvenir shops on the Costa del Sol, then the tax authorities will be interested.

There is nothing wrong with some spare-time buying and selling, or doing a bit of work on the side, provided you keep records and declare any profits.

You need to keep records even if your spare-time business *turnover* (sales in plain English) stays below £15,000 and lets you file a short form of accounts. Why? Unless you are a good record-keeper, how else do you know about your turnover figure and how do you prove it to the tax authorities?

Managing Your Record-Keeping

Record-keeping does not have to be expensive. Simple filing systems and the use of easy-to-obtain account books may be all you need. But a number of computer programs, such as Quicken or Microsoft Money, can help you as well.

Many people find using a computer easier than keeping hard-copy paperwork. But while this can lead to quicker calculations and speedier finding of information, the Inland Revenue insists you keep the hard copy as well unless you store the originals as microfilm records or use an optical imaging system. The taxman needs to be sure that computerised images are kept in a tamper-proof form and fully reflect the originals.

Always keep original copies of all records. If the original goes missing, it is not the end of the world providing you can re-create it from the original source. However, banks and many other financial companies may charge you for duplicate copies.

Part II
Tax, You, and Your Family

"The Chancellor of the Exchequer was on TV again talking about pensions."

In this part . . .

*L*ife is full of choices. And none are more significant than those we take in our personal life. Here I show you how you can legitimately arrange your tax affairs and those of your family to pay less tax.

You don't have to follow all the tips. In many cases, you won't be able to. Marriage is not for everyone nor does the married/unmarried partnership divide apply coherently across the tax board. In some cases, wife and husband are two different people entirely. In others, they are treated as an indivisible unit. And in still other cases, they are considered in exactly the same way as an unmarried couple. Help!

I also point out a potentially unpleasant surprise. You can spend all your life paying less tax only to have your savings taxed at 40 per cent when you die – so I show you the best ways to lessen the impact of Inheritance Tax. These involve more life choices.

Chapter 4

Tying the Knot – Or Not

∙∙

In This Chapter

▶ Changing your tax life when changing your marital status

▶ Making the most of your married state, tax-wise

▶ Weighing up the pros and cons of co-habiting

▶ Splitting up and sorting your taxes

∙∙

*M*any years ago, couples were given big tax breaks when they officially became man and wife. And, avid viewers of old black-and-white UK comedy films will have noticed there was even a tax-saving incentive to walk down the aisle in March. You got a whole year's married man's (yes, it was all given to the male) tax break with a March wedding. Now this annual tax allowance for married couples has withered away so only a declining number of older people still qualify.

Using all the various tax-planning devices open to married couples (and at some future stage to non-married couples) can save big money each year. But like other aspects of relationships, you have to work on it! In this chapter, I walk you down the aisle of wedded tax savings.

Getting Married

The Inland Revenue does recognise marriage as an institution. But don't expect too much, too easily, tax-wise from your wedded bliss. The days of tax relief on marriage are long gone except for those where one partner was born before April 5, 1935. And even that is not worth a great deal in hard cash terms.

Where marriage counts most is in *capital taxes* such as Capital Gains Tax and Inheritance Tax.

Married women became tax persons in their own right in 1991. Before that, they were their husband's tax chattels, with few rights. This 1991 move, known as *independent taxation,* actually increased the scope for tax-saving moves. (I provide the details in 'Maximising the Tax Benefits of Marriage' later on.)

You no longer get any income tax saving through a married couple's allowance unless one, or both, of the partners was born before 6 April 1935. (If this applies to you, see 'Looking at what's left of the married couple's allowance' a little later in this chapter.)

Becoming engaged

Your wedding can help others save tax. When you announce your engagement, you can use this hard-to-resist line to persuade parents, grandparents, and others to give you wedding presents. Tell them generous donations now can eventually save on future Inheritance Tax. Chapter 7 on Inheritance Tax has more details.

Don't forget to amend your will ahead of marriage as wills automatically stop on marriage. You don't have to wait until after the honeymoon for this. You can write a new will in anticipation of your forthcoming status change.

Anticipating changes to your tax life

Married couples benefit from the greater flexibility allowed between spouses in arranging their financial affairs.

Each person has their own tax allowances and, except for capital taxes, the Inland Revenue is not concerned whether a couple is married or co-habiting. But married partners have some advantages in passing income-producing assets such as savings accounts from the partner with the higher tax rate to the one with the lower. (See 'Maximising the Tax Benefits of Marriage'.)

Looking at what's left of the married couple's allowance

The married couple's allowance (MCA) was abolished for the majority of married partnerships in 1999. But it still remains for those relationships where at least one of the partners was born before 6 April 1935.

MCA is a tax relief, so a married couple who qualify pay less tax than a similar couple who are not married.

Seeing who can claim

The 6 April 1935 date is a fixed cut-off date, so the number of people eligible to apply for MCA diminishes each year.

The MCA goes by default to the husband. But couples can request that half, or all, of the basic amount be transferred to the wife. The wife can insist on half even if the husband says no. The decision to transfer half, or all, of the allowance must normally be made before the start of the tax year.

As the basic allowance counts against all income, it is more useful to the higher earner. It would be a gesture of mere sexual politics if a non-earner insisted on their share of the MCA.

Figuring out the allowance

The MCA has two elements:

- ✔ The **basic amount** is given as an allowance against taxable income irrespective of income levels. This is £2,280 in 2005–06, though it can change each year if the Treasury so decides. Divide that figure by the ten per cent tax allowance and it's worth £228 in cash terms.

- ✔ The **age-related amount,** which like the additional age-related personal allowance described in Chapter 6, can be clawed back by the taxman if the income of one partner falls in a higher tax band. In 2005–06, age-related MCA starts to disappear once the husband has an income in excess of £19,500. Sexist or what!

The MCA has two levels – one for couples in which the older partner was born between 6 April 1930 and April 5 1935 and a more generous tax relief level that applies for the tax year when the older partner reaches 75 years of age.

If that sounds complicated, don't worry. The difference between the two rates is not great. The lower MCA paid to the under 75s is worth a tax allowance of £5905 a year, while the higher level is £5975.

To get the allowance, couples have to earn enough to cover the amount. Then, because the tax level for the allowance is just ten per cent, the maximum value in cash terms at the lower level is £590.50 while the higher level is worth just £7 a year more in hard cash terms at £597.50. Not worth getting old for!

Connecting MCA and the age allowance

What's left of the MCA after the basic amount has been paid out (see the previous section) is subject to the age allowance trap, which affects older couples with higher-than-average incomes whose extra age allowance benefits are chipped away once their income hits a threshold. Earnings caught in the trap are taxed at 33 per cent instead of the basic 22 per cent.

When your income reaches £19,500 (for the 2005–06 tax year), the age-related element starts to fall away by £1 for every £2 your total income exceeds this level until it disappears entirely. Chapter 6 has more details on the age allowance trap.

Maximising the Tax Benefits of Marriage

If you are married, use your marital status to save tax. No one will thank you for forgoing the tax-saving opportunities I tell you about in this section.

If you want to get the best out of marriage and tax, you and your partner need to trust one another financially as well as in the usual ways. The strategies listed here generally require that couples either divide their assets up between themselves or that the better-off partner hand them over to the other.

Probably the biggest tax benefit of marriage is that you can pass ownership of money and other assets between the pair of you without tax hassles. Marriage can, for some couples, be worth ₤1,000 or more in tax savings each year. Of course, not every couple is able to save this sort of money. You need to have enough savings first of all to make it worthwhile switching the ownership from the higher-paid partner to the lower-paid one.

There are no limits to any moves of money between spouses. The taxman seems to forget independent taxation of women and goes back to a former age when a husband was responsible for the taxation of all the income-producing assets his wife possessed.

When assets are shared out, the division has to be real. The partner who gives something away cannot demand the assets back or have the income from them paid to her or his bank account. The new owner must have absolute ownership and control, including the right to sell.

Being partners at work as well as at home

Couples, whether legally married or not, who have their own business can transfer income from that business between themselves to make the best use of tax allowances and the advantages of lower tax rates.

The Inland Revenue is targeting husband and wife teams to ensure that any monies moved between the two in order to reduce their overall tax bill are wedded in reality. Where both partners are on the payroll, both have to do work to the commercial value of the payments they receive. And the earnings must be paid to the partner concerned. Sending it to a bank account in that partner's sole name is a wise move.

Also, provided it is a real job, a spouse (or unmarried partner) can employ their lower tax-rated other half. The wages paid are subject to PAYE and PAYE record-keeping unless the amount is below the national insurance minimum. Higher pay amounts, though still below the national insurance pay level, qualify for benefits such as the state retirement pension and, in particular, for the state second pension. (Chapter 17 talks about pensions.)

Sorting out your tax allowance

Each partner in a marriage, along with every other tax-payer, has a personal income tax allowance. This stands at £4,895 (for under 65s) for the 2005–06 tax year.

Some people don't have sufficient earnings from work and from interest on savings accounts to use up their personal allowance. If this is the case for you, but your spouse earns enough to use up all his or her allowance and then some, it makes sense for your partner to transfer income- or interest-producing assets to you (or vice versa if the financial situation is reversed).

Geeta earns £25,000 a year from her job, and the total of her income puts her in the 20 per cent tax band, so the £2,000 interest she is paid on her savings account costs her £400 in tax. Her husband, Vijay, has no income of his own. Geeta can transfer all her savings to Vijay so that he can reclaim the interest and the household is £400 better off.

Patrick earns £50,000 a year and is a top-rate tax-payer. The £5,000 he earns from his £100,000 savings account loses £2,000 (40 per cent) to the taxman. His wife, Rachel, earns £20,000 a year and has no savings of her own. She is a basic-rate tax-payer for whom the 20 per cent savings rate applies. If Patrick gives all his savings to Rachel, they would save £1,000 a year, the gap between 20 per cent and 40 per cent of the £5,000 interest. But Patrick needs control day-to-day over some of the money, so the couple agree to joint ownership. The result is Patrick now pays £1,000 tax on the £2,500 he earns in interest while Rachel pays £500 on her portion. The couple is now £500 better off.

Swapping your assets

Each partner in a marriage has their own Capital Gains Tax annual allowance. Capital Gains Tax (CGT) is payable when you make a profit in selling or transferring an asset to someone else – but using the allowance lets the seller have that amount of any such gain tax free.

Keeping an investment portfolio in just one partner's name means a couple can make use of only one Capital Gains Tax allowance. But dividing up the assets potentially liable to CGT, as married people can do freely, doubles the potential tax savings by giving two CGT allowances to use instead of just one.

In some cases, sharing out stocks and shares in this way also reduces the income tax payable on dividends. Chapter 14 has the lowdown on dealing with Capital Gains Tax.

Inheriting each other's assets

When a husband or wife dies, the surviving partner doesn't pay any inheritance tax on any transfer of assets between themselves whether during their lifetime or in a will. Inheritance Tax is not levied on anything that passes between spouses. Chapter 7 on Inheritance Tax has more details of what to do and what to avoid doing.

Taking a stake in a pension

Spouses can invest up to £2,808 a year into a stakeholder pension for their other halves, irrespective of the partner's income. This contribution qualifies for automatic tax relief at the basic 22 per cent level, taking the real value invested into the pension plan up to £3,600. This limit seems to be fixed in stone; it does not rise each year. The pension company does all the paperwork and increases the payment into the pension scheme in line with this tax relief.

Co-habitating instead of Marrying

Current UK law does not recognise either common-law marriages between a man and woman or same-sex relationships – but co-habiting couples are treated as though they were married for various means-tested tax credits. Any tax-planning opportunities given to married people are denied to couples who are not married.

There is, however, nothing to stop you making a gift of an asset to someone to whom you are not married. The risk is the Inheritance Tax that would apply if you failed to live seven years from the date of making the gift.

Planning recognition

Living 'in sin' should become less of a tax sin thanks to planned government moves to allow unmarried couples, whether lesbian, gay, or straight, to register their non-married relationship for tax and other purposes.

The idea is that the government will make no distinction between different ways of adults living together in long-term, consensual, relationships.

The first fruit of this is the Civil Partnership Act (due in December 2005), which will give same sex couples who register the same tax breaks as married couples. But this will not apply to different sex unmarried couples.

Unmarried couples who buy assets together are treated as though each one owned half the value on a disposal so both face any tax liability.

If you live together in unwedded bliss, make sure you each have written a will to ensure the fewest tax hassles should one of you die.

Breaking Up

A large number of marriages end in the divorce courts. But don't expect any sympathy from the Inland Revenue. There is no longer any tax relief on maintenance payments or Child Support Agency payments.

The law says that divorcing couples remain spouses until the decree absolute brings the relationship to an end. The Inland Revenue has other ideas. It only allows tax-free transfers between spouses if they have lived together for at least part of the tax year during which the asset changed hands. A couple who separated (formally stopped living together) on 30 April 2005 can transfer assets without tax hassles until that date and for the rest of the tax year ending on 5 April 2006.

I know it's tough, but if you're heading for divorce, plan ahead. Transfer assets while you are still living under the same roof or at least during the current tax year.

Sorting out the tax bill

Under present tax law, husband and wife are counted as one for Capital Gains Tax and Inheritance Tax. This can complicate the financial picture of a divorcing couple.

Ex-partners who transfer assets such as shares or property between themselves to even up the financial position as part of a divorce settlement can face an unexpected tax bill. If the partners didn't live together during the tax year, the profit made by selling an asset may be subject to a hefty Capital Gains Tax.

Paying and receiving maintenance payments

Payments you make for maintenance to a former spouse, and payments for the upkeep and education of a child of a former relationship until they are 18, or are still in full-time education, don't count for Inheritance Tax calculations if you die.

Any maintenance money you receive for whatever purpose, including maintaining a child, is tax-free whether it comes from a former spouse in this country or abroad.

Chapter 5

Taxing from the Cradle to College

*A*s you celebrate the birth of your child, someone else is celebrating too. The taxman is ready to count your infant as a new tax-payer. But it's not all one way. Along with being a potential tax-payer, your child also has tax-saving possibilities. And for most parents, that new-born will take them into the sometimes arcane, and often complex, world of child tax credit.

Becoming a Tax-payer

The Inland Revenue says that childhood officially stops at the age of 16, not the usual 18 age of majority as in other legal matters. This applies even if the child is still at school or college. You do not need to register your child with the Inland Revenue before the age of 16, but once they reach 16 they're given a national insurance number and can start paying national insurance.

So be prepared to persuade your offspring to take action to formalise their tax-payer status on or around their sixteenth birthday. If their overall income is still low enough to qualify for tax-free status on their interest earnings (if they have any) they need to sign Inland Revenue form R85.

An under 16 year old becomes a tax-payer if they earn enough to pay income tax or realise profits from sales or investments that are eligible for Capital Gains Tax.

In reality, most children's income is limited to the interest that they're paid on savings accounts. But that does not stop them (or rather you as parents) from filling in a tax form and claiming the tax back on any interest on savings.

Either you, as parents, or your child on reaching 16, has to reclaim any tax deducted from interest-earning bank accounts or investments. Preferably, you tell the bank or building society that your child is not a tax-payer so the interest can be paid gross in the first place. The most usual method of reclaiming tax is by using Inland Revenue form R85. Any savings institution can supply this form and will often pre-print the details for signature to save time. Chapter 13 has full information on how and when children can reclaim tax deducted from interest on savings.

For most children, there's a substantial, tax-saving flipside of gaining tax-payer status as soon as they are born because they also gain use of the annual personal tax allowance from that very same time. This initial tax-free income amount, £4,895 in 2005–06, can be set against any earnings from part-time jobs as well as interest earned on savings and investments. The taxman lumps everything together whether it comes from savings or hard work delivering newspapers.

Giving Money to Children

As a parent, you can give your children as much money as you want to give them. But the Inland Revenue is not stupid. It knows that many parents would happily hand over all or some of their money to their offspring in an effort to dodge tax. Don't think you can just switch money from your own savings to an account you opened for your child to avoid income tax on the interest.

The Inland Revenue distinguishes how it treats tax on the interest on gifts of money from parents. The interest, or other returns on these gifts, is considered to belong to the parent, not to the child.

You can give your over-18 offspring as much as you like without income tax worries because, unlike the under 18s, they count as legally adult. However, you can't ask for it back as the money has to be really given away and not just parked in your child's bank account to dodge tax.

The age thing can be confusing and annoying. The Inland Revenue starts to treat children as tax-payers when they reach 16 but they are only independent beings when they are 18.

Giving money as a non-parent

There is no limit on how much grandparents, aunts, uncles, godparents, cousins, any other relation, or family friends can give to children. Once they have handed over the money, it becomes the child's property, leaving the child liable for tax on the interest. The generous relation no longer has to worry about paying tax on the gift.

There is nothing to stop you giving money to your own parents (your child's grandparents). But if your child's grandparents then try to give this money to their grandchildren (your children) to avoid the £100 rule, which I explain in the next section, then the Inland Revenue can get interested and ask where the money came from originally. It won't work for your parents to say that they gave their grandchild £1,000 from their savings if you have given them the £1,000 to do so!

Taking advantage of the small amount exemption

Even the Inland Revenue has a nice side and grants parents a special exception: You can give away sums to your children and not worry about being taxed on the interest providing the annual interest on all the savings accounts does not top £100 per parent per child. It doesn't matter whether your children are natural, adopted, legitimate or illegitimate, or whether you live with your children – the exemption still applies.

Within the £100 level, the interest is taxed as belonging to your children, so they can reclaim tax deducted on it by the building society or bank (always assuming their total income falls within the personal allowance) using form R85.

Going offshore to give big sums

If you can afford to give really large sums to your children, consider off-shore roll-up funds in which the interest is not treated as taxable income because it grows within the account rather than being paid out at regular intervals. Most parents who can afford to do this are top-rate tax-payers.

The offshore fund can start to be cashed in shortly after your child's eighteenth birthday to use her or his personal allowance. If there is more than enough in the account to use one year's personal allowance, this process can then be repeated in subsequent years.

By that time your child may have found a job and may be paying income tax, so any remaining withdrawals are subject to tax. But, from your point of view as parents, this strategy avoids the 40 per cent tax rate while also allowing the interest to roll up and compound itself tax free.

Your children, or you as parents or guardians, can also reclaim half of the tax deducted if your or their income falls within the ten per cent tax band. Ten per cent tax-payers are allowed to reclaim the difference between their rate and the 20 per cent standard savings rate deduction.

With interest rates at five per cent, each parent can give each child £2,000 and stay under the £100-interest limit. If rates fell to two-and-a-half per cent, then the capital can go up to £4,000. But if interest levels rose to ten per cent, the limit that can be given would fall to £1,000 – the parent would have to ask for a refund!

One parent can give the other money to give to their child to generate up to £100 a year in interest.

The £100 is a concession, not a tax relief given as of right. Once interest tops this figure, even to £101, the entire sum is taxed as if it belonged to the parent. The only exemption to this rule is if a 16 or 17 year old marries! But that's a drastic way of paying less tax.

Keep records of where the money comes from for each account your child has. It is easiest to have one designated 'pocket money account' rather than mix up sums from you as parents with those from others. This way your child can prove to the Inland Revenue the source of each pound on which interest is earned. Of course, if your child spends all the pocket money you give or keeps it in a piggy bank, then the Inland Revenue is not concerned at all.

Saving Tax by Giving Wisely

As a parent, you can beat the £100 rule (see the previous section) by investing money in savings schemes that do not pay income or that are not liable for income tax. These tax-free savings include:

- ✔ **National Savings Children's Bonus Bonds:** You can buy these for children up until they reach 16. They have to be held for five years and pay a fixed interest rate during that time. To get the maximum benefits, they need to be held for the full five-year period. If you cash them early, you're subject to interest-rate penalties.

- ✔ **National Savings Certificates:** These come in two varieties. You can choose between fixed interest (for two or five years) and index-linked bonds whose value depends on inflation as measured by the retail prices index. Index bonds come in three- and five-year varieties.

- ✔ **Premium bonds:** These give you the chance of winning £1 million without ever having to worry about losing your initial money. If you invest the maximum £30,000, or a sum approaching that, the law of averages says you should get some small winning tickets every year to give you an income which is tax-free.

- ✔ **Friendly society plans:** These plans are intended for regular savings of up to £25 a month for a minimum of ten years. Savings grow in a tax-free environment.

Investing in single premium insurance bonds

The special tax treatment of *single premium life insurance bonds* can enable you to give money to your offspring but avoid paying tax as these bonds do not pay any income.

And because of this, they don't affect your child's personal allowance.

Insurance bonds can be complicated, so always discuss whether they are right for you and your child before buying a bond through your financial adviser.

Generally, you need to start with at least £1,000 and sometimes £5,000. Parents who are top-rate tax-payers get the most advantages from these bonds.

The Inland Revenue is currently looking for ways to stop parents benefiting from the Capital Gains Tax allowances of their offspring. But provided the children keep the investments until they are legally grown up at 18, the Inland Revenue can't do anything about the gains as they belong to the new adult. And in any case, the Capital Gains Tax rate on assets held for over three years reduces each year after the third year until the tenth year. I deal with this taper process and other Capital Gains Tax issues in Chapter 14.

Setting up a trust

A *trust* is a legal device that gives property and other assets, including cash, to a beneficiary without giving the lucky recipient full control. For most tax purposes, the gift of a trust has to be irrevocable. If you give money or property away to a child, you can't ask for it back or set conditions where it will bounce back to you.

A trust can be an ideal way of passing money to your children but preventing them from getting their sticky fingers on the cash. Most trusts are set up through wills or by gifts during someone's lifetime. Some trusts also offer tax savings because those giving money into the trust are then able to use the child's tax allowances.

Trusts can also differentiate between assets, such as shares or property, and the income they produce. So you can leave the income from a portfolio to one person and the capital assets to another person on the first person's death.

You might, for instance, want to help your child if they run into personal difficulties with a regular cash income. But the last thing you want to do is to give that child control over the capital assets that produce the income. A trust would serve this purpose.

Or you might own a substantial parcel of shares in a private firm. If you left them to your family, some might try to sell, creating problems for those wanting to hold on. A trust structure where ownership and control are separated from the income solves the difficulty.

Alternatively, you can use this device to help your offspring through college and university but then ensure they have to use their own efforts for the rest of their lives rather than live off the trust fund monies.

Setting up a trust can help beneficiaries use various tax allowances. But the Inland Revenue does not accept everything at face value. It can check to see that the arrangement is genuine and not just an attempt to profit from lower tax rates while the settlor secretly enjoys the money.

Acquiring trust vocabulary

The world of trusts has its own special words. Knowing them, and when to use them, will impress lawyers, accountants, and financial advisers as well as help you understand the ins and outs of trusts!

- ✔ **Beneficiary:** The person for whose benefit the trust is created. Beneficiaries are personally liable for tax on income they receive from the trust, but not for tax on income the trust itself owes.

- ✔ **Settler** (in Scotland, a *truster* or *granter*): A person who puts assets into a trust.

- ✔ **Trustee:** A person who administers a trust and so is the legal owner. The trustees have to file tax returns and are responsible for paying any tax the trust incurs. It is usual to have between two and five trustees.

  When you set up a trust, you can choose people you know to be the trustees or use a specialist trustee firm. Professional trustees are allowed to charge for their services, and their fees need to be taken into consideration against any potential tax savings.

Exploring types of trusts

Different types of trusts have different types of benefits, which I explain in the following list.

✔ **Accumulation and Maintenance trust:** This is the main trust vehicle for grandparents making gifts to grandchildren for regular maintenance sums such as school or college costs. The trust is subject to 40 per cent tax on the income produced from the assets, but beneficiaries can reclaim all or some of this depending on their personal tax rate.

This form of trust is not liable for Inheritance Tax, but the person who starts the trust – the *settlor* – (or their estate) is liable if the settlor fails to live seven years after passing the money into the trust.

This type of trust isn't very good from a Capital Gains Tax perspective, so it's not a choice for assets that are going to gain in value rather than produce interest or dividends. You have to be selective in the assets you put into this type of trust.

✔ **Bare trust:** Beneficiaries of a bare trust can use all their own tax breaks, including the personal allowances for income tax and Capital Gains Tax, which otherwise might not be used. If the beneficiary dies, the assets are treated as belonging to her or him rather than to the settlor.

One very basic form of a bare trust is a bank account an adult opens for a child. Suppose Sheila Smart wants to give money into an account for her grandchild, Constance Clever. The classic method would be to designate the account 'a/c Sheila Smart in re Constance Clever'. This allows Sheila to operate the account until Constance is 18 but with Constance gaining the tax benefits, including the ability to reclaim tax deducted on the bank account interest.

✔ **Discretionary trust:** The main purpose of this is to save someone who leaves assets in a will from having to be precise over who gets what. The trustees can divide up the income from the assets among various beneficiaries including, if the trust wording is right, children as yet unborn. The income is taxed at 40 per cent but each beneficiary can reclaim some or all of this depending on their personal tax rate.

A discretionary trust is also good in cases in which grandparents want to leave considerable sums of money to their grandchildren in their will – but not until the children are old enough to be responsible for the money. Many trust funds use 25 as the cut-off age between child-like stupidity and adult sensibility. Some forms of trust do not allow clauses that specify an age over 25.

Setting up a trust (usually a discretionary trust) to benefit a disabled person can help save Inheritance Tax and Capital Gains Tax. There are special rules on Trusts for the Disabled. The disabled person (or persons) must receive an attendance allowance or a disability living allowance or be considered incapable under the Mental Health Act 1983. And at least half the property within the trust must be used to benefit the person with the disability. Charities dealing with particular disabilities or illnesses are the best source of information on this very specialised aspect of trusts.

Getting Money for Children

Government-financed help for families comes in many similarly named benefit schemes. *Child benefit* is paid to all, irrespective of income. *Child tax credit* is paid to most families but at a uniform rate unless the household income is substantially below the national average. *Children's Tax Credit* no longer exists and the *Child Trust Fund* starts in 2005!

I talk about the various programmes in the following sections.

Benefiting from child benefit

The parent, nearly always the mother, of every child qualifies for a fixed *child benefit*. This is currently £17 a week for the first (or only) qualifying child and £11.40 a week for each subsequent child. Many mothers choose to have it paid monthly into their bank accounts.

Child benefit is paid tax-free to parents no matter what their own tax rate. It does not have to be declared on any self assessment tax forms.

Child benefit is paid until the September after the child's sixteenth birthday but extended up to 1 September after the child's eighteenth birthday if she or he is still in full-time education. Strangely, this means a child born on 1 September has a whole year's more child benefit than one born on the day before, 31 August. Family planning or medical techniques to delay a late August birth are outside this book's brief!

Claiming child tax credit

Child tax credit is paid to parents of children under 16 whose income is low enough to qualify. In other words, legally-speaking, child tax credit is means-tested. But the great majority of parents receive the income boost because the maximum joint-income ceiling for the credit is quite high. It is paid through salary slips – either by reducing the income tax taken or by giving back money if your tax payment is lower than your credit. See 'Counting your income for child tax credit' later on in this chapter for information on who qualifies.

Child tax credit sums are not taxed and do not have to be declared on tax forms.

You have to apply for child tax credit. You do not get it automatically, even if the Inland Revenue or your employer knows your income is below the threshold.

You can claim by

- ✔ Asking your local tax office for a claim pack and returning the paper form.
- ✔ Going online at www.inlandrevenue.gov.uk/ taxcredits.
- ✔ Calling the child tax credit helpline on 0845 300 3900 – calls are charged at the local rate.

The credit is paid up to 1 September following your child's sixteenth birthday. But if your child remains in full-time education, the credit is paid for up to a further two years. The money is usually paid directly to a bank or building society account controlled by the parent (generally the main carer).

Although the Inland Revenue has improved its act since the early days of the credit when it was making many errors, you can still end up with the wrong amount.

Use these tips to ensure you get the full amount due you:

- ✔ Remember to submit a claim form on your new-born baby as soon as possible (if you qualify). Children under 12 months qualify for higher payments.

- ✔ Check that older children still in education are continuing to qualify for a payment.

- ✔ Report all falls in earnings at once, where this either brings you into the child tax credit payment zone or gives you eligibility for the higher payments under the childcare element of Working Tax Credit (a way of boosting earnings for the lower paid through their wage packets).

- ✔ Realise that you can only claim retrospectively for three months. So if you forget to fill in the forms, your claim can only be backdated by three months.

Counting your income for child tax credit

Child tax credit is calculated and administered by the Inland Revenue. It adds up the incomes of both partners in a two-parent family, whether they are legally married or not, providing they share responsibility for the child or children. It looks at the facts of the relationship where there are two parents rather than legal niceties such as marriage certificates. This brings child tax credit into line with other means-tested benefits but runs counter to the independent taxation of married (and unmarried) women.

To determine whether you qualify to receive child tax credit, you (and your partner, if any) add up all your income from employment, self-employment, and taxable interest and dividends on investments. You do not count income from Individual Savings Accounts, tax-free National Savings, the rent-a-room scheme, or maintenance payments from former partners. You can also ignore contributions to an approved pension scheme, and any donations you pay to charity via the Gift Aid or payroll giving schemes for good causes.

Only those parents whose joint incomes add up to £58,000 or more a year (and that's increased to up to £66,000 when there is a child less than one year old in the household) will have applications turned down.

It's always worth applying for a credit. Many people who qualify get nothing because they don't bother to apply.

How much you get is normally based on your income for the previous tax year. But if your income has fallen substantially, the amount you receive may be based on the current year. You do not have to be working to claim the credit.

You have to tell the Inland Revenue if your income increases by more than £2,500 a year. Any increase less than that is ignored, although it will be counted in the following year as the start point for your family income. This buffer zone is designed so you don't have to report every single change and so that the Inland Revenue doesn't have to bill you for over-payments.

The Inland Revenue can recover overpayments – often after they have been spent! So if your income rises because one earner moves from part-time to full-time work, or an older child leaves school and starts working, or for any other reason, you must report these changes as soon as they happen.

If your income is low, you can qualify for a higher rate of child tax credit and may also be able to claim for Working Tax Credit. The exact figures depend on how many children you have, whether there are one or two parents, and other personal details. For more information on means-tested benefits, try a local council money-advice unit, Citizens Advice, or the Child Poverty Action Group.

The Inland Revenue can refuse to pay child tax credit if it considers you work or provide a service at a level which is less than the going rate. This is to prevent people (including the self-employed) artificially depressing their income so that they qualify for the credit.

Calculating how much you get

Most parents receive £545 a year tax-free no matter how many children they have. Parents with a child under 12 months are usually entitled to more. In Inland Revenue jargon, the first £545 is known as the *family element* and the extra for a child under one year (also currently £545) is called the *family element, baby addition.* The existence of this second £545 for babies means those with household incomes between £58,000 a year and £66,000 a year qualify for the baby addition child tax credit for the first year of the child's life. Households with an income above £66,000 get absolutely nothing.

But those with lower-than-average incomes, including recipients of a number of state benefits paid to those on low or no income, can receive more. Table 5-1 shows how much those on various income levels with various numbers of children are eligible to receive in child tax credit each year. The table shows key earning points and credit amounts in the 2005–06 tax year – the amounts are subject to change. The amount payable is calculated on your exact income.

Table 5-1   Child Tax Credit Amounts

Annual Joint Income	Number of Children		
	One	Two	Three
up to £10,000	£2,268	£3,962	£5,662
£15,000	£1,690	£3,380	£5,070
£20,000	£545	£1,420	£3,138
£25,000 to £50,000	£545	£545	£545
£55,000	£210	£210	£210

The Inland Revenue Web site has a calculator you can use at `www.taxcredits.inlandrevenue.gov.uk` to make a dry run to see if you qualify. The sum it produces (if any) is the amount between the date you log on to the site (deemed to be the day of claiming) and the end of the tax year.

Someone claiming on 6 December, for instance, would get a third of the sum in the table above as there are four months (one-third) left of the 12-month tax year. This is worked out on a day-by-day basis, so it can still be worthwhile claiming a few days before the end of the tax year.

Gaining a trust from the government

The government introduced a Child Trust Fund in 2005. This fund will give a £250 special bonus to every child born on or after 1 September 2002. Children born between the start date in 2002 and the introduction of the scheme in 2005 will find their trust fund earns up to £27 in extra interest depending on when the child was born.

Children born to families on lower incomes may qualify for a top-up of a further £250, for a total £500 (with the corresponding extra interest to those born between 1 September 2002 and the starting date for payments). To receive this additional sum, parents must be means-tested by the Inland Revenue, although it will go automatically to those children whose families already claim Working Family Tax Credit and certain other state benefits.

The money will be free of all taxes both to the children themselves and to their parents.

The fund will grow in a special tax-free Child Trust Fund for each child, to which anyone – including parents, grandparents, and friends – can contribute provided all contributions added together do not top £1,200 per year.

The great advantage of the Child Trust Funds is that they enable parents to give the equivalent of £100 a month to each child without worrying about their own tax position. It also gives children an extension to their tax-free allowance.

As a parent, you will be able to select how the money is invested from a range that will include shares and bonds as well as risk-free savings. You have a year from the birth of your child (or the official start of the scheme) in which to make the investment. If you do not take this opportunity, the Inland Revenue will invest the money on behalf of your child into one of a number of selected funds.

Neither you nor your children will be able to withdraw the trust fund until your child reaches 18. But once that age is reached, there are no restrictions on taking the money out or on how it is spent.

The plan is for the government to give these funds a further cash boost when the child reaches age seven. But the amount has yet to be announced.

Receiving help with childcare costs

If your income is low enough to qualify you for Working Tax Credit, you may also be able to claim help with the costs of child care. If there are two parents, both must work at least 16 hours a week unless one is incapacitated, in hospital, or in prison.

Childcare help amounts to 70 per cent of the actual costs up to an actual cost maximum of £135 per week for one child and £200 a week for two or more children. In cash terms, this equals a maximum £94.50 a week for one child and £140 a week for two or more children.

The childcare provider has to be registered or approved. This can include pre- or after-school clubs, as well as nurseries and registered childminders. It can also include carers who come to your home such as au pairs and nannies under rules coming into force in April 2005 when a new childcare approval scheme starts. The Inland Revenue conducts spot checks to look at whether the claimed childcare actually happens, as well as to verify the qualifications of the carers.

Don't try getting your mum or dad or the child's older brothers and sisters to do the caring and then expect some government help. Family members are excluded from the scheme unless they are registered childminders looking after the children of other people as well or own a registered nursery.

You might have a low income (or make a loss) when starting out in self-employment. So even though you expect to earn high sums eventually, you might be able to claim for this extra childcare help and additional child tax credits at the beginning of your self-employment. If you have set up a company of your own, you might qualify for a higher level of child-related credits and childcare help if the income you receive from the company (whether as dividends or salary) is sufficiently low. The Inland Revenue looks at your total earnings in the last complete tax year before the year in which you claim.

Chapter 6

Taxing Issues in Your Golden Years

● ●

In This Chapter

▶ Looking at retirement and beyond

▶ Taking tax advantage of pension benefits

▶ Reaping age-related perks

● ●

*N*o one owns up to being old. Euphemisms such as 'senior citizen' or 'retired' or even 'post-work person' abound. And the gap between older people and younger people in terms of culture, music, and clothes is far narrower than it was a generation ago.

These days, it seems only the Inland Revenue has very strict ideas about older people. Up to 64 years and 364 days, you're treated just the same as a person of 24 years and 364 days. But once you arrive at the tax year in which your 65th birthday occurs you are in for special, and usually better, tax treatment.

In this chapter, I fill you in on the perks of reaching late middle age and point out ways to avoid some of the tax traps.

Retiring More or Less Completely

The distinction between working age and retirement age is increasingly blurred. People often move gradually into retirement instead of working full-time one day and doing nothing for the rest of their lives on the next.

Realising when age does – and doesn't – matter

For many people, the idea of a fixed retirement age has gone out of the window. People retire at all sorts of ages – or sometimes not at all. There's a lot of choice, except as far as the Inland Revenue is concerned.

Currently, the Inland Revenue starts giving age-related benefits at age 65 for men and women. This is despite the present state retirement age for women (60), which will disappear over the coming years as the female state pension age moves upwards to 65. This affects women born between April 6 1950 and April 5 1955. All younger women have a state retirement age of 65.

Working on past retirement age

There's nothing to stop you working past the state retirement age – and your wage packet may get fatter as a consequence. Once you reach State Pension age you no longer have to pay national insurance in any of its shapes and forms.

You have to ask the Inland Revenue for a 'certificate of exemption' to give to your employer. Your boss doesn't gain on this deal: Your employer still has to pay national insurance for you until you quit working.

For employed people, the saving in tax year 2005–06 from not paying national insurance is worth 11p in each £1 earned between £94 and £630 a week. For any amount more than £630 a week, you save 1p in each £1.

If you carry on working for an employer either full or part time past your retirement age, the employer continues deducting tax under the PAYE system. But there's nothing to stop you working for yourself, maybe cashing in on a craft interest such as dressmaking or gardening.

You have to do a self assessment tax return if you have sparetime earnings from self-employment after your state retirement age just as you would before your retirement. These earnings are added to your pension payments to produce an overall figure for taxation purposes.

One difference is that you won't have to pay any national insurance on your self-employment earnings. The self-employed over state retirement age with self-employment earnings topping £4,345 a year will save £2.10 a week because they will not have to pay the national insurance Class 2 payments applicable once you pass this earnings threshold.

And those past the state retirement age will not have to pay Class 4 national insurance either. So this will save a further eight per cent of their profits between £4,895 and £32,760 compared with someone aged under state retirement age. These rates apply to the 2005–06 tax year and are likely to change in future years.

Paying Attention to Your Pension

Your pension, whether from the state, an employer, or an insurance company, counts as income. So it's taxable.

Any occupational pension is adjusted to take care of what you receive from the state before arriving at a tax deduction figure. The pension payer, usually a firm you used to work for, adds your state pension to your occupational pension to get an overall sum. The pension payer then works out your tax on that. So if your state pension is £5,000 a year and your occupational pension is £8,000, your pension payer taxes you on £13,000, sending the tax via the PAYE system.

If you do not receive the full state pension, either because you fail to qualify in part or completely or because you have chosen to defer it so that you get a larger sum each month later on, check to ensure that you are not being taxed on amounts you are not receiving. You don't want to pay tax on money you don't have!

Claiming your tax-free lump sum

Most work-related pensions, and all personal pensions, allow you to claim a lump sum paid to you out of the pension plan free of all taxes. Typically, a personal pension offers a 25 per cent tax-free lump sum.

What you do with the lump sum is up to you. You can spend it, invest it, give it away.

The flipside of taking the lump sum is a lower pension because there is less left in your pension pot after the lump sum is taken out. But even if you want a higher pension every month, you should still take the lump sum. Why? Because you can use the tax-free lump sum to buy a tax-saving annuity.

Buying an annuity to save tax

Whether it's from a former employer or from a personal pension, your income in retirement is taxed. But you can convert your tax-free lump sum (and any other savings you think fit) into an income for the rest of your life via an annuity.

An *annuity* is like life insurance in reverse. Instead of you paying premiums each month and your family receiving a big lump sum if you die, you pay over a lump sum and then receive a monthly income until you die. You obviously do better if you live for 20 to 30 years rather than 20 to 30 months.

Table 6-1 sets out definitions of the annuity types.

Table 6-1	Types of Annuities and Their Benefits	
Annuity Type	**Definition**	**Tax Implications**
Compulsory	A retirement income for life plan bought from a personal pension fund	The entire payment is taxed as income.
Purchased	A retirement income for life plan bought from any other money	Only the investment element is taxed. The repayment of your lump sum savings is tax free.

How much less you pay depends on some really complicated calculations. Everyone is different. Purchased life annuities can work better for people with short life expectancy perhaps because they are ill, or are old, because the return of capital element is greater.

The arithmetic is complicated. Obviously, the higher the investment return, the more tax is due. But the older you are when you start a purchased annuity, the more comes back to you tax free. Men, who tend to live shorter lives than women, also do better because more of each purchased annuity is treated as a tax-free return of capital rather than a taxable investment gain.

Jamil has a pension pot worth £20,000, which he turns in its entirety into a £2,000 a year pension via an annuity. He pays tax on the entire £2,000. Aleysha also has a pension pot of £20,000. She takes the 25 per cent tax-free lump of £5,000. The remaining £15,000 has to be invested in an annuity from which she receives £1,500 a year, the same rate as Jamil (women get paid less normally when they are the same age as a man, but Aleysha is older than Jamil). Aleysha can spend the tax-free lump sum how she wishes but decides to invest it in a second purchased life annuity to boost her pension income. She gets £500 a year from her remaining £5,000. Both Jamil and Aleysha started with equal pension pots and now both have £2,000 a year income before tax. But Jamil will pay more of his income away in tax than Aleysha.

Making Much of Age-Related Allowances

Irrespective of whether you are a woman or a man, and, equally, ignoring whether you are still in full-time work or now well into your retirement, the age-related personal tax allowance comes into force in the tax year when you reach 65. This is an individual allowance – it does not matter how old your spouse or partner is. You also receive this if you have dependant children.

The tax allowance goes up from £4,895 (2005–06) a year for the under 65s to £7,090 a year when you reach 65 until you're 74.

Provided you have sufficient income to use all the allowance, you save £482.90 a year in 2005–06. It is possible that all of the extra personal allowance will fall within the ten per cent lower-rate band so then your maximum saving will be £219.50 in hard cash terms. Those entirely in the ten per cent band get less because each pound of the allowance only gets them a 10p tax reduction instead of the 22p going to those on the basic 22 per cent band. And what happens to those who pay top-rate tax? They don't get the age allowance at all.

When you turn 75, the age allowance goes up to £7,220. That means people of this age get to save up to a further £28.60 (the gap between the two rates multiplied by 22p) a year. That's not too much but when there is someone in a household of that age, the television license comes for free, worth another £121 a year. So, that's a bit of compensation!

If your income, including your state pension, is too low to benefit from the age-related allowance, you can apply for a pension credit. Like all credits, this is means-tested. Your local Department of Work and Pensions office has more details. Or you can try Citizens Advice.

Losing out due to the age-allowance trap

You may notice that my calculations make no mention of those who pay the 40 per cent tax rate. That's not because I can't get my calculator to work out the sums. The real reason is that age allowance, at both 65- and 75-year-old levels, disappears for incomes that fall into the top tax rate. This *age-allowance trap* hits those with total income exceeding £19,500 a year (in 2005–06).

It's not just the very well-off older people who lose out. Many basic-rate tax-payers with incomes of little more than half to two-thirds the top rate starting level also lose out on their age allowance. Why? Because you pay a really high tax rate on each extra pound you earn once you hit the level where the age allowance starts to evaporate.

Once you top £19,500 a year in income, the age allowance goes down by £1 for every £2 of income you earn above that level until it falls back down to the same as the personal allowance for those aged under 65.

So the gap is twice the number of pounds between the under-65 personal allowance and the age-related rate. For someone aged 65 to 74, the gap in 2005–06 is £4,390, so the benefit stops entirely once your income reaches £23,890 (£19,500 plus £4,390). If you're 75 or older, the age trap disappears altogether at £24,150 (£19,500 plus £4,890). The £4,890 gap is twice the value of the 75-plus age allowance because you lose on a £1 for £2 basis.

This only affects basic-rate payers. Those not paying tax or who are on the ten per cent band don't have enough income to hit the trap. And top-rate payers are so far above the trap that they don't even notice it.

Within the trap band, every extra £1 you earn costs a 33p tax deduction. This sum is made up of the standard 22p plus one half (11p) of the 22p in tax relief that's lost for each £2. So for income caught in the trap, it's just like having a special, ultra-high 33 per cent tax rate.

Escaping the tax trap

There's not much you can do if your income comes from pensions or an employer and you fall into the age trap. But if you have income from investments or other non-work sources, you may be able to find a partial or total escape route.

If you're married and close to the level at which age allowance is reduced, consider transferring income-producing assets to the lower-earning partner.

Savings that can save tax

Income from savings such as Individual Savings Accounts, National Savings Certificates, venture capital trusts, and enterprise investment schemes are all tax free. So they don't count against your total income for age trap purposes.

Nor do withdrawals from insurance bonds, such as with-profits bonds, count provided they do not exceed five per cent of the original investment in any tax year. You can add up any unused five per cent parcels from previous years. If you missed ten years, you could have 50 per cent of your money. And if you did nothing for 20 years or longer, you could take all your original cash.

A further alternative is to use offshore roll-up accounts. These are offered by a number of banks in places like Jersey,

Guernsey, and the Isle of Man. Instead of your taking your interest every year and paying tax on it, you leave it there to grow and pay no tax until you bring it home to spend. That way, you can choose when to pay tax on it, so you could bring the interest back when you have a lower than usual income from other sources.

Capital gains don't count against age allowances, so investments that produce little or no income but aim to give capital profits can be helpful – if you want to take the risks involved. Chapter 14 explains investment vehicles.

Giving some of it away

Generous older people can reduce their income below the age-allowance trap with a Gift Aid donation to charity. You can do this with any registered charity or, if you are not too sure or want to spread the money around several, then go to the Web site of the Charities Aid Foundation, a sort of charity clearing house, at www.cafonline.org.uk.

Suppose your total income is £20,500. You are caught in the age-allowance trap by £1,000. Give £1,000 away to charity and you take all that money from the age-trap zone. If you had not given it away, you would only have £667 left to spend after the 33 per cent tax that hits every pound in the trap. But because you're generous, you give that £667 away to a good cause. And because the Inland Revenue recognises your generosity with tax relief, the charity gets the £333 tax deducted. Adding that back to your £667 means the charity gets the full £1,000. Most charities are happy to help you with the paperwork.

Chapter 7

Preparing for the Inevitable: Death and Taxes

In This Chapter

▶ Looking at Inheritance Tax

▶ Seeking to reduce the bill through spending and giving

▶ Buying an annuity

▶ Mapping out the importance of a will

'*B*ut in this world nothing can be said to be certain, except death and taxes,' wrote Benjamin Franklin in 1789. More than two centuries later, nothing has changed. We are all doomed to die. Taxes are everywhere. And, putting the two together, a large slice of what you accumulate in your lifetime is destined to go to the Inland Revenue after your demise in the shape of Inheritance Tax.

I'm not going to pretend this is a cheerful chapter, but that doesn't mean you should skip it. This chapter is the one in which I show you ways to make the most of your money in your final years and afterwards – whether you choose to leave the maximum for the next generations or to grow old 'disgracefully', spending as freely as you can and having fun with your money.

Inheritance Tax (which I call IHT from now on) has often been called a voluntary tax because you have so many ways of either avoiding it altogether or reducing its impact. Going on a spending spree is one way to take the bite out of IHT; I fill you in on heaps of other ways as well.

Passing On Inheritance Tax: Figuring the Final Take

In one way, IHT (Inheritance Tax) is very simple. When you die, your *executors*, the personal representatives who look after your estate, add up the value of everything you owned and report the total (minus some deductions) to the Inland Revenue. The Inland Revenue takes 40 per cent of what's left after the IHT allowance (£275,000 in 2005–06) – assuming anything is.

What's added in

When the Inland Revenue adds up everything, that means everything – your house, your savings, your investments (yes, even those Individual Savings Accounts that you bought because of their tax-free status), any valuables such as jewellery and artwork, your cars, your life insurance policies (many of them anyway), and any debts other people owed to you when you died.

Oh, and then just to rub more salt in the wound, the taxman counts certain gifts you made to others in the seven years before you died. (For more information on the seven-year rule, see the 'Giving money with potential' section later in the chapter.)

All these assets are valued on the date you died or when you gave them away (if that was before you died), not the day you bought them or when you wrote a will, assuming you did.

What doesn't count

After adding all your assets together, the taxman then subtracts the cost of your funeral, any debts you have such as credit card bills or mortgages, money you leave to charity and some other organisations (see the upcoming 'Being generous without pain' section), certain exemptions, and a free slice of £275,000.

Technically known as the *nil rate band* (because the rate of tax on this slice is zero), £275,000 is the deductible figure for the

2005–06 tax year. Every estate is allowed to distribute assets –
tax free – up to the threshold set by the nil rate band. It's
when an estate is valued at more than the nil rate band that
paying IHT becomes necessary.

If you give away property that, even when added to the value
of your estate, is worth less than the nil rate band, your estate
has no IHT worries. If all the estate falls under the nil rate
threshold, it doesn't matter whether any single gift or transfer
is exempt or not.

The threshold amount for the nil rate band usually goes up
each year roughly in line with general inflation. It doesn't rise to
take in big jumps in assets such as houses or shares. But then,
it doesn't go down either if property or equities slump in value.

Being generous without pain

Gifts to charities escape the IHT net no matter whether they
are made before you die or are bequeathed in your will. If you
feel like it, you can also hand over cash and other assets to
museums, libraries, and universities. Charities and other
organisations that depend on money left in wills can and will
help you out with the technicalities.

And MPs are not stupid. Many years ago, they made a special
exemption for money and other property left to mainstream
political parties. To qualify, a political party must have at least
two MPs or one MP and at least 150,000 votes for its candi-
dates at the most recent general election. Local and European
elections don't count.

Exemptions for certain service personnel

The estates of UK military personnel
are tax exempt on death if the death
is due to wounds or diseases from
active service. The death does not
have to be immediate. Old war
wounds can count. In 1978, the high
court decided that the Duke of
Westminster's death in 1967 was due
to the effects of wartime wounds he
received while on active service in
1944.

Discounting business assets

The value of a business that you have owned for at least two years does not count for IHT calculations.

This exemption applies whether the business is a registered company or is unincorporated (such as a sole proprietor or a partnership structure). This rule extends to agricultural properties such as farms and to woodlands.

It also applies to any property you operate as a business. This does not include buy-to-let properties but does include holiday properties provided you let them only for short-term lets (usually up to a month), you do not use the property yourself, you do not let friends and family stay there for free or a token rent, and that you either advertise it yourself or use a specialist holiday let agency.

Unquoted shares are counted as business assets. And this includes shares in companies listed on the Alternative Investment Market (AIM).

How the taxable total is figured

When calculating the total tax due on an estate, the Inland Revenue looks at the value of the estate, subtracts the gifts that aren't taxable and adds up the amounts of other bequests and determines whether they're under the nil rate band. Remember that the nil rate band is the first £275,000 (in 2005–06) left after the deductions. The band remains the same whatever your estate is worth – even if it's valued in millions.

When figuring the totals, lifetime gifts such as PETs (see the upcoming 'Giving money with potential') use up the nil rate band before anything else that is given away on death. The IHT rate is 40 per cent on whatever is left after the deductions – there's no starter rate or lower rate. So doesn't that mean that the Inland Revenue has it all its own way? Well, no, because there are many defensive measures you can adopt. Later sections in this chapter talk about deductions the estate can take for certain gifts you made in the seven years before death, and for business assets.

Spending Your Way Out of IHT

Most IHT advice, and there is a big, profitable industry supplying it, focuses on how to maximise the amount you leave to succeeding generations. But you don't have to bequeath them anything. Consider spending rather than saving. It's your choice whether you leave your loved ones money or spend it on yourself.

Figures from the Office for National Statistics show the typical 30-year-old woman should live to 80 while her male counterpart should make 75. And these are only averages. People with more money – those who are likely to fall into the IHT net – tend to outlive the average because more money helps pay for a healthier lifestyle. So, assuming a typical 27-year gap between generations, your children could be well into their 50s, and your grandchildren into their early 20s when you die. Ask yourself whether your children and grandchildren need an inheritance. Do they deserve one? Do they even want your money or would they rather you spent it on yourself?

If you decide to leave something to your family, consider *generation skipping* in which you leave cash and other assets to your grandchildren rather than to your children. The advantage is that youngsters have far longer to live than their parents before they have to worry about IHT (or whatever the next death-duty tax is called).

Looking at life expectancy

If you are going to have fun with the money you accumulate over a lifetime, it makes sense to know how much longer you're likely to live. Table 7-1 shows life expectancy for men and women at a range of ages.

Table 7-1	Life Expectancy by Gender	
Present Age	**Life Expectancy for Females**	**Life Expectancy for Males**
30	79 years 11 months	74 years 11 months
40	80 years 3 months	75 years 4 months
50	80 years 10 months	76 years 2 months
60	82 years 1 month	77 years 10 months
65	83 years 1 month	79 years 3 months
70	84 years 6 months	81 years 2 months
75	86 years 3 months	83 years 7 months
80	88 years 5 months	86 years 5 months
85	91 years 1 month	89 years 9 months
90	94 years 4 months	93 years 6 months
95	98 years 1 month	97 years 6 months
100	102 years 3 months	101 years 10 months

Source: English Life Tables, Office of National Statistics

The table shows typical life expectancy; your actual life expectancy could vary greatly! You have to account for a whole host of other factors such as your family situation and history, your health background, and what kind of work you do.

Of course, how long you're likely to live has nothing directly to do with IHT legislation. But if you can work out an approximation of how much money you will probably need over the rest of your life (not forgetting to add on a slice for rising prices and unforeseen circumstances as well as for living a lot longer than you expected), you can see how much, if any, you can afford to give away to your family, other people, and the causes you support.

Getting an idea about how long you'll live is important also because the tax status of some gifts depends on whether you live for seven years after you give the money away (see the later section, 'Giving money with potential').

Making sure you have a home

IHT is worked out on all your assets on death, including the value of your home. The value of a home, especially if it's paid for, or nearly paid for, often puts an estate over the nil rate band. You can make use of a few techniques to avoid your property putting your heirs into the IHT net:

- You can **downsize** your property to live in something smaller (or in a cheaper area) and spend the difference.

- You can **take up an equity release plan**. Such plans lend you money to use during your lifetime against all or part of the value of your home. The loan plus all the accumulated interest is repaid out of your estate when you die, which reduces the value of your remaining estate for IHT purposes.

- You can **give your home away but continue to live in it**. You have to pay a fair rent according to the market value, and you must be subject to a contract that gives the new owner the right to evict you providing legal notice is given (so you may end up homeless). The new owners have to account for the rent received and pay income tax on it. This arrangement is usually between parents and children. Note that such deals are coming under heavier than ever tax scrutiny to make sure they are for real and not just a tax dodge.

- If you really want to grow old in a spend, spend, spend fashion, you can **sell your house and rent** somewhere.

Giving Your Way Out of IHT

You can reduce the value of your eventual estate in many ways without incurring the wrath of an IHT charge by giving your wealth away before you die. Such gifts are known as *exempt transfers*, and in this section, I tell you how to make the best use of the available options.

The main rules of giving are that your generosity must not reduce your standard of living and it must be from your income – pensions, earnings from work, interest on bank accounts, dividends from shares, and so on – rather than from your capital – the amount you have tied up in savings, shares, and property.

Avoiding dubious deals

Accountants and lawyers (and mates in pubs) keep coming up with dubious schemes to let people have their cake, and eat it too. Most often this involves giving away property and assets to a third party but continuing to use them.

Don't follow such wrong-headed advice. Any gift has to be without reservation. You can't give something away and then ask for it back or continue to use it. Your executors have to be able to show

- ✔ Complete possession and enjoyment of the property was given over to the new owner.

- ✔ The new owner had total control over who could use the asset.

- ✔ The asset was enjoyed 'virtually to the entire exclusion of the donor'. So if you give your children your home, you can visit it from time-to-time but you can not live there, and you have to have a different permanent address. And if you gave them a valuable painting, you could look at it when you visited them but they could not lend it back to you.

The Inland Revenue actively tries to shut such schemes down. It has even backdated orders that make schemes worthless on some plans.

No set of tax rules last forever. Just in my lifetime I've seen IHT, its predecessor Capital Transfer Tax, and Estate Duty, the death tax that preceded that. All these plans had different rules. There are persistent rumours that IHT is due for a replacement, or at least, a substantial makeover. So far, this has not happened but no one can be sure.

So be wary of signing on – and paying – for schemes that could be worthless by the time you're ready to put them into action. You (or your heirs) cannot normally sue an adviser if you buy a scheme that subsequently fails to work.

Reducing your estate as you grow older

Sensible IHT planning includes giving away money or other property that you can afford to dispose of in a way that does not contravene the rules. The goal is to reduce the size of your estate when you die so less (or nothing) goes in IHT. Don't forget that some gifts can be hit by the tax if you fail to live for seven years after making them.

Spending money every day

Normal spending takes in more than just your day-to-day living expenses.

It can include paying into life insurance premiums on a regular basis. These payments can be useful because the proceeds of life insurance policies can be written in trust so as to avoid the IHT net when you die. A policy written in trust bypasses your will and goes straight to family members and isn't subject to IHT.

And you can usually count regular payments to grandchildren and others for purposes such as educational fees and living expenses. You could set up a system to give someone regular payments of your income, so long as the amount you give is over and above what you need to maintain your lifestyle. This can be variable, fluctuating from year to year. For example, say you need £10,000 a year to meet your normal expenses. Your income one year is £12,000, so you could give £2,000 to your favourite grandchild. If your income drops to £11,000 the next year, then you can reduce the payment to £1,000 for that year.

The rule about normal spending being from income and not capital or savings is accepted as a grey area. Some people, for instance, pay for holidays out of savings rather than from their regular income because it is more convenient.

Dispensing gifts

You can reduce the size of your estate by giving your assets away. In this section, I look at some of the simplest ways to do this and stay within the tax rules. If you can afford to give £3,000 away, for example, you could be saving £1,200 or 40 per cent in a future tax charge.

- ✔ **Annual exemption:** You can give a total of £3,000 a year away without any worries. And if you miss out on a year, or don't give the full £3,000 away any year, you can make up the difference the following tax year. But you can only go back one year in this way.

  There is nothing to stop one spouse giving money to the other for distribution as gifts to children or grandchildren or any others. So a married couple has two allowances a year to hand on to others, equal to £6,000, or £12,000 if they missed out in full on the previous year.

- ✔ **Small gift exemption:** You can give away a limitless number of gifts worth up to £250 without affecting any other allowance. You could give 100 people £250 each if you wanted. But you can't give the same person more than one such gift each tax year or give up to £250 to someone who has already gained from one of the other exemptions. Nor can you give £300 and expect to count the first £250 against the small-gift exemption. Once you top £250, the entire amount of that gift is then set against the £3,000 annual exemption. Someone giving £300 would have £2,700 left in their annual free slice.

- ✔ **Gifts on marriage:** You can give up to £5,000 to your child upon his or her marriage, whether the child is legitimate, illegitimate, adopted, or even a stepchild. Grandparents may give up to £2,500, while others – everyone else other than parents and grandparents – can give up to £1,000. These gifts can be in cash or in the value of goods and the present should be given before (or at) the wedding. If you leave it until later, this special tax saving does not apply so it would be back to the £3,000 a year limit.

  This exemption is for each marriage. If you are a parent and have two children marrying in the same year, you can give each one the maximum. The allowance does not have to be shared.

- ✔ **Gifts of interest:** You can lend money interest free without having to account for any tax on the interest you have given up. You can help a family member with getting on the housing ladder with a loan, for instance. There are no limits on this but it has to be returned to your estate on your death.

The gift amounts are far from generous. This is unsurprising, as they have not been updated since 1984!

Sharing with your spouse

You can transfer assets to your spouse either during your lifetime or in your will without any thought to the tax implications. You can move as much as you like, whenever you like, to your partner in marriage, provided both of you live in the UK. Anything you leave to your legally wed wife or husband on your death is IHT-free.

Notice the words *marriage* and *legally wed* in the previous paragraph. The legislation does not stretch to unmarried partners, no matter how long they have lived together or how many children they have together, or if one is wholly or largely dependant on the other. Nor does it apply to same-sex partnerships, again no matter how long established unless they register for a Civil Partnership. However, transfers between spouses who are separated, but not divorced, qualify as exempt.

Every estate is allowed a tax-free slice (£275,000 for the 2005–06 tax year). But if a spouse passes assets to their partner, taking advantage of the exemption rule on transfers between married people, then this £275,000 nil rate band does not apply on these assets in the will of the first partner to die. So if one spouse gives the other £275,000 and then dies, the surviving spouse can't claim that £275,000 is outside the IHT net because it's in the zero rate band. Tax logic says that anything that is exempt is not taxed and so does not qualify for a zero rate. The effect of this is that when the second partner dies, there is only one tax-free slice as the other is lost forever. The £275,000 counts towards the estate of the second spouse. The only way around this is for one spouse to leave the £275,000 to others. But often that is not practical as it would leave the widow or widower penniless.

Wherever possible, arrange matters to use the nil rate band to make gifts to family members and beneficiaries other than your spouse. That way, it is not lost.

Giving money with potential

Any money you give away during your lifetime that doesn't fall under the exempt transfer rules may escape IHT as a Potentially Exempt Transfer, known lovingly in the tax trade as a PET. PETs don't have limits. It's all to do with giving assets away and then living at least seven years.

The potential for a gift to be totally exempt, and hence remain outside IHT, depends on one circumstance – whether you live for seven years after making the gift.

You can give away as much as you want, and provided you die at least seven years after giving it, the amount is not subject to IHT.

Settling before seven years

No one can ever guarantee living the seven years so that a potentially exempt transfer becomes actually exempt.

If you die within seven years of giving a PET, the transfer counts for taper relief, which can reduce the tax payable. Table 7-2 shows the sliding scale used to determine tax liability on gifts given between three and seven years before the giver's death.

Table 7-2	Taper Relief for PETs	
Years after PET	*Reduction*	*Actual Tax Rate*
Zero to three years	0%	40%
Three to four years	20%	32%
Four to five years	40%	24%
Five to six years	60%	16%
Six to seven years	80%	8%

Taper relief is only of real benefit if you can also fully use the nil rate band for other transfers. Taper amounts are set against the free slice first. (See 'What doesn't count' earlier in the chapter for more on the nil rate band.)

But if you gave £100,000 away and then die four years later leaving a further £300,000 in your will, the £100,000 lifetime gift counts against your nil rate band first. So your estate would have £175,000 left in the free slice to set off against the remaining £300,000. Not fair! So your family will end up paying as much as if you had not made the transfer at all!

Taper relief is worthwhile, however, for those with large estates. Giving away £1 million and living for seven years takes the gift out of the IHT net. But if you only live for six years, the £1 million less the free slice is charged at 8 per cent tax instead of 40 per cent. Obviously, anything that is transferred through a will at death is hit with the full 40 per cent as the zero band has been used up.

If you can afford to give assets away, do so as soon as you are able so that you don't risk falling foul of the seven-year rule.

Insuring your PET

This is nothing to do with cats and dogs, of course. If you are in a position to make a sizeable PET and are worried about how long you will live, you can cover the potential tax bill with a special life insurance policy, designed to fit in with the tax taper. The proceeds of the policy can be written in trust so they are outside your estate when you die. (I talk about trusts in 'Drawing Up a Sensible Will' later in this chapter.)

Whether such a policy is worthwhile depends on the rates charged for cover. These will be based on your age, sex, and health when you start.

Turning Capital into an Income

If you have substantial savings, you could turn your capital into a regular cash income through an *annuity* – an insurance company plan that pays a guaranteed income for life in return for forgoing the lump sum used to buy it.

Buying an annuity reduces the value of your estate and so takes the original cost of the annuity out of the IHT net. You can opt for a higher income (and better standard of living) rather than leaving it all in your will to be taxed at 40 per cent.

Not living to enjoy an inheritance

Here's a bit of tax generosity, known as *quick succession relief.* There are special rules that reduce the IHT payable on assets that were inherited within the previous two to five years by the person who has died. This prevents the Inland Revenue potentially getting IHT twice over.

The value of quick succession relief is most potent up to two years. It tapers off over five years. The arithmetic can be complicated but the vital tax-saving point is to apply for it! If executors do not ask, it will not be given as there is no way the Inland Revenue could possibly know where assets come from.

Here's how the choice works. If you have £100,000 spare and leave it in a bank until you die, IHT could take £40,000 (40 per cent), leaving £60,000. Were you to buy an annuity for £100,000, taking the money out of the IHT calculation, you are only really paying £60,000 for that lifetime income so whatever rate you get is enhanced.

For example, a £100,000 annuity pays £10,000 a year guaranteed until you die. By taking that sum out of your estate, your real payment is £60,000. The lower sum would only get you £6,000 a year, so you are really getting two-thirds more! This could give you a regular income to give away.

Annuities end on death but you can guarantee the income for a fixed period so it will be paid for at least five or ten years irrespective of whether you die the next day or in 30 years' time. This can be a good idea if you expect a partner or dependant to outlive you.

Drawing Up a Sensible Will

That last will and testament is an obvious help to those who are dealing with your estate after you die. It can save tax, too.

Setting up trusts

Married couples can use wills to ensure that, where possible, only the free slice is given away on the first death, with the remaining spouse inheriting the balance. This gives the survivor more time to enjoy what is left and, possibly, use the seven-year rule (discussed in the preceding 'Giving money with potential' section) to give other assets away.

Couples can also set up a discretionary trust. Property and other assets in the trust do not count as part of the estate. This is not a do-it-yourself option so it needs a lawyer.

The proceeds of life insurance policies written in trust escape the IHT net. The life insurance company can make the arrangements for you even after you have taken out the policy. It's not a DIY option.

Setting up a trust can save tax in one way but cause tax charges from another direction. There are tax charges on transferring assets into a trust, and income generated by a trust is taxed at 40 per cent, no matter what the personal tax rate of anyone involved. Always take extreme care where two taxes can potentially interface.

Making specific bequests

Make specific bequests where possible, especially if you want to leave money to non-tax-payers such as children. A *specific bequest* is one in which you quote the source of the funds for the bequest. For example, your will may dictate '£10,000 from my savings account at ABC Bank' or 'the entire balance of my savings account at XYZ Building Society' rather than a non-specific £10,000. Making a specific bequest removes the designated money from your estate and gives it directly to your heir. That way, they can claim back any tax paid on the interest after your death.

When you die, your personal allowances against income tax die with you. So even if you paid no tax on interest from savings or were on the lower 10 per cent rate, the Inland Revenue will take the 20 per cent savings tax on interest generated from money you leave even if all the money is due to go to non-tax-payers. This rate goes up to 40 per cent if the assets are not distributed within two years.

Rewriting a will

Providing all the beneficiaries from the will are in agreement, they can rewrite a will after someone dies or write one if they died without leaving a will. This is called a *deed of variation. Wills, Probate, & Inheritance Tax For Dummies* by Julian Knight (Wiley) delves further into the processes of writing and rewriting a will.

The deed can be used to make better use of the nil rate band. Or it can help with *generation skipping,* in which money is left to a grandchild or great-grandchild. This keeps money out of the IHT for possibly six or seven decades rather than giving the money to an older child who might already be retired and face their own IHT planning problems in a few years' time.

Part III
You Work Therefore You're Taxed

In this part . . .

The vast majority of working people work for someone else. I show you why that's good news as the Pay As You Earn (PAYE) tax system makes life easy for employees. It leaves many with nothing more to do tax-wise. It's the boss who has to do most, and sometimes all, of the work. And it's the boss who has to pick up the tab if something goes wrong, even if the employee profits. Amazing.

So if employment is so simple, why bother with this part of *Paying Less Tax for Dummies*? The reason is because you have choices. You can work for yourself with big tax advantages and disadvantages. And I give you the low-down on your tax coding, show you many tax savings ranging from cycles to computers, and explain how you can take a share in your employer's business. That help comes with assistance from your friendly tax inspector. Naturally.

Chapter 8

Working for Someone Else

*P*ay As You Earn (PAYE) is a particularly British invention designed towards the end of the Second World War to collect income tax at a time when more and more people were falling into the tax net.

Today, with virtually everyone in work having some sort of Inland Revenue relationship, PAYE has become increasingly sophisticated. But it can deduct too much, especially when you change jobs. You will get overpayments back – eventually. In the meantime, you don't want the hassle. So it's best to check what's going on. And that's the main purpose of this chapter.

Delving into the Mysteries of PAYE and its Codes

PAYE (Pay As You Earn) is a tax-collecting system in which your employer deducts income tax from your pay packet and sends the money on to the Inland Revenue. It is run in parallel with the national insurance deduction scheme.

It's up to employers to collect both PAYE and national insurance on a monthly basis. This responsibility extends to casual labour and to other individuals, such as IT contractors, who prefer to be self-employed.

Your PAYE tax code tells your employer how much tax to deduct from your pay packet. If the code is wrong, you can end up paying too much or too little tax. The code consists of two parts – a number followed by a letter. The number gives the Inland Revenue and your employer an indication of the amount of your allowance; the letter shows what type of tax allowances you're claiming. This knowledge is of most use when tax allowances change.

Your PAYE code should take in a number of elements. Besides your personal allowance, which will increase if you are 65 or over, you may be able to claim on other expenses, such as pension payments, certain job-related expenses, and professional subscriptions (dealt with more fully in Chapter 9). In addition, there are a number of other allowances you may be able to claim such as payments to a friendly society for death benefits or the blind person's allowance for you or your spouse if she or he does not earn enough to benefit. You're charged for perks such as a company car, private medical insurance, and most state benefits such as the State Pension and jobseeker's allowance.

You should also receive extra tax relief if you donate to Gift Aid and you are a top-rate tax-payer. Although, if you give more to Gift Aid than you have paid in income tax or Capital Gains Tax, then the nice people at the Inland Revenue will claw back tax relief on the charitable donation through the coding system. That's not very charitable!

Finding out what the numbers mean

The tax code number is your tax-free allowance divided by ten with fractions ignored. If you have the full personal allowance (£4,895 in 2005–06) your code is 489. Someone over 65 but under 75 has a £7,090 basic allowance, giving them a 709 code if they have a full personal allowance.

Your allowance may be reduced if you have taxable perks or receive taxable sums from investments or a spare-time job.

Someone starting with the full 489 code with a $1,000 valuation of their car benefit will end up with $3,895 in allowances or a 374 code. Add in $500 tax due on spare-time earnings and $500 in tax on savings and investments not deducted at source and the code falls to 289.

Looking at the letters

The second part of your tax code consists of a letter or combination of letters. These give those concerned with your PAYE status a quick indication of the general level of your tax allowances. They mainly help when the government announces changes to tax allowances.

The following list tells you what the most commonly used letters represent:

- ✔ **L:** The basic personal allowance.

- ✔ **P:** The allowance for those aged 65 to 74.

- ✔ **V:** The allowance for the 65-to-74 age group plus the married couple's allowance, which you qualify for if you're married and were born before 6 April 1935.

- ✔ **Y:** The personal allowance for those aged 75 or over.

- ✔ **A:** The basic personal allowance plus one half of the child tax credit. It's used if you pay the basic tax rate and share the child tax credit with your partner.

- ✔ **H:** This is similar to A; it's the basic allowance plus *all* the child tax credit.

- ✔ **K:** The code used when the total allowances you are due are not as great as the total deductions. The preceding number is negative: the higher it is, the more you pay.

  Someone who is due the personal allowance starts off with $4,895 (in 2005–06) or code 489. If they have a car benefit worth $4,000, medical insurance worth $505, extra savings tax of $500, and spare-time earnings worth $1,000 in tax, they end up with $6,005. Subtract that from $4,895 and they end up with a negative K code of 111 to reflect the $1,110 they owe. It works out the same as if they earned $1,110 more than their salary without any deductions.

T: The code you get if you ask the Inland Revenue not to use any of the others. You may, for instance, not wish the wages department to know about your other sources of income. It's also used for some special cases.

✔ **OT:** No allowances at all but tax deducted normally at the highest rate applicable to your earnings. Used usually when you have a second income source that uses up all your allowances.

✔ **BR:** The code for those whose allowances are used elsewhere. Every pound is taxed at the basic rate, currently 22 per cent. This code may be used if there is some doubt about your tax status. It's less severe on you than the OT code.

✔ **DO:** This is generally used if you are a high earner who has more than one job and have been fully credited with your allowances elsewhere. Every pound you earn is taxed at the top rate, currently 40 per cent.

✔ **NT:** No tax, usually because you are not resident in the UK for tax purposes.

Checking Your Deductions

Everything you earn from your employment, whether called wages, salary, commission, bonus, or even, for vicars, a stipend, is known as an *emolument* in Inland Revenue-speak. It does not matter whether you are paid weekly or monthly or whether you're paid in cash, cheque, or straight into a bank. All emoluments are subject to PAYE.

So, too, are many pension payments from past employers and other schemes. You can't necessarily escape PAYE by retiring. Many pension payers lump the state pension into the overall payment. That way, it is added in and subject to PAYE. But if all you have is the state pension, you don't pay any tax as your earnings are below the tax threshold.

Payments of expenses and perks (technically known as benefits-in-kind) are not in PAYE even if they are taxable. The next chapter (Chapter 9) deals with tax issues related to perks.

Checking your pay packet

All tax and national insurance deductions made by your employer should be accurate to the last penny. But you should check your pay cheque to see that nothing is wrong, especially when you start a new job or receive a salary boost (or reduction). There is always the chance of data being incorrectly input into the computer program or a small business employer getting confused with the PAYE manual.

Arriving at a ball-park figure for take-home pay

Following the steps in this sidebar gives you an estimate of how much money you'll take home each month: This formula is designed to work across tax years as it pays no attention to minor changes in personal allowances. It ignores pensions, the 10 per cent income tax starter rate, workplace charitable donations, and other deductions. But it works surprisingly well for people earning up to around £32,000 a year, which is more than 80 per cent of the employed population. Chapter 18 on self assessment shows you how to come up with an exact figure for the year. This rough formula should work with your monthly salary slip.

1. Subtract £5,000 a year from your gross salary.

   As an example, start with a salary of £23,000 a year gross. Subtracting £5,000 gives you £18,000.

2. Divide what's left by 12 to give a monthly figure because you're paid once a month.

   Dividing £18,000 by 12 gives £1,500.

3. Take away one-third of this new figure – 22% for income tax and 11% for national insurance.

   A third of £1,500 is £500; subtracting that gives £1,000.

4. Add back the £5,000 you took off at the start but divide it by 12 to turn it into a monthly figure. This sum roughly equals the money you have to spend, known as *net pay*.

   £5,000 divided by 12 gives you around £400. Adding that to the £1,000 in Step 3 gives you £1,400, which is roughly the amount your employer should deposit in your bank account each month. (The exact figure for 2005–06 is £1,439, but that takes a whole load of calculations to work out – my way is much easier! And you've actually got a £39 bonus to tide you over the end of the month!)

Meeting your national insurance obligations

Employers have to deduct national insurance where appropriate at the right amount. And they have to pay their own contribution. Failure to do so can bring similar penalties to failing to send a PAYE cheque.

Your boss should deduct national insurance at the time they issue your pay packet. They cannot normally chase you later if they forget.

Paying in

When national insurance started in 1948, everyone in employment paid a stamp at a flat rate. This payment provided you with certain benefits such as a retirement pension and payments during periods of unemployment. Today, national insurance is effectively a tax on earnings from employment until you reach the state retirement age, currently 65 for men and 60 for women. You won't get anything more by offering to pay more through PAYE!

Many benefits are tied to certain minimum payment rules that required you to contribute for a minimum number of weeks each year at the lowest level applicable to that year.

Because national insurance is under the control of the Inland Revenue, it comes under the purview of this book. After all, you need to know what you can claim and hence increase the amount you receive from the state in return for your tax pounds when you are in need.

What you pay as an employee depends on what you earn, but for most people the combination of basic rate income tax with national insurance takes 33p from every additional pound they earn after their personal allowances and the 10 per cent tax band.

By comparison, top-rate tax-payers lose 41p from every extra pound they earn once they reach the 40 per cent tax band. This is because the main 11p in the pound stops before the top tax band. The only extra national insurance anyone in the top band has to pay is a one per cent surcharge, making 41p in the pound in all. *Surcharge* is just another name for tax. And you don't get any benefits from it.

Taking out

Some state benefits are linked to national insurance, but generally to amounts based on the minimum weekly payment rather than what you might actually have paid. A *minimum payment* is the lowest level that can be taken for one week in any one tax year. But because some benefits are expressed as so many times the equivalent minimum, these can tot up faster if you pay more on higher earnings. The maximum is usually around five times the minimum, so if you pay the highest possible amount, you gain the benefit five times faster.

You have to claim many of these benefits as they are not paid automatically. Rates, which can be complicated, change from time to time. You can get more information from the Inland Revenue Web site at www.inlandrevenue.gov.uk, at local advice centres, or from charitable organisations such as Citizens Advice and the Child Poverty Action Group.

The benefits include:

- **Bereavement allowance:** Paid for one year to widows and widowers over 45 who were below pension age when their spouse died. The dead spouse would have had to have paid the equivalent of 25 minimum payments.

- **Contribution-based jobseeker's allowance:** Paid to those who are out of work up to a maximum of 26 weeks. You need to have earned enough to have paid the equivalent of at least 25 payments of the minimum weekly amount in any tax year plus at least 50 payments of the minimum weekly amount in each of the last two complete tax years as an employed person before your unemployment started. National insurance paid as a self-employed person does not count.

- **Incapacity benefit:** Paid to those with long-term illnesses or disabilities. The contribution requirements are similar to those for the contribution-based jobseeker's allowance but the self-employed can apply.

- **State retirement pension:** Currently paid to men at age 65 and over and to women age 60 or over. (The age for women will rise to 65 by 2015 on a stepped changeover from April 2010 onwards. This affects women born after April 5, 1950. It will be gradual so that a woman born in 1952 will have to wait until she is 62, one born in 1954 will have to wait until she is 64, while all of those born after April 5, 1955 will have to wait until they reach 65.) Either you or a late spouse (or former spouse) must have paid 52 times the minimum contribution in any tax year. And you have to have paid at least 52 times the minimum weekly contribution throughout your working life, although you are allowed to miss out one year in every ten. If you don't meet these minimum requirements, you may get a percentage of the full amount depending on how far you fall short.

✔ **Widowed parent's allowance:** Paid to widows and widowers with children. The contribution rules are similar to those for the state retirement pension.

If you have a period away from work, check with the Inland Revenue to see if you can have your contributions credited (usually for family care duties) or if it is worth your while buying Class 3 voluntary contributions to maintain your record.

The Class 4 contributions paid by the self-employed do not qualify for any benefits at all as this is a pure extra tax-raising exercise.

Noticing when your employer gets it wrong

Along with basic PAYE deductions, employers have a duty to check on any expenses paid without a tax deduction. For instance, someone who normally works in Manchester and is sent to London for the day can claim travelling expenses. But someone who is normally based in Manchester and is told to work in London for six months cannot claim travelling costs.

There are obviously many grey areas. But unless an employer can show the PAYE error was made in good faith (usually a polite way of saying the employee or someone else tried to pull a fast one), then the employer has to pay up.

Employers sometimes tell casual staff who demand full-time staff benefits that they will report them to the Inland Revenue for keeping their self-employed status. But any boss that does that will shoot themselves in the foot. The Inland Revenue attitude will be that the amount paid is net and the employer will be liable for tax and national insurance on top of the money already paid.

 There are very few, and very special, circumstances when the employer can go back to the employee and ask for extra tax money. Always check with an accountant, Citizens Advice, or a trade union before agreeing to such a deduction from your pay packet. Bust bosses have been known to loot pay packets before disappearing!

Pleading confusion or ignorance is not a defence for the boss. Employers who fail to pass on PAYE deductions face interest charges and penalties.

Considering Special Jobs and Special Situations

If your job falls into a special category or if you work for yourself, your PAYE requirements are a bit different. The next sections tell you how different.

PAYEing people in special jobs

If you're paying off student loans, work in the IT or buildings industry, or are employed by an agency that supplies temporary workers, your PAYE situation is out of the ordinary. The following list tells you how:

- **Agency workers:** The agency who sends you out on a job is normally responsible for your PAYE unless the firm or organisation for which you work has the same control over you, and your hours of work, as it does over full-time employees.

- **Former students with outstanding loans:** The employer has to deduct sums owed to the Student Loans Company. Employers receive notices from the Inland Revenue telling them when to start, vary, or stop deductions.

✔ **Building industry contractors:** Many of those who work in construction are referred to as 'labour-only sub-contractors'. Payments to such people can now be made on the same basis as if they were on full PAYE; or under the Construction Industry Scheme where a flat rate 18 per cent is deducted to holders of certificate CIS4 after an allowance for materials, any VAT, and any industry training board levies; or paid gross under another Construction Industry Scheme. The Inland Revenue wants to do away with all these complex schemes and replace them with one fairer and easy to understand system.

✔ **IT contractors:** Most information technology contractors who have personal service companies which provide nothing other than the services of that company's share-holders are now paid under PAYE rather than gross. They are known as IR35 workers.

Those on IR35, such as IT contractors, can deduct amounts for certain expenses they would have been given had they been the full-time employee of the firm where they are working. This can include travel to another site when ordered to do so by the firm.

PAYEing when you're on a contract or a casual worker

Part-time, casual, and contract workers have to pay PAYE and national insurance in just the same way as those on normal full-time contracts. From the government's point of view, there is no difference.

The Inland Revenue is clamping down on firms that try to pay casual and contract workers on a self-employed or freelance basis.

Losing or Leaving Your Job

A tiny number of those who lose their jobs every year end up featured in one of those newspaper 'finance-for-failure' stories that dissect once high-flying executives of major companies who collect millions after they are sacked for being useless. Don't shed too many tears for them. They are rich enough to hire lawyers and accountants to help minimise any tax take.

For mere mortals who lose their jobs due to changing economic circumstances or shifting employer needs, post-termination life is likely to be a bit less rosy. In these sections, I tell you how to cope successfully with the tax issues.

Don't forget to claim jobseeker's allowance if you are out of work but trying to find a new job. You pay for this benefit through your tax and national insurance payments, so don't ignore it. At £55.65 a week for six months (in 2005), it's not a fortune. But it will help pay for stamps to send off application forms and expenses in going to interviews.

Making the most of the magic number

The magic figure for payoffs, redundancy, or termination payments (or whatever the current euphemism may be) is £30,000. The first £30,000 of any redundancy payment is tax-free. This £30,000 includes any statutory amount you receive under the Employment Protection (Consolidation) Act 1978, which is tax-free anyway.

To calculate the statutory amount if you're between the ages of 20 and 63, you multiply your weekly pay up to £270 by one-and-a-half times the number of years you worked. So if you worked ten years and earned £250 a week, you would be entitled to 15 times (1.5×10) your £250, giving you £3,750.

The statutory payments are not that high and cannot reach the £30,000 tax-free limit. Many about-to-be-former workers manage to negotiate higher non-statutory amounts. Additional amounts should normally be paid tax-free, providing:

- You have been in the job for at least two years.

- Payments are made to all employees in the same situation and not just to a select few or part of the group.

✔ Payments are not excessively large in relation to salaries paid and length of service.

This point can be contentious. But it's designed to stop bosses paying you very little while you are working there and then sacking you with a huge redundancy payment.

The sum of £30,000 has remained unchanged for many years. But, under a complicated formula, the £30,000 exempt figure can be increased if your employment included a spell overseas. This is rarely applicable but the Inland Revenue Web site (www.inlandrevenue.gov.uk) has the complicated details.

If your redundancy payment tops £30,000, the excess is taxed as income in the normal way.

If you have to leave a job through illness, disability, or injury, try to negotiate a payoff. It will normally be paid tax-free.

When you leave an employer for whatever reason (including a voluntary resignation when quitting may be a blessed relief), you receive form P45 to take to your next job. The P45 details your earnings in the work you are leaving and helps your new boss with the PAYE computation. Check your P45 to make sure any termination payment you receive isn't included.

If you are in your fifties or older, make sure that any redundancy payoff, or golden handshake, is structured so that the Inland Revenue cannot claim it is effectively an early retirement sum and then hit the amount with a tax bill. Early retirement can include people near their normal retirement age leaving jobs to take care of aged relatives.

Heading off to temporary retirement

You might be bundled out of your workplace by an unsmiling security person with your belongings in a bin-liner. But for many employers, that is not the end of the salary story.

To stop you moving to a competitor the next day and taking up-to-date knowledge with you, your employer may structure your departure with payments in lieu of notice (known in the tax trade as Pilons).

With a *Pilon,* you receive your regular salary for a period but you do not work, and you cannot work for someone else. All you can do is to tend your garden (or go fishing or watch daytime television or do whatever else turns you on).

The good news is that you don't have to get out of bed in the morning. The bad news is that Pilons are usually taxable because the Inland Revenue argues they are a regular income from your employer, that you cannot work elsewhere, and that the payments are in line with your contract which will probably have specified a period of notice on either side.

Welcoming a golden hello

Many firms now pay *golden hellos* to induce people to leave another employer and sign on with them. The amounts paid are normally taxable as income but can escape income tax in some circumstances. These can include:

- ✔ Payments which would not have to be returned if the recipient did not turn up at work or did not work there for very long.

- ✔ Payments that have no linking to future earnings.

- ✔ Payments made to someone who has had to abandon a partnership (typically lawyers, accountants, architects) or give up self-employment to join the new employer.

- ✔ Payments made to recompense someone for tuition fees for a course or qualification that will be useful to the new employer.

The more points you can tick off in your own golden hello circumstances, the better. But as sums involved can be large, it is worth the tax authority's while to challenge them wherever there is a chance of hitting someone with a tax bill. It can be worthwhile taking specialist advice first.

Chapter 9

Paying on the Perks

● ●

In This Chapter

▶ Looking at how the extras at worked are taxed

▶ Working through the tax collector's help with your transport

▶ Discovering a range of tax-free benefits

▶ Finding out how work-related expenses can be tax-free

● ●

*Y*our employer can provide you with a wide range of extras ranging from private healthcare plans to company cars to workplace parties to the occasional free breakfast if you cycle to work.

All these non-cash items – anything that comes from your boss but not through your pay packet – are known by tax officials and accountants as *benefits-in-kind*. They're more generally called *perks*. Some are taxable; some are tax-free; and still others are partially tax-free. This chapter looks at the wide variety. Persuading your boss to give you some or any is then up to you!

Taxing those Little Extras

If you receive perks from your employer (a company car and healthcare scheme are probably the biggest), you most likely have to pay tax on their value. This value is added to your regular earnings. So, someone with a £25,000 salary and £3,000 in taxable benefits-in-kind is treated as though they earn £28,000.

Workplace perks split into three categories: Those that are taxed, those that are tax-free and the essentials – expenses which are free of income tax because they are 'wholly, exclusively, and necessarily in the performance of your duties.'

The Inland Revenue always talks about taxable charges. These are not as big as they sound. The *taxable charge* is not what you pay but a factor added to your other income and then taxed at your highest rate. So someone paying 40 per cent tax on their income who has a perk with an annual £10,000 taxable charge value has to find 40 per cent of that sum (or £4,000) in cash when it comes to finalising their tax bill for the year.

In normal speech, you never hear the word emoluments, but it's an important word in taxmanese so watch out for it. *Emoluments* are the total value of all you get from your job including the worth of all the perks. And because the value of these perks counts for your overall taxable emoluments, they can push someone from the basic-rate tax band into the top-rate tax band. A tax-payer on £35,000 a year is within the basic zone; add in £5,000 worth of taxable benefits such as a company car and the top slice of their total emoluments is taxable at 40 per cent.

Don't turn your nose up at a perk just because it is taxable. Employers can often negotiate far better deals than you can as an individual on benefits such as healthcare plans because buying for hundreds or thousands gives them bulk purchasing power. In any case, if you bought the benefit personally, it would come out of your taxed income.

Taxable perks are known in the tax trade as *P11D benefits* after the Inland Revenue form your workplace gives you once a year if you receive any taxable perks.

The P11D lists the amount it cost the employer to provide the benefit less any amount you contribute yourself from your taxed salary (I talk about the special rules for company cars and vans in the next section). Some employers, for instance, offer gym membership but insist that the employee pays a percentage to show that they are serious about exercise.

Perks on which you have to pay tax are listed on this form. You can either pay the amounts through the self assessment system or elect to pay for them through PAYE (Pay As You Earn) deductions from your regular salary if the annual tax on the perks is no greater than £2,000. If the tax tops £2,000, you have to pay separately through the self assessment system every six months. So, if this fits you, you need to put cash aside (or have a helpful bank manager!).

Looking at the way it used to be

Serious taxation of benefits-in-kind was introduced in 1979. At that time, the top tax rates were far higher than now so employers worked around the tax rules by paying their staff in tax-free goods. Besides company cars, employees would receive free suits, free holidays, free luxury food hampers, free insurance, and a host of other freebies.

When the 1979 rules came in, they applied to directors and 'higher paid employees'. There was an exemption for 'lower paid employees' who continued to receive their perks tax-free. Lower paid was then defined as 'under £8,500 a year'. This sum included the value of the perks to prevent someone paying £8,499 a year and then adding on loads of free goodies.

The £8,500 a year limit has never changed, but the designation of those earning more than £8,500 as 'higher paid employees' has long disappeared. More than a quarter of a century later, it is impossible for a full-time employee to earn so little due to minimum wage legislation. There are, nevertheless, a few part-time workers who slip below the threshold. They have the value of their perks listed on form P9D.

Travelling To and For Work

One of the biggest costs of working is getting there in the morning and coming home at night (or vice versa if you work shifts). Your boss may help you with some of these expenses.

Your employer can provide tax-free help, including the cost of hiring cars and hotel bills, if your normal travel arrangements are impossible due to a rail strike.

Counting the cost of a company car

The company car is Britain's biggest employer-provided benefit. Its popularity dates from years of *tax breaks* (special tax relief for special situations). And though many tax advantages have been eroded, a company car remains a potent, if taxable, status symbol.

You no longer have to visit clients in both Land's End and John O'Groats at the end of the tax year to boost your proportion of business to private mileage. You're taxed as long as you can use the car privately, no matter what the proportion is.

Working out the tax

The annual taxable benefit of most workplace-provided cars depends on two factors:

- ✔ The car's full list price including the full value of any accessories (excluding a mobile phone and anything to help drivers with disabilities). Any discounts, or extras such as 'free' hi-fi upgrades, air-conditioning, or metallic paint that a private buyer can obtain, are ignored. So the taxable value is likely to be more than the cost would be to you as an individual.

- ✔ The car's CO_2 (carbon dioxide) emissions. The greener the car, the less you pay. The Inland Revenue computes a factor deriving from carbon emissions to give a percentage of the car's original cost. The taxable amount can range from 15 per cent of cost for the cleanest cars up to 35 per cent for the least atmosphere-friendly vehicles. This figure gives the taxable value.

There are special rules for older cars, and other vehicles which do not have an emission figure. Those who drive valuable vintage cars are now assessed on the vehicle's current market value if it is over £15,000 and not the original list price. So, there's another loophole gone!

Under the present rules, the maximum value of any car for these calculations is £80,000. Going over this only applies to a few people but it's useful to know if you are really ambitious about that Ferrari, Lamborghini, Bentley, or Rolls-Royce!

Considering other ways to pay for driving

In many cases, you might be better off negotiating a pay rise and giving up the company car benefit. Employers can pay you a tax-free and national insurance-free amount for every mile you drive on workplace duties.

This is currently

- 40p per mile for the first 10,000 miles
- 25p per mile for each subsequent mile
- 24p per mile for motorcycles
- 5p per mile extra for each passenger carried on work-related journeys

If you are reimbursed for mileage at less than these rates, you can claim the balance (but not the 5p per mile passenger extra) against your taxable income. For instance, if your employer gives you 30p per mile for 1,000 miles, you have a 10p a mile shortfall so you can claim £100 against your taxable income.

A number of lease packages effectively duplicate the company car experience by including insurance, repairs, regular maintenance, depreciation, and other expenses in an overall monthly sum.

Alternatively, you can just go out and buy a cheap second-hand car or, if you want, a really flash sports car. Or you can decide you do not need a car at all.

The sums involved can be horrendously complicated, with every case different, but if your employer is willing to swap your company car for extra cash (there is no obligation to do so), ask your personnel department or a benefits consultant to work out the sums for you.

Checking what counts as business mileage

The big exception to business mileage is the daily commute from home to work and back again. The Inland Revenue defines regular commuting as travel to a location you report to on 40 per cent or more of your working days.

But if you have to go for work purposes to a location that is not your normal place of work, you may be able to claim business mileage on this *triangular travel*. (I bet you thought triangular travel was when you tried to sail against the wind!)

Suppose you live in London and regularly commute to your workplace in Brighton. This is not business mileage. But if you're told to go to Birmingham for the day, this mileage would count. You can not, however, count somewhere directly between London and Brighton such as Gatwick Airport. Nor would it count to anywhere within ten miles of the normal journey.

You can also claim costs involved in *site travel,* in which you have to go to and from a location that isn't your official place of work. You may also be able to claim tax relief on *subsistence costs* such as buying yourself a midday meal when you are not at your normal workplace. You can't do this forever, however. After 24 months, the Inland Revenue says the site is now your normal workplace.

Fuelling concerns

You have to pay an additional tax charge for private petrol provided free-of-charge. This is calculated by multiplying the CO_2 percentage (see the previous 'Working out the tax' section) by £14,400. So if the percentage is 20, the tax charge for petrol is £2,880. For a basic-rate tax-payer, the after-tax cash equivalent is £633; it's £1,152 at the top rate.

The charge is the same whether you take 2 litres or 2,000 litres, so once you've paid it makes sense to use as much free petrol as possible.

Your employer can give you a tax-free fuel allowance if you pay for fuel used for business travel. This ranges from 9p per mile for smaller diesel cars (under 2,000cc) to 14p a mile for larger petrol cars (over 2,000cc). There are lower rates for cars using the cheaper liquid petroleum gas, ranging from 7p to 10p a mile.

Driving a van can save tax

From April 2005, driving a van can save you loads of tax. But this only applies if it's the right sort of journey and, from April 2007, the right sort of van.

In the past, anyone who was allowed to use their company van for private use was given an automatic £500 tax charge (reduced to £350 for old vans), so the actual cash cost was £110 to the basic-rate tax-payer and £200 to the top-rate tax-payer.

That charge no longer applies if the van is only used for business, journeys to and from work, and other 'insignificant' usage:

> ✔ Insignificant usage *can mean* making a slight detour every morning on the journey to work to buy sandwiches or a newspaper for the day, calling occasionally at the

doctor for medical reasons, and using the van once or twice a year to collect flat-pack furniture at the local DIY shop.

✔ Insignificant usage *does not mean* going to the supermarket for the weekly shop, using the van as a holiday vehicle, or as a party vehicle to go out socialising at night or weekends.

Drivers who use their van for these other uses face a continuation of the present £500 (or £350 for old vans) tax charge until April 2007, after which they will have to pay £3,000.

Van drivers who want to use the car for significant use occasionally can opt to pay a daily £5 tax charge – £1.10 in cash terms for basic-rate tax-payers and £2 for those on the top rate.

Some firms offer double-cab vans to staff as an alternative to a company car. These vans are often luxurious, with leather steering wheels and alloy rims. From April 2007, they will be treated as cars for tax purposes.

Cycling – two wheels are better

The government is keen on green commuting. And it's willing to subsidise pedal-pushers through the tax system. In general, any cycle benefit has to be made available to all employees from the most senior to recent school- or college-leavers.

Employers can provide cycles, cycling equipment, and cycle facilities such as bike sheds and showers to employees without employees incurring any tax or national insurance liabilities.

Employees can use these bikes for journeys to work and for some leisure use. The Inland Revenue knows that if tracking down van use (see above) is hard, then deciding on who cycles where and why is just about impossible, so in reality, you're free to use a work-provided cycle whenever you like.

Those who use their own bicycles for business use can claim a 20p a mile tax-free 'approved mileage allowance payment' from their employers. If the firm pays less, or nothing at all, you can claim that 20p per mile mileage allowance relief via your employer, through writing to your tax inspector, or on your self assessment form. So if you cycle 1,000 miles a year and receive nothing from your employer, you can deduct £200 from your taxable income. However, you can't claim the 20p per mile if your bike is being bought under the Green Transport Plan (see the sidebar 'Having the tax collector help buy your bike').

Employers who encourage staff to cycle by holding 'cycle-to-work' days can provide a tax-free breakfast to those who pedal on up to six days a year!

Having the tax collector help buy your bike

Whether it's a boneshaker costing under £100 or a top-of-the-range model at £4,000 plus, you can get a new bike and all the extra bits such as locks, lights, and pannier racks with help from the Inland Revenue.

It's called the Green Transport Plan. You persuade your employer to either buy or lease the bike (which is chosen can depend on your boss's tax and cash position). There are specialist firms that do all the paperwork. But a good local dealer will be able to do this as well, especially if it means selling a few dozen machines!

The employer then loans the bikes to the employee in return for a monthly amount, deducted from their salary. The employee's gross earnings are cut (which can have pension and mortgage application repercussions).

The employer can reclaim the VAT, so a £270 bike immediately becomes £40.20 cheaper (and that's not counting doing a deal with the bike shop because so many extra bikes can be sold). That brings the cost down to £229.80. Employers then arrange a

repayment period, perhaps over 24 months. So the employee sacrifices £9.57 a month.

The £9.57 is free of employees' national insurance and income tax, for most people equal to 33 per cent. So the real cost is £6.39 a month or £153.36 over the 24 months. This includes interest-free credit worth perhaps £20 on the bike's original selling price. All in all, you have so far paid around half the real cost (it would be even less if you were a top-rate tax-payer).

After two years, the employer sells the bike to you. This will normally be a nominal sum – perhaps £20 in this case.

You are supposed to use the bike for commuting but commuting also includes where you use the train for long distances while riding at either end. You can also use it for leisure purposes.

Amazingly, this benefit also extends to electric bikes so you don't have to be that athletic to apply.

Getting to work the green way

Employers who want to reduce pollution can set up *Green Transport* or *Travel Plans,* which are voluntary government initiatives whose goal is to encourage cleaner travel, and claim tax relief against their profits. And that's always an incentive!

Getting on the works bus

Employees who are offered a free or subsidised works bus to get them to and from their workplace are not charged income tax or national insurance on the perk. The bus has to seat at least nine passengers, so limousines are ruled out. The employer can also offer free or cut-price travel on public buses to help staff avoid tax.

Going home late

You can have a tax-free taxi to take you home after 9 p.m. as long as no public transport exists or it would be unreasonable for you to use it. This does not apply if you have to regularly or frequently work past 9 p.m.

Helping those with disabilities

Assistance with travelling costs between home and work for those with disabilities is not taxed. This can include public transport and a specially adapted car as long as the car is only used for commuting.

Taking up season ticket loans

Your employer can offer an interest-free or low-interest loan of up to £5,000 so you can buy a railway, bus, or river-bus season ticket. There is no tax or national insurance to pay on the interest benefit provided the loan is repaid in full and the total outstanding amount of all loans from your employer does not exceed £5,000.

Where loans for all purposes exceed £5,000, you're taxed on any interest saving on the whole amount, not just the balance over £5,000. The Inland Revenue has an official interest rate to decide if the loan is subsidised or not. This usually stands at around 1 per cent over the Bank of England base rate.

Getting Non-Transport Perks

There is a huge variety of benefits employers can give as part of an overall remuneration package. The following sections talk about many of them.

Housing: from the vicarage to the lighthouse

If you are offered low- or no-rent accommodation as part of your overall pay package, expect to pay income tax and national insurance on the benefit. However, in certain situations, your housing benefit is tax-free. Such circumstances may be because:

- ✔ You have to live in the housing to fulfil your duties properly. You may be a caretaker, or a gamekeeper who needs to be close to the birds you're looking after. This exemption also includes lighthouse-keepers, and many staff members of boarding schools such as housemasters and mistresses.

- ✔ Living in on-site housing helps you perform your duties better or such accommodation is customary. This may include some farm-workers in the first category and vicars in the second. It can also include pub managers and caravan-site managers.

- ✔ You have to live in specific accommodation due to a special security threat to you. This can include members of the armed forces and those in the diplomatic service.

The tax freedom only extends to the rent. You can be charged a P11D-style amount on the value of furniture and equipment within the house. This is usually calculated at 20 per cent of the market value of the furniture when it was first installed. So any charge would be negligible if the furniture was second-hand.

Paying for childcare

Firms can offer childcare (such as a nursery or a pre-school or after-school club) free of national insurance and income tax, providing:

✔ It is not in a private home.

✔ It meets local authority guidelines.

✔ It is concerned with care rather than education – it must be a nursery not a school.

A new scheme from April 2005 allows employers to pay up to £50 a week free-of-tax and national insurance towards childcare arrangements other than those listed above. These can include registered childminders.

The money will normally be in the form of vouchers or go directly to the childcare provider. This scheme must be made available either to all employees or all employees at a particular location – employers can't offer the benefit just to a few people.

Realising other tax-free perks

Your firm can provide an amazing range of perks tax-free designed to keep you happy.

Enjoying your lunch tax-free

Providing a free or subsidised canteen or staff restaurant is a tax-free benefit. It does not have to be on the premises but if it is elsewhere, it must be in a separate part of the outside restaurant or hotel from where the general public is barred. Higher-paid staff can have a separate room as long as the food they get is no better than that served to others.

Employers can provide luncheon vouchers up to the amazing value of 15p a day tax-free for each working day. The sum has stayed unchanged for some 40 years when it was three shillings in pre-decimal money (15p in decimal money) and you could buy a proper meal for that sum! It's worth about £7.50 for a basic-rate tax-payer a year. So it's just about enough for half a pint and a sandwich for two to toast the Inland Revenue's continuing generosity!

Playing games tax-free

Free or subsidised sports or social facilities such as football fields or a darts club do not count as a taxable perk. But company membership of health clubs or other outside fitness venues is taxable under the P11D mechanism unless those facilities are available to employees only.

Making calls and paying less tax

Private use of mobile phones supplied by your employer escapes the tax net altogether.

Moving home with Inland Revenue assistance

You can receive up to £8,000 a move from your employer and not pay tax on it when your company forces you to relocate or when you take up a new job which compels you to move home.

The tax-free expenses can include removal costs and the legal and other expenses of any house purchase that fails. You do not have to sell your old home.

Profiting from the suggestion box

Unless it is part of your normal job to come up with brain-storming ideas, you can get tax-free cash if suggestions made into schemes are adopted. The amount is related to the financial gain to your employer. The limit is an award of £5,000 – anything above this is taxable. You can also have up to £25 tax-free if your suggestion is a bright concept but is not implemented.

Enjoying a party

Your employer can spend up to £150 a year per employee on staff parties. This does not have to be a Christmas party; it can be any time of the year for any purpose. Your boss can also hold a summer and a winter party and split the cost between the two. The party must be generally open to all staff or all staff on a certain site; it cannot be open just to senior executives. This sum does not cover the cost of inviting any outside guests.

Getting your gold watch tax-free, too

Long service awards are tax-free as long as the recipient has at least 20 years with the same employer and there has been no similar gift in the past ten years. The gift can be worth as much as £50 for each year of service. It cannot be in cash.

Going online at home – tax-free

The Home Computing Initiative is a government scheme to give employees tax-free computers for use in their homes.

Employers, usually through specialist firms, offer staff a range of machines which they buy over a period, often 36 months, using gross salary rather than the money in their pay packet which they would use at an electronics store. The deal can also include software, printers and other extras.

To purchase a computer under the scheme, you agree to a monthly reduction in your gross salary. This money buys the computer. For instance, someone on basic-rate tax and national insurance contributes £40 a month from their gross earnings. Over a three-year period, this equals £1,440 so, under the scheme, that person can have a computer package worth £1,440 (not counting the value of the interest-free loan).

But the cash outlay from what would normally be their net salary is just £964.80, so they get a much better computer for their cash using this scheme. It works even better for the top-rate tax-payer, who gets £1,440 worth of computer goodies by spending £849.60 from net salary over the three years. Who makes up the gap between what you spend and what you get? Why, it's your friends at the Inland Revenue.

At the end of the loan period, the employer charges a small amount to end the loan deal. This is usually £10 or under, although some home computing initiative paperwork allows for anything from £1 to £49.

The computer does not have to be used for work. And any member of the family can use it.

There is a £2,500 limit on machines supplied under the scheme.

Taking financial advice

You can have up to £150 worth a year of financial and pensions advice tax-free when it is provided by your employer.

Free eyesight tests and glasses

Health and safety legislation demands that employers offer regular eye checks to staff who use computer screens. This is a tax-free benefit, as is any fixed amount you are given towards buying glasses. This is usually enough to purchase a basic pair of spectacles.

Explaining Expenses: The Wholly, Exclusively, and Necessarily Rule

The self-employed have substantial freedom in deciding the expenses they can set against earnings, and so remove them from the income tax net. Not so, those who work for others. They have to convince the tax inspector that any expenses they receive from their employers are 'wholly, exclusively, and necessarily in the performance of their duties'.

These are very strict guidelines. Pass them, and the money your employer gives you is tax-free. Fail them and you face tax and national insurance on the amounts, just the same as if they were part of your salary packet. There is, of course, nothing to stop your employer picking up the tax bill on your behalf.

Examining expenses that qualify

There is no tax to pay on:

- Travelling expenses when you are ordered by your employer to make the journey.

- The cost of meals when you are away from home on business.

- Travelling to a temporary workplace for up to 24 months.

- Personal expenses when you are away from home on business of up to £5 a night in the UK and £10 a night elsewhere.

- Payments of up to £2 a week for expenses when you have to work at home.

- The cost of two return journeys a year for your spouse and children to a location outside the UK if you have to work overseas for a continuous period of at least 60 days.

- Medical treatment if incurred overseas when on business.

✔ The cost of entertaining customers, contacts, and clients. Earlier Inland Revenue attempts to split the bill so the guest's food and drink was tax-free while you paid tax on your consumption resulted in a farce as hosts claimed they had one glass of water while guests tucked into big meals.

Eyeing expenses you pay tax on

Here are some examples of claims when tax inspectors were not convinced of wholly, exclusively, and necessarily:

✔ Ordinary every day clothing

✔ Travelling costs to work at a normal site

✔ Costs of domestic help at an employee's home

✔ Meal expenses paid out of meal allowances

✔ Phone line rental costs when the phone is not used wholly, exclusively, and necessarily for work (but claims for fax lines at home have been more successful)

✔ Courses to improve your background knowledge of the subject – for instance, an architect cannot claim a tour to see the architecture of Ancient Rome

✔ Costs incurred by a teacher in keeping a room at her home for marking work

✔ Diet supplements for professional sports people

✔ Newspapers read by journalists – these may be 'wholly and exclusively' for work but the Inland Revenue will argue that they are not 'necessary'

Special deals for special jobs

The Inland Revenue allows you to deduct the cost of subscriptions to various professional organisations that are essential if you are to continue with your work. In some cases, only part of the amount is allowable as the balance covers non-essential items such as lobbying. There is also a long list of flat-rate deductions that can be claimed by people in various manual jobs requiring special clothing or tools. But don't get too excited. The sums are relatively small, have not been updated since 1996, and the cash savings are small – in most cases,

33 per cent (the basic tax rate plus national insurance) of the amounts shown in Table 9-1. Most employers in these industries arrange for automatic deductions, so you may not have to claim.

Table 9-1	Deductions for Certain Jobs
Agriculture	£70
Banking – uniformed employees	£40
Carpenters	£105
Electrical supply workers	£90
Fire Service	£60
Glass workers	£60
Healthcare – ambulance workers	£110
– nurses	£70
Leather workers	£40
Police officers	£55
Printers	£70
Police	£55
Prison officers	£55
Railway workers	£70
Textile workers	£60
Wood and furniture workers	£75

The Inland Revenue's *Extra Statutory Concessions* booklet has a complete list with full descriptions, including unusual jobs such as artificial limb makers (they get £90 but £115 if the limbs are made of wood – don't ask why!). You can download this booklet from the Inland Revenue Web site at www.inland revenue.gov.uk or get it from your local tax office. It's quite a hefty publication so if you print if off from the Web site, make sure you have about 150 sheets of paper.

Chapter 10

Sharing in Your Firm's Fortunes

*M*any employers operate schemes that give employees a chance to share in the firm's ups (and sometimes, regrettably, downs) by offering them a share stake in the company.

But to get the tax incentives to take a stake in your employer, and then work harder to increase the value of what you have, you must work for a firm that issues shares. If you work for the government, for a local authority, for a charity, for an institute, for the National Health Service, in education, or any other employer who is not a company, you have no chance of getting these benefits. And there is no compensating tax-saving mechanism, either. Sorry. So if you fall into one of these categories, either skip this chapter altogether, or read it, and then resolve to move to an employer with a staff share plan.

Offering Share Schemes – Who and How

In a *share scheme,* the company's directors offer employees an opportunity to invest in the company by buying shares in the firm or by offering options to buy shares. An option is a sort of one-way promise. If the shares go up, you can take up the option but if they go down or you can't afford them, you can tear up the option and not suffer any penalty.

Different share schemes have differing rules on how much you can put in, what your boss can add, when you can take your investment out, and how much (if any) tax you pay on any profits you make. So read on, and if your employer has shares, you should find a plan that's suitable.

Your employer can offer you a *share incentive plan* (SIP) and a *Save As You Earn* (SAYE) scheme at the same time, entitling you to extra benefits.

Working out who offers what to whom

There is no obligation on employers to offer a share scheme. Companies that offer their staff share plans reckon it is well worth the cost of issuing the shares as employees tend to be more motivated, work harder, and remain loyal when the carrot of a big pack of shares with tax benefits is dangled a few years in front of them.

Schemes are most common in large quoted companies. Schemes are rarer in smaller companies, where the shareholder list is likely to be restricted to members of the family that owns the firm. There is no bar against overseas companies offering access to their foreign-quoted shares to their UK employees.

With the lone exception of free share incentive plans (SIPs), these schemes must be available to all employees whether full- or part-time and however exulted or lowly their salary level or job status. In Save As You Earn schemes and some SIPs, the firm can impose a qualifying period of up to five years' work for the firm providing it applies equally to everyone.

Treasuring the tax savings

Company share schemes can be worth over £1,000 a year in tax savings. Most of these incentive plans include tax-saving possibilities. The exact amount of tax savings depends on how much you go in for and what happens to the shares. You get the tax savings at the end of the scheme period. And, of course, the shares have to go up for you to realise any tax savings at all.

To get tax advantages, share schemes have to be properly structured. A straight gift of shares from your employer counts as a taxable benefit. You will have to pay tax based on the shares' market value on the day you receive them. If you pay part of their worth, you will be taxed on the gap between what you paid and their stock market value.

Listing the types of schemes

To benefit tax-wise, the shares have to be issued through one of a number of schemes. These schemes are normally Inland Revenue-approved but there are also non-approved schemes. Non-approval does not imply they are illegal or total tax dodges, but it often means the scheme is complicated and may be intended to boost the earnings of senior persons rather than being available more generally to employees. Non-approved schemes can be more difficult to set up. But they make big money for specialist tax lawyers! I address some non-approved plans in the 'Going Beyond Approval' section later in this chapter.

The great advantage of approval is that your employer can just slot a scheme into a pre-existing blueprint. That makes it really easy to set up. The biggest approved scheme is SAYE (Save As You Earn) but there are also SIPs (share incentive plans). Sorry about more alphabet soup.

There are three main routes into employee shareholding: I go through the details of each later in this chapter.

- ✔ Free shares where the employer gives you a handout.

- ✔ Option plans where the employee has the right, but not the obligation, to buy shares at a fixed value (known as the 'strike price') on a set date or dates in the future. You can walk away from an option without penalty if the shares trade below the strike price.

- ✔ Schemes where you buy shares at their current value, or at an 'undervalue', in the expectation that there will be a gain, which will be advantageous from a tax point of view as well.

Saving with a Save As You Earn Scheme

Save As You Earn (SAYE) is the most popular share incentive scheme. Through a SAYE plan, employees contract to save a set amount from £5 to £250 out of their pay packet each month for a set period of time – three or five years. A further option is to leave the money in the account for a further two years after the fifth year.

Be sure you are comfortable with the amount you agree to pay into a SAYE account. You cannot increase or decrease the amount during the term of the plan. Decreasing or permanently stopping payments ends the plan.

You are allowed to delay up to six monthly payments during your SAYE plan. This extends your contract by the number of missed months. Once you go beyond six missed payments, the plan is terminated.

You may have the choice of saving for three years, five years, or seven years. In the latter case, you save for five years and then leave the money saved for another two years. Employers can offer (and many do) a choice of these periods or you may only have one option.

The money you pay into your SAYE plan every month goes into a special SAYE account with a bank or building society, chosen by your employer. It earns tax-free interest and a tax-free interest-related bonus.

You do not acquire any shares yourself with each monthly payment. But you can buy them with the proceeds of your SAYE account at the end of your SAYE period at the pre-set option price.

When you start a SAYE plan, the company sets the share value anywhere in a range between the current stock market value or 20 per cent lower. This is your starting price. You compare the price at the end of the scheme with this to see if you have made money on the shares. If not, walk away. You pay no income tax or national insurance on these undervalued shares.

You can have more than one scheme with your employer providing your monthly contribution total does not exceed £250. Many firms have regular offers, each with a different option price, to reflect ups and downs in the stock market.

If your SAYE scheme works out well and you take up the shares, why not use another tax-saving plan to protect further growth against Capital Gains Tax? You can do this by transferring your shares into an Individual Savings Account (ISA). There is an annual tax year limit of £7,000 on all money put into an ISA. So if you have used your allowance for other investments or savings, you can't put your share-scheme money into it. And even if you put just £1 into a mini-cash ISA, your annual shares limit falls to £3,000. There are strict rules about not exceeding your ISA limits. If you do it accidentally, you have to pay any tax you otherwise avoided. (Turn to Chapter 14 for details about ISAs.)

Looking at how SAYE accounts grow your money

The interest you get is set at the time you sign up for the SAYE plan. Banks and building societies compete mainly on service to employers and rarely on interest rates. You do not have a choice in the SAYE account provider; it is up to negotiations between the bank and your employer.

At the time of writing, if you opt for the three-year plan, your money is refunded on maturity plus a bonus equal to 1.9 monthly contributions. So, someone paying in £100 a month would receive £3,600 plus £190, which comes to £3,790. Opting for the five-year plan gives a bigger bonus equal to 6.1 monthly payments – in this case, a £100 a month investment yields a repayment of £6,000 plus £610 to give a tax-free £6,610. If you opt for seven years, you pay no more after five years. You would then, at current rates, receive 11.5 times the monthly payment at the end. In the £100 a month example, this gives a tax-free £1,150 bonus.

You receive no interest at all if you stop within 12 months of starting the scheme. And the return is limited to a miserable 2 per cent simple interest if you fail to finish your contract.

SAYE plan rates and bonuses go up and down with Bank of England base rates. But they are fixed for the life of the contract at the time you sign up.

Feeling safe with SAYE

SAYE shares are win-win for employees. If the shares go up, they gain. And if share values drop, there is the fall-back of the tax-free interest in the bank or building society account.

Your monthly savings and their tax-free growth belong to you no matter what happens to the share price. If the shares go up, you can keep them or sell them. If they go down, as they did in the first few years of the present decade, you can get your savings back, plus interest (see the previous section for information on interest). Either way, there is no income tax or national insurance to pay on the gains.

Cashing in

If it's worthwhile for you to take the shares, your employer issues you with the paperwork to prove you own them.

Sharing a SAYE success story

Suppose the shares of your company trade at 100p when you start. You are given an SAYE option at 80p, the maximum 20 per cent discount.

You save £100 a month for five years, which, including the tax-free interest, gives you a fund of £6,610. This will buy you 8,262 shares no matter what has happened to the price of the shares over the period of your contract. I'm ignoring the 40p left over.

If the price of the shares is over 80p, you can make a profit by exercising the option with the money in the account and then selling the shares. This profit will be liable to Capital Gains Tax on the amount between the present value and the option price. But don't forget you have an annual zero rate allowance. And you don't have to sell. You can keep all the shares for the future or sell some to make the best use of your annual Capital Gains Tax allowance.

It's your choice what you do with them. You can keep them and hope they go up or sell them through a stockbroker. Some firms have in-house schemes to help you find a broker. Your bank will be able to help as well.

Chapter 14 can help you decipher Capital Gains Tax issues.

Leaving before your shares' time

SAYE schemes finish if you leave the company before the end of the contracted period of the scheme that you signed up for whether that is three, five, or seven years. You get a refund of your savings, though, with interest, but without the attractive interest-rate bonus which is automatically paid at the end of three years on all plans.

However, if you have to leave your job before the scheme finishes due to retirement, illness, injury, or redundancy you can still exercise your options if they are worthwhile. You have a six-month window to do this. If you die within this timeframe then your family can exercise your options on your behalf, in which case the period of taking the option is extended to 12 months. There are also special rules if the firm (or the part where you work) is taken over.

Discussing Share Incentive Plans

Share incentive plans (SIPs) offer more (sometimes much more) in the way of tax-saving benefits than the SAYE plan I explain in the preceding sections. SIPs used to be called All Employee Share Ownership Plans, with the whimsical acronym Aesops, but SIPs is pretty jaunty in its own right.

Share incentive plans come with higher risks than SAYE schemes. You buy actual shares from the start instead of accumulating options. The shares you buy are not like options you can abandon if the stock market price falls. So if the share price goes down, you will take a loss.

You do not receive the shares when you are awarded them. Instead, they are held by trustees in a plan for three to five years, depending on the specifics of the scheme. If you leave the firm, other than for disability or death, you may forfeit your tax-saving arrangement (see the earlier 'Treasuring the tax savings' section).

Share prices in your company may fall along with share prices generally in the stock market no matter how hard you and your colleagues work! There is no tax compensation if you have to sell out at a loss.

Share incentive plans come in three flavours: Free shares, partnership shares, and matching shares. Which type you receive is up to your employer. Some go for the free shares route; others will take the partnership (and possibly matching shares) road. I talk about each type in turn in the next sections.

Keep full records of all SIP share transactions for five years. You can face an income tax charge if you withdraw your shares from the plan within five years of joining it.

Getting something for nothing with free shares

Free shares are obviously the best deal because they cost you nothing. Unlike other work-related perks, there is no income tax or national insurance to pay. And as employers can give up to £3,000 in any one tax year, that's worth up to £999 in tax benefits for basic-rate tax-payers and up to £1,230 for top-rate payers.

You can receive free shares according to performance measures, salary, or length of service. These targets must be publicised ahead of your signing up for the scheme and cannot be changed midway. And the highest performance-linked handout cannot be greater than four times the non-performance figure.

This is an all-employee scheme so it must be available to everyone in the company, including part-timers. But firms can set a qualifying limit of up to 18 months' employment before letting someone join.

Turning a SIP into a SIPP

No, this is not alphabet soup gone mad, just a way to take your share incentive plan (SIP) investments and transfer them directly to a *self invested personal pension* (SIPP). Doing this turns each 78p of SIP shares into £1 of SIPP for a basic- or lower-rate or non-tax-payer. A top-rate tax-payer can turn 60p of SIP into £1 of SIPP. The SIPP provider has to be happy with accepting the shares so they will probably have to be equities in stock market-quoted companies. Once within the SIPP, they can be sold without tax concerns.

This SIP to SIPP transfer must be made within 90 days of withdrawing the shares from your employer's plan.

These shares are held on your behalf in a trust. If you leave the firm within three years of your starting the scheme, then you generally lose your rights to the tax benefits on free shares. If you take your investment out of the plan between the three- and five-year period, you may face a tax charge on the difference between the value on the day you acquired them and the day you took them out of the plan to spend the proceeds. The exact rules depend on the company and the way it has set up the trust. But you cannot lose your tax savings if you have to leave through injury, disability, illness, retirement, or redundancy. And, if you die, your heirs can make use of the tax savings.

Going into partnership with your employer

Partnership shares in a SIP give you the chance to back your firm with your own cash. You buy shares at market value with money that is free of income tax and national insurance deductions. There is an annual limit of £1,500 (or 10 per cent of your gross pay after pension plan contributions, and any workplace charitable donations if this is lower). The £1,500 maximum is worth up to nearly £500 for basic-rate tax-payers and up to £615 for top-rate tax-payers.

If you withdraw partnership shares from the trust within three years of joining the plan, you pay tax based on the market value at the time you take the shares, not the original value, which may, of course, be lower or higher. After five years, you can take them out of the plan and sell them without any income tax worries.

As long as you keep your shares in the plan, they grow free of Capital Gains Tax bills.

Matching shares with employer generosity

You cannot be forced to buy shares. But the matching scheme may make them hard to resist. A firm can give up to two matching shares for each partnership share an employee purchases. This gives a maximum £3,000 a year in shares which are free of all income tax and national insurance charges.

Matching shares have to be given to all employees on the same basis so if the senior managers get a two-for-one offer, the most junior staff must have the same deal.

Divvying up the dividends

Dividends from SIPs are taxable. But most employers offer a dividend reinvestment scheme so you can buy even more shares instead of receiving cash dividends. Dividends that are reinvested are tax-free. You can re-invest up to £1,500 a year in this tax-saving way. The tax freedom lasts as long as you keep your shares within the plan.

Going Beyond Approval

A number of employee share incentive schemes are deemed 'not approved' by Inland Revenue, yet are still worth consideration in certain circumstances. Being *not approved* means that, unlike approved schemes in which all the rules are laid out, precise details are not checked out by the Inland Revenue. These schemes are generally offered by small companies and are intended to help retain key staff members.

Getting a reward for enterprise

Enterprise management incentives (EMIs) can add up to big tax savings for employees, usually senior staff, in smaller companies.

Firms with assets worth up to £30 million can give share options worth up to £100,000 per employee in the scheme. Options are not shares; they're a promise you can buy a set number at a pre-set price on a future date.

The options can be issued at or below market value. Most are issued at market value; this allows the recipient to cash in the options without paying income tax or national insurance on their value.

The only tax charge is Capital Gains Tax. But this is only paid when the shares are sold. And it can be managed by selling shares over a number of years, so making use of several annual exemptions.

Picking out particular employees with a CSOP

A CSOP is a *company share option plan*. It can give employees selected by the firm the right to buy shares worth up to £30,000 on the day the option is granted. Provided the options are held for at least three years, the only tax will be income tax on the gain, if any, between the option price and the value of the shares on the market on the day the option is exercised.

Chapter 11

Working for Yourself Can Be Less Taxing

• •

• •

*A*ccording to the Federation of Small Businesses, around four million people in the UK work for themselves. But whatever the exact headcount, the Inland Revenue taxes all these businesspeople. This chapter looks at dealing with the tax authorities as the owner of your own business instead of as an employee in someone else's.

Doing your taxes correctly can put your new firm on the road to success; messing them up is a sure-fire road to commercial oblivion or even bankruptcy. In this chapter I show you the tax advantages of self-employment and steer you away from some of the dangerous pitfalls.

Defining the Terms

Most people who strike out on their own, even if they go on to become multi-billionaires, often start as *sole traders* – the technical term for working for yourself, being a one-person band, or working as a freelancer.

For some, being self-employed means running a full-time business complete with commercial plans, business bank loans, staff, and public-liability insurance. If that's you, then, one day, you may hope to be a really big company and even float the company on the stock market. Lots of quoted companies started off as ventures run from an entrepreneur's dining room table.

Some sole traders offer the skills they have, such as plumbing, management consultancy, car mechanics, or writing books about money, directly to the client or end-user. Most of these businesspeople will never be big firms but they enjoy the freedom (as well as the responsibilities) of self-employment.

And for a growing number, it's all about part-time boosts to their earnings from a paying job that can be anything from regular wheeling-and-dealing on online auction sites to being a buy-to-let landlord.

Whatever category you are in, you are in business. And that puts you firmly into the tax-paying net even if you already pay income tax because you work full-time for an employer.

Some small businesses decide to become companies rather than sole traders. The advantages, and tax implications, of limited company status are dealt with in the next chapter.

Meeting the Inland Revenue's standards for self-employment

The Inland Revenue applies basic tests to determine whether you are really self-employed rather than working for someone else. Pass them and you can be on the way to tax savings! The standards are that:

- ✔ You work for more than one customer – and preferably several.
- ✔ You work from your own premises, or, if you don't, you work from several locations. If you're a writer, for example, you probably work from your home; however, if you're a plumber, you travel to your customers' premises.

- You're in control of what you do and the hours you work. You must be able to turn down work you do not fancy, and you should set your own prices.

- You have a business address – often your home – from which you carry out some business functions, if only message taking.

- You supply and maintain your own vehicles, tools, computers, and/or other items of equipment needed for your trade or profession.

- You correct bad work in your own time and at your own expense.

- You are legally liable for your mistakes.

Some businesses have acquired a reputation for turning people whose main function is selling their labour into self-employed workers when they should be employed under PAYE. Some examples are computer consultants who work for one company, sub-contract builders who work for others on sites, and hairdressers who rent the chair and basin space in the salon. The Inland Revenue makes big (and usually successful) efforts to deny such people self-employed status and the tax savings that can go with it.

Delving into the grey area: Sole trader or simple seller?

Most know when they start as a sole trader. They do work for customers in return for a commercial rate of reward. But there is a grey area where you may not know if you are trading or simply selling something.

One activity the Inland Revenue is targeting is selling via online auction. Proceeds from these sales are not, as some believe, always outside the tax net. Nor are car boot sales. Tax inspectors look for evidence of trading.

If you buy goods, either from wholesalers, or from other auctions, or from junk or charity shops with the intention of selling these things on at a profit, you are *trading* and so face a potential tax bill.

If you're clearing out the loft or spare room and have a one-off sale as an alternative to carting the lot to the charity shop or dump, then you are not trading, so there are no tax hassles. Although, should you find a Picasso in your loft and sell it for wads of money, you can face a Capital Gains Tax bill on the proceeds! (See Chapter 14 for more on capital gains.)

It is your responsibility to register, so find out about your status if you are in doubt. You cannot argue against a fine or penalty by saying you did not know or that you were waiting for the Inland Revenue to contact you.

Testing your wings whilst staying employed

These days, the Inland Revenue insists that the newly self-employed register within three months of starting up their activity. But, in practice, someone on PAYE who earns a one-off payment, perhaps for contributing to a publication or a one-off consultancy payment, does not need to register as self-employed although the remuneration they receive for this must be declared for tax. No absolute rules govern this – if you're unsure of your status, make sure you register with the Inland Revenue.

Formalising Your Status

Just as no job is complete until the paperwork is done, neither can you start a business without filing forms with the Inland Revenue and deciding when your tax year runs. The following sections tell you what you need to do.

Registering your new business

The self-employed have to register as such with the Inland Revenue. This procedure includes making arrangements to pay national insurance contributions, which you will probably have to make. The upcoming 'Scanning National Insurance' section covers this issue.

You can register by:

✔ **Calling** a special helpline on 0845 915 4515. It's open between 8.00 a.m. and 8.00 p.m. seven days a week (except Christmas Day and one or two bank holidays).

✔ **Filing** form CWF1. Find it in Inland Revenue leaflet PSE1 *Thinking of working for yourself?* Or download it online at `www.inlandrevenue.gov.uk/forms/cwf1.pdf` **or** register online at `www.inlandrevenue.gov.uk/starting up/register.htm`.

Failing to register within three months of starting self-employment can bring a £100 penalty. In some cases, the business's exact start date may be debatable, so it is best to register as soon as you can.

Larger penalties can be imposed if tax is paid late because an unincorporated business failed to register by 5 October of the following tax year in which it was set up.

Choosing your tax year carefully

Most businesses have an accounting year that runs alongside the tax year from 6 April to 5 April, though you may find it more convenient to use 31 March as the end date for your tax year. If you use 5 April or 31 March as the last day of your year, you're opting for *fiscal accounting,* so-called because your business year is the same as the tax, or fiscal, year. Fiscal year users account for tax by the 31 January following the end of their year.

You can use any other date for your year-end. Choosing a different date can give you longer to file and more time to keep the tax earning interest in the bank, which sounds like a great tax-saving idea. However, while many accountants still recommend choosing a different date, there are drawbacks.

Filing your first two returns

If you don't opt for a fiscal year-end, you have to meet extra requirements when filing tax returns for your first two years of operation. Your first year's tax bill is based on profits, if any, from the start of trading until the next 5 April – even though that's not the year-end date you chose. So, depending on when you start your business, your first tax bill may cover a matter of a few days or virtually a whole year.

Taxes for the second year are based on either the 12 months trading that ends on the date you chose in that year or your first 12 months of trading. You have to use the second option if the selected year-end date is less than 12 months after the start of the business.

Jessica starts her business on 1 August 2005 and decides on a 31 July year end. She makes a regular £2,000 a month profit. Under the start-up rules for the first two years, she has to account for her business from her 1 August 2005 start-date to 5 April 2006 on her 2005–06 tax return due in by 31 January 2007. She has to declare profits of £16,000 for these eight months because her selected year-end date is less than 12 months from the start of her business.

So far, so good. But her second year-end date is after her first 12 months of trading, so she has to account for the full 12 months from 1 August 2005 to 31 July 2006. Her profits here will be £24,000. Now for the really bad bit, which sounds like something out of *Alice in Wonderland*.

Even though Jessica has had to pay tax on her first eight months, she also has to pay tax on the first year. Now these overlap to a big extent. So, although she has only 12 months of trading to earn her money, she is assessed for 20 months of tax payments. On her £2,000 a month profits, she has earned £24,000 but she has to pay as though she has earned £40,000 (that's 20 months or 12 months plus eight months).

Of course, no one who is self-employed has exact months like that all the time. But I selected the same amount each month to make a complicated overlap a little simpler.

Lessening the effects of overlap

Having to pay tax on profits you haven't yet made is known in the tax trade as *overlap*. And you ignore it at your peril. For most small businesses, overlap is something to avoid. The answer is to align your business year with the tax year.

You can change your accounting year-end during the life of your business to lessen the effect of overlap if you need to. You can elect for a year-end change by notifying the Inland Revenue on a self assessment form or sending your tax inspector a letter.

If you don't cure your overlap while you are in self-employment, you only get your excess tax payment back when you cease trading. Such an event can be many years in the future, and the overpayments you made on starting will not be adjusted for inflation or changing tax rates.

If you have to borrow extra cash because paying overlap tax takes cash out of your business, you can claim the interest against a future tax bill.

Those setting up a business where the costs of the first year or so of trading are likely to be greater than their earnings obviously need have less fear of overlap as there will be no profits to tax.

Signing on for and paying VAT

Whether you are a self-employed sole trader, a partnership, or a limited company, you have to register for VAT once your annual sales top a threshold amount (£60,000 in 2005–06) determined by the Chancellor of the Exchequer. This threshold tends to rise each year roughly in line with inflation. (For the current VAT threshold, go to HM Customs and Excise Web site at www.hmce.gov.uk.)You also need to register if your earnings in any one quarter are such that, multiplied by four, they would exceed the threshold.

The VAT threshold is determined by *total sales* – not total profits. You can make a loss and still need to be VAT registered.

Once you register for VAT, you have to charge VAT on all the work or goods you supply to customers (other than VAT-exempt goods and services) and account for these amounts. But then you can also deduct VAT on goods and services you have to buy in for your business.

Most goods and services are charged standard rate VAT, now 17.5 per cent. But some items are different. Supplying electricity to people's homes has a 5 per cent rate. More importantly, a number of everyday items – fresh food, children's clothes, books, magazines, and newspapers, for example – have a special 0 per cent rate. This is called *zero rating*. You must be VAT registered even if all the goods you supply are zero rated providing your sales top the VAT threshold.

Register with Customs and Excise within 30 days of being aware that you will exceed the threshold. Failing to register brings a fine, which is the greater of £50, or 5 per cent of the VAT owed, if registration is made within nine months of when registration should have taken place, 10 per cent where it is between nine and 18 months late and 15 per cent in all other cases. All these figures are on top of the VAT itself.

You can register for VAT even if your sales are below the threshold, and you may actually save tax by doing so. If you buy a £100 item for your business as a non-VAT trader and pay VAT on it, you have £117.50 (£100 plus 17.5 per cent VAT) to set against your profits for income tax. As a basic-rate tax-payer with a 22 per cent rate, that cuts your bill by £25.85 as you can take off 22 per cent, so the asset costs £91.96. But if you were registered for VAT, you would reclaim the £17.50 *input* (the technical VAT term for anything you buy in for your business) and still have £100 to set against profits. Taking off 22 per cent gives a £22 tax reduction. In this case, the actual cost is £78. So, registering for VAT can be useful if your main clients are organisations that can reclaim VAT themselves.

VAT-registered businesses supplying goods and services to private individuals are at a disadvantage to their non-registered counterparts as they have to boost every bill by 17.5 per cent. If you supply goods or services, you may be able to keep below the annual VAT threshold by supplying labour only and getting your clients to buy the goods needed themselves. For instance, a decorator can ask a customer to buy the paint and wallpaper from the local DIY store. The customer still pays VAT on these items but not on the decorator's labour, so reducing the decorator's turnover.

Paying the VAT bill

The VAT return asks for two figures: your *output* – the amount you take in for selling goods or supplying services shown on your invoices to customers – and your *input* – the value of goods or services you buy in to help carry out your business shown on invoices you receive from suppliers.

In the past, you had to report your output and input on a quarterly basis. Accountants charged substantial sums for dealing with this work even for relatively small businesses. Some businesses, though, like the discipline of quarterly returns which make sure they get on top of their affairs and don't leave things to fester for up to a year.

But you can ease the VAT paperwork burden (and account-ancy bills) through one of the following three options:

- ✔ **Cash accounting:** You pay tax according to what actually happens in your business. With this method there is no need to go through the complicated business of reclaim-ing VAT on a bad debt. You still pay quarterly.

- ✔ **Flat rate scheme:** This plan is aimed at businesses with taxable sales of up to £150,000 a year. In following this scheme, you bill customers in the normal way at 17.5 per cent. But instead of paying this amount, less your input, you agree a percentage of your turnover with Customs and Excise and pay it. This percentage varies from 2 per cent for food and children's clothing retailers up to 13.5 per cent for builders and contractors who only supply their labour. You don't have to figure out your outputs and inputs, so it's a lot simpler, but you can end up paying more than you would have had you claimed for your inputs. To join, submit form VAT 600 (FRS), which you can download from the Customs and Excise Web site at www.hmce.gov.uk.

- ✔ **Annual accounting:** This system is used for businesses with turnovers of up to £660,000 a year. You make one VAT return a year but make nine monthly interim esti-mated payments. The annual return allows you to bal-ance your monthly payments either with another payment or asking for money back if you have over-esti-mated your sales. This is just like the way many pay for gas and electricity – 11 fixed amounts plus a balancing payment in the final month.

Deregistering for VAT

If your sales fall to below the VAT threshold (£58,000 in 2005–06) you can opt to deregister. This drop takes you out of the VAT net. But you don't have to deregister.

If you anticipate that your business downturn is temporary and if charging VAT does not harm your relationships with customers, stick with it if you can stand the paperwork as you'll only have to reregister when your sales go up again. And keeping a VAT number means you can continue to offset all the VAT on goods and services you buy in.

Keeping Accounts to Keep Everyone Happy

Here's a scary thought: The biggest single cheque you'll ever write out may well be to the Inland Revenue. In this section, I show you how to minimise your tax bite legally. And, in keeping with this book's theme of making sure that you don't give up all the tax you've saved by sending it all back, and, even worse, paying penalties, I focus on how to stick to the rules.

You need to keep records of transactions, not only to make your business run smoothly but in order to fill out your self assessment return. You can make use of a number of computer packages available for both record-keeping and accounts. And consult *Starting a Business For Dummies* by Colin Barrow (Wiley) for tips on setting up an accounting system.

You have to keep records of your business for five years following the final filing date for your trading year. Someone with a trading year ending on 31 March 2006 will file by 31 January 2007 and needs to keep the paperwork (or computer records) until 31 January 2012.

Filling out Schedule D can pay dividends

Self-employed people have to fill in the basic self assessment tax form and also the self-employment pages (downloadable from the Inland Revenue at www.inlandrevenue.gov.uk/ sa/index.htm or available via the Inland Revenue helpline on 0845 9000444). (Chapter 18 offers help with the self assessment form.)

If you are self-employed, you will end up being taxed under what the taxman and accountants used to call Schedule D (which we'll still use as shorthand). Being on Schedule D can make your personal bank balance happier, most importantly because you can claim many expenses against what you earn. (See the following section.)

Those who work for someone else on PAYE can claim business expenses against tax only if those expenses are 'wholly, exclusively, and necessarily' incurred in carrying out their contract of employment. That definition is really tough to meet. But when you are on Schedule D, the 'necessarily' part of the PAYE definition goes. The reason? No outsider can define 'necessity'. Do you actually need to advertise your services in one particular way? Do you necessarily need a new vehicle when you can do the work using a clapped-out pushbike? Is your computer over-specified and do you need one at all?

All these choices are open to big companies and small firms alike and all the expenses can be set against the company's tax or your personal self assessment form.

Counting your credits

You have a lot of freedom as a self-employed person. You can choose how you'll carry out your business and money spent wholly and exclusively for your business can be set against your earnings.

The tax authorities are not idiots. Don't try putting the costs of a Rolls-Royce down against tax claiming it is a vehicle you use 'wholly and exclusively' for your business, unless, of course, you run a wedding limousine hire firm.

The Inland Revenue is always on the lookout for exaggerated expenses, but you don't have to exaggerate to minimise your tax bill. Just make sure you deduct everything you're legally allowed to, including:

- ✔ The administrative cost of running the business against your earnings from it. This sounds elementary, but many people with start-ups or those who have a small business on the side still have the mindset of working for an employer who picks up all the costs of running the business. All those little items such as postage stamps, fuel, mobile and fixed telephone charges, and even heating and lighting for your workplace add up over a year and are legally deductible.

- ✔ The cost of equipment including computers, machinery, and other big items. I explain how to deal with big items in the next section. Cars have rules of their own and are covered in the next section.

✔ Bank charges on business accounts and interest on loans for your business

✔ A proportion of the costs of running your home if you use part of your property as a base. There are no specific rules for this. It's a question of common sense. If you have a house with six rooms and use one fairly regularly for your business, then look at your domestic bills and take a sixth-part.

Obviously, if you use other premises solely for business, then you can deduct all the costs.

Always make sure you say the rooms you use are 'non-exclusive' and don't claim mortgage interest or council tax for that portion of your property otherwise you could run into Capital Gains Tax problems when you sell the home and incur a business rate from the local council.

✔ Accountancy and legal fees and the costs of debt collection.

✔ Pension contributions can count against self-employment earnings.

✔ Publications, stationery, postage, wages and other costs of employing people, insurance, travel, subsistence, gas, electricity, water – all the way down to the batteries in your calculator.

Accounting for big business items

Big expenditure items such as plant and machinery, cars, and computers are not counted against your profits in the same way as the goods and services you buy in to make your business work. With these big items, you can claim capital allowances against your profits. A *capital allowance is* a proportion of the purchase cost that you can set against profits each year as long as you own the item. The result is that tax relief against the expenditure made on these items can be spread out over several years.

The following list explains capital allowances for major items:

✔ On most **plant and machinery,** you can claim 40 per cent of the value in the first year, and then 25 per cent of the balance each following year. So something costing £1,000 has £400 (40 per cent) offset against tax in the first year, and 25 per cent of the £600 balance, or £150, offset in the second year. The starting figure is £450 for the next year, and goes down by a quarter each year. You never get to zero!

✔ **Cars** qualify for a 25 per cent capital allowance each year with a limit of £12,000 on the value of the car. Using this ceiling, the maximum allowance in the first year is £3,000, then 25 per cent of the remaining £9,000 (£2,250), and so on.

Low-emission vehicles benefit from a 100 per cent allowance for the first year. The vehicle manufacturer will tell you if your vehicle qualifies as less noxious – printing the rules in full would take up a large part of this book.

Capital allowances are available against the actual cost of the asset. You set the costs of any bank loan or other financing against business expenses.

You cannot claim capital allowances greater than your profits. But there is nothing to stop you claiming less than your maximum and then carrying the remaining amounts into a subsequent year.

Claiming extra help as you start up

Money you spend before you start can be counted against your profits once you set up. This expenditure may include the money you paid for a computer and other machinery you already possess and the cost of feasibility studies into your hoped-for business. These sums will normally be counted against your first year's profits. But if you make a loss, you can count them against the next year (and so on, for a total of four years if you fail to make a profit).

Accounting for loss making

With the best will in the world, your self-employment could result in a loss. In such a case, you have two tax options, which I explore in the next two sections.

Deducting the loss from other taxable sums

Provided you have earnings from a PAYE job, a pension, from dividends or interest, or from taxable capital gains, you could set your loss off against these amounts. This is a good route for a self-employed person whose business is part-time. Someone earning £20,000 from a PAYE post, and losing £2,000 on their business would end up with a tax bill based on £18,000.

If you make a loss in any of the first four years of a new business, you can offset this loss against tax on your salary in the three years preceding the establishment of your business. You may have to prove you intended to make profits during this period: Tax inspectors look out for loss-making 'hobbies' whose main function is to dodge tax.

You have to inform the tax inspector within 12 months following the 31 January after the end of your loss-making business year.

Subtracting the loss from future earnings

If your losses exceed your taxable sums, you can carry forward the loss against future profits. You can do this for as many years as you need – there is no limit. But you have to tell the Inland Revenue within five years of the 31 January following the end of the tax year in which your personal accounted year finished.

In most cases, it makes sense to offset your losses against earnings, dividends, interest, and capital gains from elsewhere. But if you expect your self-run business to be very remunerative in the future and take you into the top tax band, then consider subtracting early losses from future earnings.

Scanning National Insurance

As a self-employed person, profits you make from your business are added to other earnings, pensions, dividends, and interest for income tax. National insurance is different. There are special rules for the self-employed and two sets of payments you may have to make.

Complicating the classes

National insurance comes in four classes, numbered one to four. Class 1 is for employed persons. The self-employed have to look at Classes 2 and 4, which I do in the next sections. And in case you're wondering, Class 3 is voluntary – it's paid by people who do not work but who wish to keep up their record to qualify for the state retirement pension and other benefits.

Class 4 is collected through the annual self assessment return. It is the only national insurance to be collected in this way. Most people pay Class 1 via their salary packet, while Class 2 and Class 3 are paid usually with a direct debit.

Paying Class 2

As a self-employed person you have to pay a fixed £2.10 a week (in 2005–06) in national insurance. This maintains your payment record for the state pension and health-related benefits – but not jobseeker's allowance.

If your earnings from all self-employment are below the Class 2 threshold (£4,345 in 2005–06), you are exempt from Class 2.

Paying Class 4

Class 4 national insurance is effectively an additional tax on the self-employed. It does not provide any benefits, but that doesn't mean you don't have to pay it if your profits (what you take in less your costs) are at least £4,895 in a year. If your profits are below that figure, you don't have to worry about Class 4.

But if you do have to pay, it is currently (2005–06) charged at 8 per cent of your taxable profits from £4,895 a year to £32,760. The 8 per cent stops there. But there's a 1 per cent surcharge on all sums above that. So if your profits were £42,760, you would pay 1 per cent on the £10,000 above the upper profits level.

Putting a cap on national insurance

Someone with a mix of self-employment and employment could end up paying Class 1, Class 2, and Class 4. The bad news is that many pay more in national insurance for the same amount of income if it comes from a variety of sources, such as self-employment and employment, than they would if it all came from one source. The good news is that there are ceilings on payments.

If all your income comes from being self-employed, then you cannot pay more than £2,346 (in tax year 2005–06) in Class 2 and Class 4 together. The Inland Revenue Web site (www.inlandrevenue.gov.uk) or your local tax office can give details of future rates. And if you have earnings from employment as well, there is a chance you have paid a lot more than you should when you add up all the sums from your job and your self-employment. But you cannot pay more than £3,065 in a tax year (again, according to 2005–06 limits). So you could claim a refund from the Inland Revenue if you have paid more than this amount.

None of these limits includes the new 1 per cent national insurance surcharge on earnings over £32,760.

If you know, or reasonably suspect, that you will hit the overall national insurance limit, you can apply for Class 2 and/or Class 4 payments to be deferred until you know the outcome of the year's earnings pattern. You should do this before the start of the tax year, but the Inland Revenue, which runs the national insurance collection, often allows later applications.

Hiring Helpers

Being a sole trader doesn't mean you have to work on your own. It's a tax definition, after all. You may need to pay for help on a part- or full-time basis or to hire someone to help out every now and again. If you have family, you may want to make the most of the tax advantages you can reap by employing them. The next sections tell you how to look at employees as ways to lower your tax.

Employing your family

You can employ your family in the business and thereby take advantage of the lower tax rates your spouse or children fall under to reduce your household's overall tax bill.

You do have to keep a few rules in mind, though:

- ✔ You have to hire your relative to do real work at commercial wage rates. You cannot get away with paying a small child £100 an hour for taking telephone messages!

- ✔ Local authorities have rules on children working. This will not apply to a few hours working in the home. But if you want to employ a child under 16 in other circumstances, always check with the council first.

- ✔ Family members who earn more than £94 (in 2005–06) in any week are liable for national insurance payments. As the employer, you also have to pay national insurance on their behalf. This is called the *national insurance lower earnings limit.* Accountants call it the LEL.

Your teenage children might have no income to offset against their personal allowance. Or you might be a top-rate tax-payer and have a partner whose maximum is at the basic or lower rate.

You set up a computer repair service working from a small shop. Your 16 year old helps you at your premises for four hours a week at £5 an hour. That's £20 a week – say £1,000 a year, allowing for holidays and some overtime. You can offset the £1,000 against your profits. And, if your teenager has no other income, he or she does not have to pay tax at all as the £1,000 is well within the personal allowance limit. Had you done the work yourself and not used your child, the £1,000 would have been taxable as profits at up to 40 per cent, so the household would only have £600 instead of the full £1,000.

You have to pay the money for real, of course. The taxman can ask for the audit trail to see how the payment goes from your business to the family member concerned.

Establishing a partnership with your partner

If you and your spouse or partner are both involved in running a business, it could be worth exploring a partnership structure. There are legal concerns such as each partner being liable for debts incurred by other partners. For tax reasons, it is best to have a partnership contract which sets out how profits will be shared.

Starting a Business For Dummies by Colin Barrow (Wiley) sets out who should and who should not set up as partners. You need to work out whether you are better off with a partnership but, more importantly, whether your relationship could stand it. And that's outside the scope of *Paying Less Tax For Dummies.*

The Inland Revenue is on the lookout for phoney partnerships, established solely with the aim of reducing a couple's overall tax bill. If you have a business partnership with your spouse, you may have to show that both work in the firm and both contribute work according to the proportion of the profits you each earn. This is a measure to prevent couples sharing profits on a 50-50 basis to use up tax allowances of the non-worker when only one works.

Paying employees

If you hire employees, you are in the same situation as any other employer. You have to sort out any PAYE tax and national insurance contributions they owe.

Giving Up Work

Stopping work is easier than starting. You should inform the Inland Revenue if you intend to stop working in your business. And if you were caught by overlap, now is the time to claim it back. Your final accounts can also take care of what happens when you sell plant, machinery, vehicles, or stock.

The reality of self-employment is that most businesses cease entirely when the self-employed person retires or goes back to working for someone else. A few businesses have a future value. The chapters on Inheritance Tax and Capital Gains Tax deal with any implications where you sell your business for a profit to a third party.

Chapter 12

Considering Your Company's Status

*T*urning the business you run into a limited company has never been more popular. As well as awarding yourself the title of company director, and enjoying the separation of business and personal life that limited company status can provide, low rates on corporation tax, the tax companies pay on profits, are really attractive.

After all, what can be better than the zero per cent corporation tax rate payable on the first £10,000 of profits? And there are 101 ways (well, not quite as many, but a good number anyway) of using loopholes to reduce tax even further.

But turning your business into a limited company for tax benefits is not a one-way game. For starters, if there are 101 ways of using a company to save tax, the Inland Revenue knows 102 ways to stop inappropriate use of these methods. And it is increasingly using this muscle, some would say controversially, to stop its tax take leaking away. So before you opt for company status as the automatic road to tax savings, weigh up the advantages and disadvantages.

Informing Yourself about Incorporating

The basic choice, once you decide to work for yourself, is between being incorporated or unincorporated.

Being incorporated is not as scary as it sounds. *Incorporation* is when you decide on the legal (and therefore tax) framework of a limited company. It's essential for a firm that is going places big time. But it can turn out to be a bad deal for you in your early trading days, or if you never intend growing past the status of a one-man or a one-woman band.

Looking at reasons to reject the company route

Company status can be a really bad option for many small businesses. So start with looking at some negatives to see if corporate life rather than self-employment is really such a good idea. If you tick two or more of the disadvantages in the following list, you may be better off staying unincorporated. Go back to Chapter 11 on self-employment status, and use the time you would have spent reading this chapter on growing your business instead!

It may sound great to have *Co Ltd* after your firm's name; and to be able to put up a brass plate. But here are some pointers as to why it can be a bad idea:

- ✔ There can be complications where your personal tax dealings and those of your company interface.

- ✔ You generally have more flexibility in dealing with the Inland Revenue over income tax and national insurance as a self-employed individual than you do as a company director.

- ✔ The additional legal and regulatory costs involved with incorporating and complying with company law may outweigh tax savings.

✔ It can be difficult to escape paying accountancy fees to audit the accounts you have to file with the Inland Revenue.

✔ You have to file details of your business once a year with Companies House. These details such as share ownership, home addresses, and some financial details are available to the public so your competitors (or even nosy neighbours) can find out some things about your business affairs. However, small companies do not have to file full accounts.

✔ You have to make national insurance payments as both an employer and an employee. If you are self-employed, you make only one set of payments.

✔ Tax rules make some company pension plans less flexible – and often more expensive to administer.

✔ The Inland Revenue is clamping down on what it considers to be the abuses of the company structure by what are essentially one-person, personal service businesses (see 'Steering clear of the big tax clampdown' later in this chapter). If you are caught by this, you can get the worst of both company and self-employed status.

Taking advantage of company status

Incorporating can appear to be a no-brainer option. There's the zero per cent tax starter rate and lower tax levels compared to working as a self-employed person as the company grows. And there's the glamour of the brass plate outside your premises proclaiming your existence.

Becoming incorporated means you pay zero per cent tax on the first £10,000 of your profits . . . provided you plough this money back into the company.

Some reasons you may want to turn your small business into a limited company are:

✔ You have the ability to plan where profits go. This can bring big tax benefits to a growing company.

✔ You only need two shareholders with one share each – the minimum per share investment is £1.

✔ You can repay people who back your venture, but who do not have any part in the operation of the business, by giving them *dividends* (payments once or twice a year decided by the directors which depend on profits).

✔ Selling or passing on an incorporated business when you retire or die is often less complicated tax-wise than the same procedure for an unincorporated business.

✔ You may be able to raise money for your business through the Enterprise Investment Scheme (EIS), which gives a number of tax-saving deals to those who put their cash into your firm via a share issue. The EIS is complicated, so take advice from a stock broker and accountant.

Oddly enough, the list of reasons for becoming a company is shorter than the list for not going for incorporation. But don't worry. The tax and other plus points in favour of company status are powerful even if they are not too long!

Setting up a Limited Company

Setting up a limited company is easy. You can do it yourself with forms from Companies House (www.companieshouse.gov.uk), the organisation that controls all of Britain's 1.8 million companies. But most people buy an off-the-shelf company from a firm specialising in company formations at a cost of around £100 to £200. An *off-the-shelf company* essentially gives you the go-ahead for company status. You can change the name of this company and take off the original directors and replace them with names of your choice. It's quicker than having a company set-up specialist establishing a company just for you.

Minimising tax on death

Provided you owned your business in whole or in part for at least two years, your heirs can deduct 100 per cent of its value from the value of other assets you leave behind when you die.

This does not apply to companies that are set up for dealing in shares or other securities, or for dealing in property. And the assets have to be real business assets. You can't stuff the valuable jewellery and priceless works of art that you intend leaving behind into your bike repair company.

However you set up a company, don't forget that the initial setting-up costs involved, as well as the continuing costs such as the £15 annual filing fee with the Registrar of Companies and accounting and auditing fees, can all be set off against your profits and so reduce the business's tax bill.

As a company, you can give as much as you like to your favourite charity! The amount is tax-deductible from the firm's profits so it's free of corporation tax. But your company must not derive any significant benefit from the donation. The glow of doing good is fine but insisting that your generosity appears plastered all over town as an advert is not.

And don't forget a company can always cease trading and the owners revert to the self-employment option in some circumstances.

Steering clear of the big tax clampdown

The Inland Revenue is determined not to allow small businesses to choose between self-employment and company structure just to reduce income tax and national insurance. Its first move was against *personal service companies,* the technical name for one-person firms (plus one other share-holder, usually a spouse or partner) that supply nothing other than labour.

Most personal service companies work in the information technology business. The proprietors became limited companies employing themselves because many did not qualify for self-employment status as they worked full-time for one employer. Becoming companies, and having a supply contract with a big company whose computers they looked after, resulted in them paying less tax and national insurance than being employed by those companies.

The Inland Revenue argument is that most of these firms do nothing more than work for bigger companies on a series of fixed-term contracts. So the company structure is an artificial means of dodging tax. IR35 people (named after the number of the Inland Revenue circular that authorises the crackdown on these companies) do not use their own materials, nor work from their own premises, nor are they able to set their own hours or other terms of work – all signs of business independence. So the Inland Revenue says they should be treated as employees and be on PAYE.

But not all IT contractors are caught by IR35. Those who genuinely work for a number of people, have invested in their own equipment, can control their own working hours, and risk making a loss continue to qualify as companies.

Making use of family to lessen the tax bite

You can use members of your family in your business to help reduce the overall tax bill of your household.

As the director of a company, you have control of your business. As a tax-payer, you can manage your takings from your company to lessen your tax bite.

Transferring money to your spouse is a well-known and perfectly legal method to minimise the tax your family pays. You can pay family members dividends or hire them to work for your company (I talk about the issues related to hiring family in Chapter 11). In this section, I give you some hints on how to make the most of your earnings by paying the least possible in tax.

Suppose a company owner wants (and can afford) to take £50,000 a year from the firm. This is well over the top-rate threshold so whether it is paid as salary or a dividend, there will be a 40 per cent tax bill on the top slice of this money.

But if the owner has a spouse who earns very little, and the company is structured in such a way that the low-earning spouse owns 99 per cent of the shares and hence gets 99 per cent of the dividend payouts, the £50,000 can be divided up so the owner gets £30,000 in salary, putting this person easily into the basic-tax band.

The other £20,000 from the £50,000 is paid in dividends. This would divide up as £200 (1 per cent) for the owner and £19,800 (99 per cent) for the spouse. So neither would pay top-rate tax. The dividend tax would be 19 per cent (£3,800 on the £20,000), but that's a lot better than paying up to 40 per cent.

An alternative would be to pay the spouse £20,000, declaring no dividend or just a tiny one. This would work out at a combined income tax and national insurance take of £4,734, more than the dividend route but still saving a good few thousand compared with the working spouse earning £50,000.

The Inland Revenue is increasingly questioning these 'husband and wife' company arrangements. It checks to see if a paid spouse really does work to the value of the salary – doing one hour a week for £20,000 a year won't wash if that's far less than the commercial rate of employing someone else.

And it is looking at dividends. It might question, for instance, where the capital came from to buy the shares in the first place.

Deciding How Best to Pay Yourself

Once you set up as a limited company, you still have to work out your profits in just the same way as you did when you were just a self-employed person – by taking costs away from your earnings from customers. So if your customers paid you £40,000 and your total expenditure was £10,000, you end up with £30,000 in profit.

It's what you then do with your profit that matters. These profits can be distributed in three different ways, all with their own set of tax rules:

- ✔ **Keep profits within the company:** Cash you keep within the company to fund further expansion; research or marketing is subject to corporation tax.

- ✔ **Pay salaries:** In most small companies, the directors and their family or friends are likely to be the only employees. Profits paid as salaries are subject to PAYE income tax and national insurance.

- ✔ **Distribute dividends:** This does not attract national insurance payments and once the company itself has paid corporation tax on it, there is no further tax to pay for basic-rate tax-payers.

This three-way split gives companies a number of tax planning opportunities as well as a number of tax disasters. Directors can, for instance, decide between keeping money in the company to fund the future and raising a bank loan. And, more importantly for tax saving, they can decide between paying themselves a salary or paying themselves through dividends.

Leaving the money in the company

Money you leave in the firm after paying out salaries has a special tax rate. And it is zero – yes, zero per cent – for the first £10,000. A lot of people decided to incorporate as a result of this seeming gift. But if you pay this £10,000 out as a salary rather than leaving it in the business, you get hit by income tax and national insurance. And if it's paid as a dividend, the tax rate jumps to 19 per cent. Not much zero about either of those.

Paying yourself a salary out of the profits

Paying yourself (or other directors) a regular salary means accounting for the PAYE and National Insurance, too. Despite this, a regular salary does have advantages – you need to have a regular salary if you apply for many types of personal loan, including most mortgages. Until new rules kick in (in April 2006), the amount you can pay into a pension plan is also governed by your salary.

However, the biggest advantage of paying yourself a regular salary is that the Inland Revenue will not question these arrangements, as salaries represent the biggest possible take for the tax inspector.

Taking dividends versus taking salary

The main advantage of taking dividends instead of a salary is that dividends are not liable to national insurance payments. Not paying national insurance can save the company 12.8 per cent and the recipient up to 11 per cent. And the special tax rate at 19 per cent is lower for dividend recipients who pay income tax at the basic rate (currently 22 per cent).

The disadvantages to paying yourself with dividends are you have less money on which to base pension contributions and a lower salary for purposes such as impressing the bank or building society when you want to take out a mortgage.

How it all works

When you set up your new business for real, you need to decide how to structure it. You have a choice of:

✔ staying self-employed and not bothering with a company
structure

✔ establishing a limited company and paying yourself a
salary out of the profits

✔ going down the limited company route, but paying yourself mostly through a dividend

Each has its own set of tax rules; and each produces quite different amounts of cash for the firm's owner, especially in the
early years.

I can't pretend the choice is easy. It's not. Or that understanding the rules is a piece of cake. It's not. But if you take your
future business seriously, you'll need to make up your mind,
although it's always possible, if costly, to change your decision later on.

So bear with me and look at how Ali, Ben, and Charlotte's big
ideas progress. These are just outlines, but they should give
you enough information to help you in coming up with the business plan your bank manager or other advisers will demand
to see.

Ali, Ben and Charlotte all set out in business on the same day.
All three are interior decorators and designers with ambition.
All three need £115,000 to kick-start their businesses. And all
three turn out to have the same earnings from customers and
the same outlay on materials and other expenses (hey, this is
just an example, after all!). They make just £1,500 profits each
in their difficult first year; and £20,000 profits in their second
year when they are more confident. So are they all equal?
Absolutely not:

✔ Ali stays self-employed, and is technically a sole trader

✔ Ben has a limited company but largely pays himself
through dividends from his profits, with the balance
as a salary

✔ Charlotte will take all her future earnings from her limited company as a salary

So read on and see how they progress from start-up to long term going concern. I round the sums of money so you can see how it works without worrying about slight changes of tax rates each year. The gaps between the three are gigantic, anyway.

Ali's Alluring Interiors

Ali is self-employed. He borrows £100,000 from the bank at 6% to start his business and puts in £15,000 from his own savings.

In his first year, Ali makes £1,500 from customers but after paying his £6,000 bank interest he loses £4,500. He can claim this loss against his other income either in the current year or in preceding years. He does not have to pay national insurance because he does not earn enough.

In year 2, his business earns £20,000 after costs. This all goes down on his tax form so he ends up with around £15,600 to take home after tax and national insurance.

In year 3, he expands. He can now offset part of the money he spends on his new premises against his earnings.

Many years later, he decides to sell up. He will be liable to capital gains tax on any profit he makes but at the business asset rate so he could get away with a 10 per cent rate.

Ben's Beautiful Homes

Ben borrows £100,000 from the bank but uses his £15,000 to create shares in his limited company. He decides on a minimal £5,000 a year salary and to take the rest in dividends when his profits grow.

The first year is poor and he makes just £1,500. And after paying himself £5,000 and bank interest of £6,000, he makes a £9,500 loss. He can't offset this against any other earnings present or past. So he has to wait until the company does better. He has very little tax or national insurance to pay so he can take home over £4,950.

In year 2, he makes £20,000. He still takes £5,000 as a salary. Now, because it's profitable, his company has to pay corporation tax – around £2,550. The balance of around £12,450 is paid to Ben as a dividend. As this has already been taxed through corporation tax, and as Ben is a basic rate taxpayer, he has no more income tax to pay on his dividend. So his take home is roughly £17,450.

Looking further ahead, Ben will be able to claim allowances against profits for capital spending and by doing so cuts his corporation tax bill. But he must not forget that dividends can only be earned from taxed profits. And dividends do not count for pensions, or for most mortgage loan applications.

When Ben decides to sell up, he faces capital gains tax on the increased value of the shares at the business rate. But this future change of ownership has no effect on the company itself.

Charlotte's Classy Décor

Charlotte borrows £100,000 from the bank and then adds her own £15,000 to turn the whole £115,000 into shares. She wants a steady income as a salary from her company.

She has a tax-saving idea. Because her company has five or fewer shareholders, it's what accountants call a *close company*. This allows her to offset the £6,000 bank interest against her earnings. So her £20,000 taxable pay is cut to around £12,500 after national insurance and the loan interest deduction. The company, however, loses £18,500 in its first year because it pays her £20,000 salary but only earns £1,500 from customers. This loss can be offset against future profits.

In year 2, the £20,000 profit has to pay not just her salary but also the employer's national insurance contribution of around £1,725. She has to pay national insurance and income tax on the £18,275 over giving her a take home pay of around £14,100.

As she becomes more successful, she will have to juggle raising her salary and not having enough profits to offset against her spending on expansion, or restraining her salary, and having enough profits to set against tax. She will also have to weigh up the pros and cons of paying corporation tax on profits against income tax and national insurance on her salary. She might then start to take part of her money in salary and part in dividend.

When she wants to quit, she does not sell the company. Instead, she decides that selling the assets is a better idea. This way, she pays corporation tax on the profits, possibly a better deal than the capital gains tax she might have had to pay. She may, of course, pay no corporation tax as she might still have losses from previous years to set against the amount she gets for the firm's assets.

Setting Up Special Pension Plans

As a director of a limited company, you can use the tax saving on paying into a pension plan to reduce the amount of your hard-earned cash that the Inland Revenue takes. Pensions qualify for tax relief on the contribution at your top rate, grow in a tax-free fund, and offer a tax-free lump sum when you decide to retire.

Directors can set up personal pension schemes (like the self-employed) or contribute to stakeholder plans (again like the self-employed. For many, one of these options is the easiest route. You can pay in up to the percentage limit for your age (this is due to be replaced in 2006 by a lifetime pension fund limit).

You can subtract the costs of setting up and maintaining a company pension plan from your profits.

Starting your very own company scheme

You can set up your very own company pension scheme, just like those operated by really big companies. But you can limit it to yourself, or to yourself and fellow directors, if you don't want to extend it to any staff you hire.

One big advantage is that money spent on pensions for directors and other staff comes off your profits so there is no corporation tax to pay. And to top that with another bonus, employers do not pay national insurance on company pension contributions.

You cannot count money you receive as dividends for your own pension purposes. But the tax rules say you can use it to pay up to £3,600 before tax relief (£2,808 net) into a stakeholder pension for someone in your family.

Looking at limits on how much you can pay in

Your pension scheme will probably invest in a fund, just like those on offer to personal pension plan purchasers. But while as an employee you can only pay in 15 per cent of your salary to your plan, putting on your other hat as a controlling director, you can invest far larger sums into the pension as an employer contribution.

The maximum percentages depend on the age of the director when the plan was started. The figures, set out in Table 12-1, are really weird! But they are correct.

Table 12-1   Employer Limits on Pension Contributions

Age on Starting	Maximum Per Cent of Salary
25	27.66
30	33.60
35	41.95
40	54.54
45	75.60
50	117.84
55	244.79

Source: Inland Revenue

By balancing the sums you pay yourself as a salary and the amount of your profit, your firm can save a fortune in national insurance and you can save personal tax and national insurance as well.

You start your new company when you are 50. Instead of paying yourself the £60,000 you can afford as a salary, you decide to earn £30,000 and get the company to pay in a £30,000 contribution to the company pension plan on your behalf. The result is your firm only pays employer's national insurance on £30,000 and not £60,000. This saves £3,840 (£30,000 times the 12.8 per cent national insurance rate). As an employee, you save 11 per cent national insurance on the slice between £30,000 and £32,760, which is worth £303.60 (£2,760 times 11 per cent), and you save 1 per cent on the £27,240 balance – another £274. And you can put in another 15 per cent – £4,500 – of your salary as well as your own personal contribution and keep that out of the tax net as well!

Some small company pension plans known as Small Self Administered Pension Schemes let you choose the investments yourself. In some circumstances, you can sell your company premises to the scheme as a contribution and then pay your plan a commercial rent. Because this is a pension plan, that rent will not be taxed. Make sure you know what you're doing, though, as these plans can be costly and complex. They are not for DIY pension buyers!

Selling Up and Tax Rules

Stopping your business can have as many tax implications as starting it. There are a number of options, which I lay out here. But before you read them, a word of advice. No two companies or two people are the same, so it is always worthwhile seeking individual help from an accountant before acting. However, I can give you some general advice.

One route when you decide you want to cash in on your company is selling the shares in your business to another person. This is worthwhile if the company's business and reputation have a value.

In general, you will be liable for Capital Gains Tax on the difference between what you paid for the shares (or what they were worth when the company started) and what you get for them. But while Capital Gains Tax can hit you for 40 per cent, you will get *business asset taper relief*, which means you pay over no more than 20 per cent of the gain if the business asset was held for one year and no more than 10 per cent of the gain if it was held for two or more years.

Or you can sell the assets and shut the company. This can be more complicated, involving corporation tax on any gains plus tax when you take out the money from the company to pay it to yourself.

If your company is worth something, then it is worth hiring an accountant to tell you the best way of disposing of it. In some cases, you might consider stretching the sale over more than one tax year.

Part IV
Save on Your Savings and Investments

"Under gifts, you seem to have made several large donations to the poor starving bank managers of the Cayman Islands."

In this part . . .

Save right and you pay no tax. Save wrong, and up to 40 per cent of what you make goes to the tax authorities. But saving for tax-breaks can be an investment disaster.

In this part, I show you how tax works on your nest egg from basic savings to big risks to retirement planning. The lesson? There are no correct answers. It all depends on you, your family, and what you need.

And don't forget, some financial advisers have their own agenda. They want you to buy investment packages from them. They know putting 'tax-free' in the biggest typeface available will pull in loads of commission-paying punters. That doesn't mean it's good for you. Be warned.

Chapter 13

Minimising Tax on Your Savings

- -

In This Chapter

▶ Working out how interest is taxed

▶ Getting a rebate

▶ Filing a retro-claim

▶ Looking at children's savings

▶ Considering tax-free savings

- -

*Y*ou work really hard for your money. And it's taxed all the way. But you've managed to scrimp here and economise there so you have some money tied up in interest-bearing savings accounts with a bank or building society. You feel good about this – as well you should. But if your money is earning interest, the Inland Revenue wants a share, even though you paid tax on the money in the first place.

Tax applies to all accounts whether operated by a branch-based passbook, by post, by phone, or online. You pay tax whether you save with a bank or building society or even with some accounts from the government's National Savings and Investments. And don't think you can escape just because the interest rate is a measly 0.1 per cent rather than a healthy (at the time of writing) 4 to 5 per cent. The taxman still wants even this tiny ounce of flesh.

This chapter shows how the system of taxing savings works and how the Inland Revenue collects tax without so much as a by-your-leave. It also points out ways you can get your tax deductions back easily and speedily.

Taxing Interest

Suppose you have £1,000 in savings. You find an account which pays 5 per cent – and you're proud of yourself because that's a comparatively good rate at the time. You reckon you don't even need a calculator to work out that you're going to earn £50 in interest for the year. You get top marks for arithmetic. Your old maths teacher would be proud of you. But if you think you can budget to spend that £50 at the end of the year, think again.

The stated annual interest rate, whatever rate it might be, is the rate your money earns – the *gross interest* amount – and indicates the sum you would get if there were no such things as taxes. However, the final amount that actually gets paid to you, or gets paid back into your account, is the gross interest amount minus the income tax the Inland Revenue takes for taxes. This final amount is the *net interest.*

The following sections talk about how this system works.

Paying tax without effort (or intent)

Under long-standing arrangements, the bank or building society you invest your savings with automatically diverts some of your interest to the Inland Revenue. You may be able to prevent this – see 'Recovering money with form R85' later on – but for the great majority, tax comes off willy-nilly.

From your point of view, this automatic deduction can save you a lot of bother paying the tax later. And by taking it away before you can spend it, this method prevents the embarrassment of having to scrimp, steal (metaphorically, anyway), or borrow to find the money at tax time.

From the Inland Revenue's point of view, this tax-gathering process is super efficient. The bank or building society does the Revenue's work for it. It knows that this deduction makes it impossible for savers to 'forget' about paying.

You must keep all the paperwork, including any notices you get from the bank or building society, which shows interest paid. In some cases, this comes in the form of an entry in a savings passbook. You must keep this for a minimum of 22 months after the end of the tax year.

Shelling out at the special savings rate

Currently, the tax rate on savings is 20 per cent, a nice round sum (as well as just a little less than the basic tax rate). Most basic-rate tax-payers need do no more – they need not fill in any forms or pay any more tax. But the statement your bank or building society sends shows your interest in two parts. The bigger amount is the net interest your account is credited with; the smaller amount is the tax deducted. Adding the two back together again produces the gross interest. Table 13-1 shows how various interest rates affect £1,000 in savings.

Table 13-1	Interest and Taxes on Savings of £1,000		
Interest Rate	*Gross Interest*	*Tax Deducted*	*Net Interest*
6%	£60	£12	£48
5%	£50	£10	£40
4%	£40	£8	£32
3%	£30	£6	£24
2%	£20	£4	£16
1%	£10	£2	£8
0.5%	£5	£1	£4
0.1%	£1	£0.20	£0.80

Doing the sums yourself

For most basic-rate tax-payers, the deductions in Table 13-1, which turn gross interest into net interest, are the end of the matter. But the Inland Revenue concerns itself with all your income, not just your savings. So, before you breathe a sigh of relief and think that the savings rate deduction is all you have to worry about, you need to do some arithmetic.

Your savings interest, added to other sources of income (such as employment earnings, self-employment, or pensions) can push you into the top tax bracket, which currently starts at £37,295 for someone with a standard personal allowance. The personal allowance is dealt with fully in Chapter 4.

Top-rate tax-payers, and those whose interest from savings pushes them into the 40 per cent tax bracket, have to pay more income tax on their savings earnings. If this applies to you, you do this by declaring your savings interest income on the self assessment form and then paying the extra tax on the due dates or via PAYE (Pay As You Earn) if the sum is small enough. The self assessment form is considered fully in Chapter 18.

The process works like this: You add the gross interest from all your interest-bearing accounts to all your other earnings and then you calculate the top rate – 40 per cent – of this amount. Remember, the bank or building society has already deducted tax at the 20 per cent special savings rate and the self assessment form makes allowance for this deduction.

For example, if your income from your job in 2005–06 is £35,000 then it is well within the basic 20 per cent rate tax band, and comfortably below the threshold of £37,295 for paying 40 per cent. However, if you're lucky enough to win £100,000 on the lottery (lottery winnings are tax-free) and you invest the money in a safe, sensible bank account earning 5 per cent (or £5,000 gross interest) then your bank deducts 20 per cent (£1,000) of the annual gross interest, leaving you with £4,000 net to spend.

And if you think that's the end of the matter, think again. You have to add the gross interest sum (even though you receive only 80 per cent of it) to all your other earnings. Unfortunately the total now pushes you into the higher 40 per cent rate band. So, when you file your self assessment form be prepared to pay tax over and above the amount already deducted at source. And make sure that you read the next section on how bank and building society interest impacts on top-rate tax-payers.

Adding your £5,000 gross interest to your work earnings of £35,000 gives you a total £40,000, assuming you have no other source of income. So everything over and above £37,295 falls into the top tax band. In this case, you have to pay extra tax beyond the standard rate on the sum of £2,705 – the difference between the £37,295 where the 40 per cent top rate starts and your £40,000 total income.

You have become a higher-rate tax-payer. As 20 per cent of the difference has already been taken off by your savings provider you need to find a further 20 per cent that, in this case, works out at £771.

Giving the taxman double

The bottom line, if you're in the higher 40 per cent tax bracket, is that you have to pay 20 per cent more on the interest you earn. So, if your savings interest from all sources adds up to £1,000, then £200 – 20 per cent – has already been taken off by the bank or building society, leaving a further £200 for you to pay.

Once you pass the top-rate tax threshold (where you go from being a basic-rate payer to a top-rate payer) you pay 20 per cent extra on every pound of interest you earn.

At current rates, all you have to do is to look at the first deduction and duplicate it. Easy, providing you have put the cash away to meet the self assessment bill!

Top-rate tax-payers may think it is unfair that basic-rate tax-payers, who normally pay 22 per cent on their earnings, get away with a reduced 20 per cent on savings whereas there is no such reduction for those on the higher rate. But as I've said elsewhere (and often!), don't expect the system to be logical or fair.

Adding up all your income sources

Include every interest-bearing account in your calculations, no matter how small the interest rate may be. However, perks such as free travel insurance, reductions on hotel rates from premium bank accounts where you pay a monthly fee, or rebates from credit cards do not count. The Inland Revenue says these deals are merely promotional discounts or other marketing ideas. You do not earn a fixed sum from these (whatever the glossy promotional literature might promise!) so there is no tax to pay. An additional factor is that you have a choice whether to accept these discount deals and give-aways so there is no contractual arrangement.

Making the most of joint accounts and sharing savings

Many people have joint accounts with spouses or partners to simplify their household finances. The notion that a married woman was dependant on her husband for tax returns died in the early 1990s. Now each holder of a joint account is consid-ered a separate person. And the rule is that each signatory to an account earns an equal share of the interest. So, if there are three signatories, the account is divided three ways.

Each partner must work out if they qualify for gross interest in their own right. For example, if the total gross interest earned is £200, divide that by two and add the resultant £100 to each holder's income to see if they can ask for a rebate.

The Inland Revenue doesn't care if you qualify for the rebate and your partner does not. Nor does it matter if one of you qualifies completely and the other one only partially qualifies because their earnings are a little above the cut-off point set at the personal allowance level. As far as the Inland Revenue is concerned, you each have your own account with your share of the total interest.

Married couples have the absolute legal right to transfer sav-ings between themselves without any taxation consequences. So it makes sense to put as much savings as possible into the name of the partner with the lower tax rate. So, if one spouse is a non-tax-payer in their own right, or pays the lower 10 per cent tax rate (see 'Looking at people in the 10 per cent band' later in this chapter), or pays the basic-rate tax while the other partner is taxed at a higher rate, then transfer savings to the partner with the lower income. Doing this can, if your savings are large enough, save you several thousand pounds a year.

So if one partner has £10,000 worth of savings producing £500 interest a year gross, she or he will pay £200 in tax if taxed at 40 per cent. By transferring the £10,000 to a non-tax-paying spouse, the interest can be paid gross, saving £200.

The Inland Revenue treats transfers as gifts and counts interest or other income from such transfers as income for the recipient, not the giver.

Tax savings can add up if you and your partner arrange things correctly. For example, if one partner is a higher-rate payer and the other a basic-rate payer, and the higher-rate payer earns £500 gross interest, then this amount is reduced to £300 with the 40 per cent tax rate, handing over £200 to the Inland Revenue. Transferring the same capital, and the £500 gross interest, to the basic-rate tax-payer reduces the tax rate to 20 per cent or £100 – a saving of £100.

The same neat bit of arithmetic and the same £100 savings occur if one partner is a basic-rate payer and the other is a non-tax-payer. The basic-rate payer has 20 per cent or £100 deducted. The non-tax-payer suffers no such deduction (thanks to the wonderful R85; see the upcoming 'Recovering money with form R85' section) or can claim the £100 back later.

But take care, having savings in one partner's name has several ramifications, and not all of them work for every couple:

- ✔ Only the partner in whose name the account is can access the money.

- ✔ The extra interest may push the new account holder into a higher tax band, making the transfer a waste of time.

- ✔ Each partner has to trust the other financially! There's no point transferring your life savings to your partner only to have him or her spend it all or run off with your wealth! Read *Relationships For Dummies* by Kate M. Wachs (Wiley) to find out more about the effect that arguing about money has on domestic bliss. It's probably the biggest single cause of partnership stress and break-up.

Looking at people in the 10 per cent band

People with incomes just over the tax-free band do not go straight to the basic rate. Instead, there is a small slice of income (£2,090 in 2005–06), which is taxed at 10p in the pound.

Given this 10 per cent tax band, it would be unfair to tax someone at 10 per cent on earnings and 20 per cent on savings. So if your total income ends up in the 10 per cent zone – if you're under 65, that starts at £4,896 a year for 2005–06 – you can reduce the 20 per cent savings rate to 10 per cent.

You can reclaim in two ways: You can use a self assessment form, though it's improbable that you would need one as your tax affairs are unlikely to be that complicated if your income is this low! Or you can reclaim via form R40 – a more likely route as it's much shorter and easier to fill in than the self assessment form!

An example may help make this clear. Say Maria's only income is bank interest from her savings in one account. In 2005–6, she earned £5,000 gross, which was reduced to £4,000 net after the 20 per cent tax deduction. The gross amount, however, is higher than her personal tax allowance of £4,895 so she cannot fill in form R85.

Using R40 (see the forthcoming section 'Getting money back with R40'), she claims

- ✔ Gross bank interest of £5,000
- ✔ Total income of £5,000
- ✔ Less personal allowance of £4,895
- ✔ Equals taxable income of £105

Maria must pay 10 per cent on the £105, or £10.50. But she paid £1,000 through having it deducted from her savings account, so she gets back £989.50 (£1,000 less her tax bill).

Asking for a Tax Rebate

It's not all one-way traffic. Although the Inland Revenue always has its tax-raising eye on the 20 per cent of bank and building society interest you earn, it does not have an absolute right to the money. This is in sharp contrast to the deduction of tax on income earned from dividends on shares (dealt with fully in Chapter 14) where the deduction of tax rights is absolute.

Literally millions of savers can apply to get £1 in every £5 of their interest deduction reversed and, legally, keep all the interest. In other words, you keep the gross interest amount instead of the net figure after 20 per cent is paid to the Inland Revenue.

The following sections tell you whether you qualify and how to apply for a tax rebate.

Checking your rebate qualifications

A large proportion of people who can apply for a tax rebate do not. They needlessly hand over cash that's theirs by right. Sadly, these people are often those who can least afford to pass up cash. They are on low or no income at all, and it is because their earnings are so low that they can escape the tax net.

Even the Inland Revenue has a conscience about this. Every so often, it mounts a publicity campaign for people to check whether they are receiving their full entitlement from their savings interest.

The main groups who qualify for tax rebates include pensioners, non-working spouses, and children. Broadly speaking, anyone with a low income can avoid paying tax on savings interest.

Recognising reasons people don't ask for their own money back

Check to see whether the reasons (or excuses) savers let the tax authorities end up with several hundred millions in extra tax each year apply to you:

✔ You had no idea that tax was automatically deducted and that this situation can only be prevented by filling in a tax form.

✔ You thought that tax did not apply to you as your income was so low.

✔ Your bank or building society did not explain your rights.

✔ You knew about the deduction but you thought the amount was too small to bother about.

✔ You were frightened to apply.

✔ You do not like filling in forms.

✔ Your previous arrangements to receive interest gross stopped because you reached 16.

✔ You had a period on no or low pay a few years ago but you now earn good money. Those in this position can apply for a rebate for up to six years in the past.

✔ You have a joint account with a spouse or partner and your other half is a high earner.

If any of these points apply to you, now's the time to get applying.

The basic rule is that if your gross interest from all your interest paying accounts plus all your earnings from employment or pensions (including state pensions but excluding any pension credits) total a sum below the personal allowance level (see Chapter 5 for information on allowance levels), then you should be paid gross interest rather than net on your savings. So, if you're under the age of 65 and have an income of less than £4,895 (in 2005–06), you qualify.

Savings firms such as banks and building societies don't sort your tax out for you automatically – they don't know your overall tax position unless you tell them about it. So, even with the best will in the world on their part, you have to start the ball rolling. The upcoming 'Recovering money with form R85' section tells you how.

Recovering money with form R85

If your total earnings from work and interest on savings fall below the personal allowance level, this section tells you how to claim your tax rebate.

The easy way of ensuring that you keep all the interest you earn is by filling in the very wonderful form R85. You can get this from a bank, building society, or from the Inland Revenue. You can print it from the Inland Revenue Web site at www.inlandrevenue.gov.uk.

In filling out form R85 and sending it to the Inland Revenue (your bank may do this for you), you're saying that your total income is below the tax-paying level, and therefore the bank or building society is authorised to pay you gross interest. You only have to fill in one form for each particular bank or building society but you must list separately and in full all the existing accounts you have with each financial institution. If you open a new account, or take your money out of one account and transfer it to another with the same bank or building society, make sure you fill in a new R85.

Your R85 declaration continues from tax year to tax year until you rescind it by telling the savings institution that you no longer qualify. You can also rescind the form by informing your tax inspector. You need to do this when your income grows to tax-paying levels. The one exception to this rule is for children reaching 16 – the special rules for youngsters' savings are considered in 'Caring for Children's Bank Accounts' later in this chapter.

The best way to get form R85 is to ask for it when you open an account at a bank or building society. Many savings firms give you an R85 ready-printed with details such as your name and address, that of the bank or building society, and the account number so all you have to do is sign it. By doing this, you get paid gross interest from the very start.

Don't expect the person behind the counter necessarily to volunteer an R85 form. You will probably have to ask for it. The bank clerk cannot know your circumstances such as whether your £100 deposit is all you have in the world or is just a small part of your wealth. And even if they did, they would not know details of any other income you might have.

Most people register for themselves. But parents or guardians can register for a young person aged under 16 and there are special facilities for those with power of attorney or other legal methods of managing money for someone who is not capable of doing so themselves.

Getting money back with R40

If you failed to fill in form R85 (see the preceding section) – perhaps your expected income fell so you became a non-taxpayer, or you simply forgot to ask for the form – don't worry. The tax is not lost.

Using repayment claim form R40 (available at your local tax office or as a download from the Inland Revenue Web site at www.inlandrevenue.gov.uk, or sometimes at a bank or building society), you can ask that your overpaid tax be refunded.

Using R40 is a little more complicated than filling in form R85 and depends on your keeping good records of how much interest you earned in each account as you will need to list this. You may need to ask the bank or building society for a duplicate certificate of tax deducted or a copy of your passbook.

You do not need to send this paperwork to the Inland Revenue along with the form but you must be able to show the claim is genuine – a number of claims are checked.

With R40, you have to put down all your income including interest from savings to show that some, or all, of your interest falls into the tax-free band.

Getting money back up to five years later

You have five years from 31 January after the end of the tax year for which you are claiming to file for a refund of taxes you have already paid. It may come as a surprise that you can go back on what you might have thought was a closed book, but the Inland Revenue does not consider it odd for people to go back all these years. So if you realise in January 2006 that you paid tax unnecessarily, you can ask for your money back for all the years back to 6 April 1999.

To do this, you complete form R40 (see the preceding section 'Getting money back with R40') and send it to the relevant Inland Revenue office. In some cases, you may need to ask for seven R40 forms as you have to fill in one for each tax year in which you believe you overpaid.

R40 claims are dealt with by five special Inland Revenue offices. The office that handles your R40 claim may not be the one nearest your home. For example, residents of some London postcodes have to deal with an office in Leicestershire while some other Londoners have to send their forms to Glenrothes in Scotland. But don't worry about this – your local tax office has the list.

Caring for Children's Bank Accounts

From the moment the midwife says 'it's a girl' or 'it's a boy' or twins or triplets or even more, those little bundles of fun are potential tax-payers. Children born with a lot of silver spoons in their mouths face an Inland Revenue liability from day one. They will be taxed on their income – just like their parents.

Less well-off children are also in the tax net. But provided their total income (including earnings from work) falls below the personal allowance line, they can *usually* reclaim tax deducted on any bank or building society savings they may hold.

If you start a savings account for your child, make sure that you sign form R85 on behalf of your offspring so that the interest is paid gross without tax deduction. If you fail to file form R85 with the Inland Revenue you can always use form R40 later on.

In England, Wales, and Northern Ireland, a parent, guardian, or trustee has to sign on behalf of anyone aged under 18. In Scotland, the age at which a young person can sign for themselves is 16. The signing restrictions apply whether the account is held in the child's name or in that of the donor. Many grandparents for instance will give sums of money but not want the child to spend it while they are young. So, Tom Jones, a child, might have an account from his granny, Angela Smith, in the form of 'Angela Smith in re: Tom Jones' – this is legally a form of trust.

Considering the source

A child's savings can come from a variety of sources such as earnings from a part-time job, presents, pocket money, an inheritance, and a trust fund.

Most savings youngsters have, though, come from adults who give them cash. Provided that the money in a child's savings account comes from any source other than the parents, the amount and the number of generous givers is immaterial. There are no problems if that cash comes from grandparents, aunts, uncles, older sisters and brothers, cousins, godparents, or the next door neighbours – in fact anyone other than parents.

However, the Inland Revenue wants to stop better-off parents using the personal allowance of their children to dodge tax.

To stop parents dodging tax on savings accounts by giving money to non-tax-paying children, the Inland Revenue has a special rule that applies to each parent separately.

Each parent can give a child a sum that earns up to £100 in gross interest each year. If the child's account earns more than the £100 maximum allowed, all the interest is taxed at the parent's rate and considered part of the parent's income.

If the interest from a parent's contribution to their child's account is more than £100, the entire tax-free amount is lost – not just the excess over £100.

To keep your parental contributions in line with Inland Revenue requirements, keep these tips in mind:

- ✔ Make sure any money comes evenly from both parents wherever possible to maximise the amount that can be given.

- ✔ Explore tax-free savings such as some National Savings products (see 'Opting for Tax-Free Savings' later on in this chapter).

- ✔ Remember that once a child reaches 18 – or gets married – the £100 rule ceases.

- ✔ Don't be tempted to give cash to a grandparent so the grandparent can appear to make a gift to the child – the Inland Revenue can track money.

- ✔ Go for riskier investments such as certain types of shares where the capital grows and there is little or no income. Another of my books, *Investing For Dummies* (Wiley), explains more on this.

- ✔ You can invest up to £25 a month on a child's behalf into a *friendly society plan,* a special form of insurance policy. But costs are high and can often outweigh the tax savings. Also, the minimum contract length is ten years. So, like all other tax-linked investment tips, think twice to see if the tax savings are really worthwhile.

Noticing when R85 stops

When you open an account for a child, the R85 continues until it is either rescinded by withdrawing it at the bank or building society, by telling the Inland Revenue (because the child is earning too much), or by the child reaching the age of 16.

According to the Inland Revenue, a 16 year old is old enough to go out to work so they are old enough to lose their tax-free account.

Many parents fail to notice this. But the R85 facility does not end. It can be renewed by getting the 16 year old to ask for a new form and starting all over again! And once it is renewed, it continues to apply for that account even when the child legally becomes an adult at 18.

Just two days a week work at the national minimum wage will use up most of the personal allowance – so students doing evening or weekend work will have to do their sums to see if they are still within the R85 zone.

Opting for Tax-Free Savings

Some savings plans pay interest free of tax. These include premium bonds from the government's National Savings and Investments (you can get information at your local post office).

Weigh up your personal tax rate against the fact that these investments tend to have lower interest rates.

Considering tax-free savings plans

The best deal is the *mini-cash ISA* (Individual Savings Account), in which adults can invest up to £3,000 in each tax year into an interest-bearing account where no tax is deducted. This benefit is lost if, in the same tax year, the saver also invests into a maxi-ISA (which concentrates on stocks and shares) because the rules preclude having both types of ISA for the same tax year.

Anyone with a matured *Tessa* – an old tax-free savings scheme which is no longer available – can save up to a further £9,000 in a Tessa Only Isa or Toisa. The exact amount you can save depends on the value of the money put into the Tessa during its life. Nothing can be added to a Toisa.

Children aged 16 to 18 can buy a mini-cash ISA but the money has to come from their own earnings and not from parents.

Betting on premium bonds

Premium bonds don't actually pay interest but give out prizes –
you might land £1 million! Going for a big holding – the maximum is £30,000 – means you have loads of chances of winning
each month so, statistically, you should get enough prizes each
year to make your stake worthwhile.

At the moment, the prize fund is calculated at 3.2 per cent of
the total in the bonds. So if you have £30,000, you should earn
an average 3.2 per cent of that sum per year – £960. But as
that sum is tax-free, a higher-rate tax-payer would otherwise
have to earn £1,600 gross to get £960 in their bank account.
The equivalent gross interest rate would be 5.33 per cent. For
basic-rate payers, the 3.2 per cent tax-free return turns into
4 per cent gross. This percentage tends to go up and down
with interest rates.

Chapter 14

Taxing Investments

. . . .

In This Chapter

▶ Considering stock market basics

▶ Examining tax liabilities

▶ Sorting out Stamp Duty

▶ Delving into Dividends Tax

▶ Capping Capital Gains Tax

. . . .

*P*utting money into stocks and shares – the main investments quoted on the London stock exchange and other stock markets across the world – has soared in popularity over the past two decades or so. But whether your portfolio is worth £100 or £100 million, each investment you make has tax implications, and, unfortunately, the different ways of making (or, if you're unlucky, losing) your money on the stock market all have their own tax rules.

Some gains and losses, and regular payments, such as dividends, have to be declared on self assessment tax forms. Others can be ignored. Some investments have advantages for those in the top tax bracket whilst some give benefits for those who pay no tax at all – and others treat all investors identically.

In this chapter, I explain the tax implications of various types of investments and how to use investments to improve not only your financial bottom line but also your tax profile.

Considering a Trio of Taxes

Three taxes can hit your investment return – Stamp Duty, income tax, and Capital Gains Tax. The next sections talk about each in turn.

Doling out Stamp Duty

Stamp Duty doesn't only apply to philatelists – it's basically a tax you pay on legal transactions. And, because buying and selling stocks is a legal transaction, you pay Stamp Duty on your stock market investments.

Stamp Duty, technically called Stamp Duty Reserve Tax, is one of the oldest taxes around. Documents literally had (and often still have) government revenues stamps embossed or stuck onto them.

Forking out small amounts frequently

Stamp Duty is no respecter of people. You pay the same percentage on the day you buy whether you're dealing in a £100 or £1 million lot of shares. The basic rule is that every time you buy a share the government charges you 0.5 per cent as Stamp Duty. You can't avoid it on transactions where it applies. And you can't ask for it back.

The more often you buy shares, the more stamp duty you pay overall. For frequent traders those 0.5 per cent slices really add up. You may need to make 5 per cent or 10 per cent gains each year just to overcome Stamp Duty deductions.

The good news is that you don't have to do anything to pay Stamp Duty. The stockbroker charges you when you buy shares (and that includes investment trusts whether you purchase them from a stockbroker or through a special savings scheme).

Licking Stamp Duty

Some stock market transactions don't attract Stamp Duty. These include:

- **Cash accounts,** including National Savings and mini-cash ISAs.
- **Bonds,** whether issued by the government or a company.

✔ **Derivative funds,** which are funds based on stock market performance but do not own actual shares. Instead, they invest in complicated vehicles called futures, options, swaps, and swaptions (please, don't ask!). The most common form is the stock market guaranteed fund where you are promised at least your money back no matter how far the stock market may fall.

✔ **New shares** issued by a company in an initial public offering (often called a *flotation*).

✔ **Exchange Traded Funds,** which are special investments based on a parcel of shares such as the *FT-SE100 Index* (the *Financial Times* Share Index covering the top 100 UK public companies, usually referred to as the Footsie) and traded on the stock market.

✔ **Contracts for difference, spread bets, traded options, and warrants,** which are specialist ways of buying into shares, often designed for very short-term investment or professional share punters. *Investing For Dummies* by your humble author (Wiley) has details of all of these.

✔ **Gifts and transfers of shares,** which includes transferring shares out of your name to someone else, such as a family member; transferring shares under a will; and transferring shares on a divorce settlement.

Declaring your dividends

Dividends are payments from shares, unit and investment trusts, which, investors hope, are not only regular (usually twice a year) but also rise over time to reflect the company's (or trust's) growing fortunes. Dividends are taxable as income.

The good news is tax on UK share dividends is deducted before you get it. If you are a basic-rate tax-payer, you don't have to do anything else. Non-tax-payers and 10 per cent tax-payers don't need to do anything either. But there's bad news here: You can't reclaim the deducted tax under any circumstances. Even though it's called a tax credit by the Inland Revenue, I refer to it as a deduction to save confusion.

Top-rate tax-payers have to declare dividends on their self assessment form and have the cash ready to pay the gap between the 40 per cent rate and the tax deducted.

Whether you get income from unit trusts, investment trusts, or individual shares, look at the date the dividend was declared and ignore the period for which the dividend applied. A 10p a share dividend for the year ending 31 December 2004 declared on 1 May 2005 and paid on 1 June 2005 counts as part of your 2005–06 return, not the 2004–05 calculation.

If you invest for long-term growth in shares that pay low or no dividends, you'll less income tax. But don't forget these shares tend to be riskier. And you can get hit for Capital Gains Tax on your profits (see the upcoming 'Dealing with Capital Gains Tax' for information on that subject).

Don't forget if you are near the top of the basic-rate ladder – earning around £35,000 a year – your dividends can push you into the top tax bracket. For instance, if you earn £35,500 and have £3,500 of dividends you'll be over the £37,295 (in 2005–06) basic-rate tax limit for a person aged under 65.

The sums can be complicated. So either use self assessment software or get your form in before 30 September so the Inland Revenue will do the calculations.

Receiving dividends from foreign shares

Dividends from stocks traded in foreign markets can be tough to deal with. You may have to convert dividend payments into sterling as well as account for them separately.

You need to fill out the *foreign income* pages of the self assessment form. The UK has *double taxation agreements* with most foreign countries. The effect of these agreements is to cap the tax due on foreign-sourced income so you are no worse off as a result of possibly being taxed twice.

Re-investing dividends

Many stock market companies have schemes by which shareholders can opt to receive new shares to the value of their dividends rather than a dividend cheque. Even if you choose this option, you still have to declare the value of the new shares and any balance carried forward in cash because it is not large enough to buy a share. You're liable for tax on re-invested dividends in just the same way as a cash dividend.

Dealing with Capital Gains Tax

Capital Gains Tax (CGT) is paid on profits you make on selling a number of assets including shares and properties (but not the house you count as your main residence.)

You pay CGT only when you sell an asset – keep it and you have nothing to pay or declare.

Counting the things that don't count

You pay Capital Gains Tax on a lot of profitable items, including shares and buy-to-lets. The following list reminds you of some items that aren't subject to CGT, even though they may make you money when you sell them:

✔ Your only or main home (not counting anywhere you rent). If you have more than one property, you can choose which one is out of the CGT net – it will usually be the more valuable. Unmarried couples can each have a home provided they live in them.

✔ National Savings including certificates and premium bonds.

✔ UK government bonds (gilts) and most corporate bonds.

✔ Bank accounts and deposits.

✔ Personal Equity Plans (PEPs) and Individual Savings Accounts (ISAs).

✔ Life insurance policies (but these have internal CGT charges so effectively you pay whether you want to or not).

✔ Investments in forestry and woodlands.

✔ Classic cars.

✔ Tangible moveable property with an expected life of 50 years or under (this may cover some of the more controversial artworks such as sharks and sheep pickled in alcohol!) and all tangible moveable property worth under £6,000.

✔ Profit from selling your own medals for valour.

✔ Shares held on behalf of employees in share incentive schemes up to the date the employee gets full ownership.

✔ Shares in special schemes such as the Business Expansion Scheme, the Enterprise Investment Scheme, and Venture Capital Trusts.

The CGT bill is calculated at either 20 per cent or 40 per cent of the gain. Which rate you pay depends on your other income for the year. Your CGT bill is added to your other taxable income and you pay accordingly. If the grand total keeps you in the basic-rate band, you pay 20 per cent. Otherwise, you pay at 40 per cent. You could, of course, pay part in the basic band and part in the top band.

Someone who earns £20,000 salary and has capital gains of £10,000 has a total of £30,000 in income, which is well within the basic-rate tax band. This tax-payer is liable for 20 per cent taxation, or £2,000, on the £10,000 capital gain part of their income. A £40,000 earner – already in the 40 per cent band – who makes the same £10,000 gain ends up with a total £50,000, well into the 40 per cent end of the tax world and has to pay £4,000 to the Inland Revenue.

Reducing your CGT bill

You can do a lot to reduce your bill – perhaps all the way down to nothing – by remembering a few CGT basics.

- ✔ You're entitled to an annual free slice – the first £8,500 (in 2005–06) of capital gains is tax exempt. Keep in mind that this exemption is good only for the current tax year. You can't go back and make claims for past years. It's a use it or lose it deal. The amount usually changes from year to year – so far it has always increased.

- ✔ You pay only if you make a profit. You can deduct costs such as stockbroker commission and any legal expenses connected with property or share purchases. And don't forget to deduct selling costs as well.

- ✔ The longer you hold on to a taxable asset, the less you have to pay as a percentage of the gain (see the 'Cutting the tax with rising prices and the falling taper' section later in the chapter for more information on this).

Swapping shares to claim the tax exemption

You are not allowed to sell a share and then buy it back the next day (or within 30 days) to create a gain so that you can use your free slice. But you can sell one share and buy another, perhaps one with a similar profile such as selling Bank A and buying Bank B. You don't have to be a stock market genius to know companies that are similar to each other tend to go up and down together.

One half of a married couple can sell shares to use the free slice, leaving the other half to buy the shares at the same time. But this has to be a genuine transaction with each side paying the stockbroker costs involved and not merely a paper change of ownership or a precise swap. It doesn't work if the shares were jointly held in both names. Selling and repurchasing shares in this way establishes a new, higher, starting price for subsequent calculations.

Another great way of using the annual exemption to the best effect is to spread sales of shares over two tax years – sell half on 5 April and the rest on 6 April if you can. Doing this enables you to claim the tax exemption for two years.

Using your married status to best advantage

A married couple can split assets such as shares and each can set £8,500 (in 2005–06) against their gain. And if one partner pays top-rate tax while the other pays a lower rate, then it's worthwhile transferring the assets to the lower-rate tax-payer.

Married couples can transfer assets between themselves without taxation worries.

Cutting the tax with rising prices and the falling taper

To figure your capital gains liability, you add the original purchase price and any associated fees and selling costs together and subtract them from the final sale price.

CGT works by subtracting the original purchase price and any costs from the final sale price to give the tax liability. And until April 1998, that could be further adjusted to take account of inflation. If you bought before 5 April 1998, your starting figure is now the inflation-adjusted cost of your asset between the date of purchase and April 1998.

A buyer of shares in ABC Enterprises for £10,000 in January 1987 would find there was a 65 per cent increase in the cost of living by April 1998. So the new starting price for the shares would be £16,500 (a 65 per cent gain).

The Inland Revenue publishes a table of CGT indexation allowances on its Web site at www.inlandrevenue.gov.uk.

But inflation is nowadays far lower. A new scheme came in force in April 1998 – the CGT taper. So from April 1998 onwards, you have to move the taper system I describe here. So you can find you have to do two sets of sums; one for the asset up to April 1998 and one for the subsequent period.

Here's how the taper works. The taper reduces your taxable gain on most assets after you have held them for three full years from the date of purchase. You then cut 5 per cent off the profit for each year until ten full years are passed and you reach a 40 per cent deduction. It only applies to non-business assets. The taper for business assets is far shorter, as shown in Table 14-1.

Table 14-1	The CGT Taper
Non-Business Assets	
Number of complete years	***Percentage of gain charged for tax***
0	100
1	100
2	100
3	95
4	90
5	85
6	80
7	75
8	70
9	65
10 or more	60

Assets bought before 17 March 1998 get a bonus year. They earn 35 per cent after eight rather than nine years, for instance, and hit the final 40 per cent one year earlier.

Holding loan notes

What if you're forced to sell a substantial holding because the company whose shares you own has succumbed to a takeover bid?

Don't worry. Most big company takeovers offer 'loan notes' as an option to cashing in your shares

there and then. *Loan notes* pay interest and stretch out your gains with an annual payment typically made over three to five tax years. The disadvantage is you can't invest your money tied up in the loan notes anywhere else.

Looking at the Tax Implications of Investing

It's obviously important for you to know where your investments stand in the tax pecking order. It's vital you don't get trapped in an investment whose special tax status is just plain wrong for your circumstances.

There is one even more essential rule: Never, never, never invest your money on the basis of any stated tax advantages. There are many investments that offer special tax treatment that they push as 'tax savings' or 'tax freedom'. But a government-backed tax-favoured status is not a guarantee of profitable performance. And if your investment fails, the Inland Revenue will not ride to your rescue and restore your losses.

Saving hassle with unit and investment trusts

A portfolio of shares managed by a professional organisation such as a unit trust (often called an open-ended investment company or OEIC) or investment trust is a great idea for the tax saver. Such investments can save tax, and just as importantly tax hassle.

The manager of a unit trust takes care of paying Stamp Duty for you – otherwise it would be charged at 0.5 per cent of the purchase price. How do they do that? They build it into the price they charge for a unit. But you do pay stamp duty as a separate item when you buy into an investment trust, even on regular savings schemes in which you invest as little as £20 a month.

And investment trusts and unit trusts don't pay Capital Gains Tax on profits they make a-wheeling and a-dealing. So the managers can swap and change portfolios without worrying about tax. So when does the Capital Gains Tax hit you? Only when you sell the units or investment trust shares yourself.

You may still have to pay Capital Gains Tax, but you have some control over when and whether you pay as you only become liable when you sell the unit or investment trust.

You only have to put down one entry for each trust on your tax form each year, even if the trust itself holds hundreds of different shares.

Buying bonds

Bonds are loans to companies and governments. A bond is essentially a promise to pay a set sum of interest (known as a *coupon* if you want to be technical) every six months and to repay the face value of the bond on a set date in the future. The face value may be more or less than you paid for it.

Bonds, which are traded on the stock exchange, are pretty simple to deal with from a tax perspective – they act like cash accounts. The regular payments on most UK bonds, including government stocks (known as *gilts*), are paid with the basic savings rate (20 per cent) already deducted. So if you're a basic-rate tax-payer, you don't need to do anything more (unless the payment nudges you into the higher rate). Those who don't pay tax and those who pay at the 10 per cent rate can reclaim all or part of the deduction. Higher-rate tax-payers have to pay the difference between the 20 per cent rate and the 40 per cent rate.

Some bonds, including a number from the government, are *low coupon,* meaning that the regular payment is lower than normal. The payment is lower so the tax you have to pay is less. But you don't lose out – you get a bigger bonus when the bond matures, and that gain is tax-free.

The opposite also applies. You can pay more than the face value of the bond because you want a higher income. But when it matures and gives you less than you paid, you can't offset the loss.

The dividends on War Loan bonds and government stocks bought through the National Savings Bank Register are paid gross without deducting any tax, which is good news for non-tax-payers who don't want the hassle of reclaiming.

Examining the benefits of ISAs

It can be worthwhile looking at Individual Savings Accounts (ISAs) if you're investing in shares or bonds. But ISAs (and their predecessors PEPs or Personal Equity Plans) investing in shares or share funds such as investment or unit trusts are not as worthwhile from the tax point of view as they once were.

Share-based ISAs give you freedom from paying income tax on dividends and Capital Gains Tax on profits. The flipside is that if you make a capital loss on an ISA (and millions have done just this!), you can't claim it against gains elsewhere. And, thanks to the complications of the tax credit on shares (see 'Declaring your dividends' later in this chapter), basic-rate tax-payers now do not get any rebate on dividends. If you're a basic-rate tax-payer, the only benefit with a shares ISA is not facing a Capital Gains Tax bill. But you still gain from tax relief on bond funds you bought into.

With an ISA, you don't have to do anything. The ISA management company you use deals with all the tax hassles on your behalf. You don't even have to tell the taxman about your ISA.

Higher-rate tax-payers may still benefit from investing into shares through an ISA, though, because they pay no additional tax on the investment. Why? Well, as you don't list ISAs on your self assessment return, there can't be any additional tax to pay.

Put in cash terms, a higher-rate tax-payer investing the maximum £7,000 allowed in the 2005–06 tax year for ISAs into shares, or unit or investment trusts, with a typical 3 per cent yield, will be about £53 better off inside an ISA than outside one (assuming there is no extra ISA cost).

ISAs are due to end in 2010. But there is a review in 2006, which may extend their life or offer a new tax-saving deal.

You can get more out of your ISA whatever your tax level if you stick to bonds and bond funds. There is no dividend tax credit arithmetic to worry about. If you put £5,000 into a bond fund yielding 10 per cent you get the full £500 each year whatever your tax rate. Outside an ISA, a basic-rate tax-payer would lose £100 of that in tax while a top-rate tax-payer would have to pay £200 of the £500 in 40 per cent tax to the Inland Revenue. Funds that hold both shares and bonds must have at least 60 per cent in bonds to qualify for this treatment.

Rewarding risk takers

A number of schemes investing in high-risk assets have special tax-saving characteristics. I go through them in the following sections.

Financing stage and cinema

Some Enterprise Investment Scheme's hopes ride on the success (or otherwise) of a film or play – it's often otherwise! And there are some very complicated schemes for saving tax by investing in British films. You can save big bucks even if the film is a total box-office disaster.

These investment opportunities are aimed at the ultra-rich and are normally only sold by specialist accountancy firms.

Taking AIM

AIM stands for *alternative investment market,* a vehicle for trading shares in smaller companies – although a few of the companies are now very big. The companies are listed in newspapers and you buy and sell shares through stockbrokers in the normal way.

But as far as the Inland Revenue is concerned, shares invested in AIM are on a different planet. Because they are not fully listed, the Inland Revenue considers them *unquoted* (even if they're quoted everywhere!). Trading in unquoted shares is to your advantage. AIM assets count as business assets rather than shares. And business assets have a super-fast taper. Hold them for just one complete year and the Capital Gains Tax is cut by 50 per cent. Sell them after two years and your taper relief is 75 per cent. This means the 40 per cent tax-payer has an effective 20 per cent rate after one year and just 10 per cent after two years.

The same rules apply to shares listed on OFEX, the even further off-the-main-stock-exchange market. OFEX stands for *off-exchange* because the shares are not traded or in any way regulated on the London Stock Exchange.

AIM and OFEX shares are far more volatile and more likely to make losses than blue-chip stocks. To repeat a warning I made earlier this chapter, NEVER invest just on the basis of potential tax savings.

Venturing ahead with VCTs

Venture capital trusts (VCTs) are investment vehicles that invest in small, usually start-up, companies. VCTs offer big tax incentives for investors prepared to back a fund of unknown, untested, and generally unprofitable companies. The hope is that, while many will flop, a few will become the Microsoft, Google, or Ryanair of the future. VCT promoters claim the few winners will more than make up for the failures and the go-nowheres.

If you are willing to accept these risks, plus the high charges in many funds, the Inland Revenue will help you on your way – you can invest up to £200,000 per person in a tax year into a VCT. You must hold the shares for at least three years.

Here's what you get for your courage:

- ✔ 40 per cent tax relief when you buy a new VCT issue (they come out every year, usually around November to January). You get this rate even if you're not a top-rate payer provided the tax you paid at least equals the rebate.

  Suppose you pay £5,000 in tax this year as a basic-rate payer. The £5,000 is 40 per cent of £12,500 so you can invest up to £12,500 into a VCT and get up to 40 per cent back – up to the £5,000 you paid in tax.

- ✔ Tax freedom is given on dividends paid out both to new holders and to those who purchase existing shares. You don't even have to put the dividends received down on your tax form.

- ✔ No Capital Gains Tax liability when you sell – hopefully at a profit.

If you don't want to venture into the totally unknown, AIM-listed shares count as VCTs as well. Fund managers create AIM funds to take advantage of this loophole. (See the previous section for more on AIMs.)

Sheltering gains with EIS

If you made a capital gain in the past three years and are willing to take a big risk with that gain to avoid paying Capital Gains Tax, then maybe the Enterprise Investment Scheme (EIS) is for you.

EIS investors put their money into one small company that often has no track record, let alone a profit or dividend. What they get in return is a shelter from their Capital Gains Tax (CGT) bills from the previous three years. If you're rich enough, you can put in £200,000 a year! There is no minimum, but most EIS companies don't accept less than £1,000. And you can, of course, put your money into a number of EIS companies each year if you wish.

So, if you have £20,000 of Capital Gains Tax to pay, you can put £20,000 into EIS companies, hold the money there for the required three-year minimum and watch your CGT bill evaporate.

On top of offsetting your CGT, you get 20 per cent income tax relief on all EIS share purchases. Add the possible 40 per cent CGT saving to the 20 per cent income tax credit, and you get 60 per cent – so you are only risking 40p for each £1 you invest. If you make a profit you do not pay any CGT on the gain. But obviously, you can't have it both ways! If you make a loss (and this is ever so likely) you cannot offset this against gains elsewhere.

Taking account of losses

You don't really want to read this bit, and I hope you never have to make use of the information here. But life has been tough on the stock market since early 2000, and there are a lot of ways to lose money as well as to gain it. This section talks about dealing with losses.

The one bright spot in selling shares for a loss is that you can set that loss against capital gains you make elsewhere – either now or in the future.

You can use part of your losses for the current year and hold over the balance – there is no time limit.

You can't, however, use the indexation on assets bought before April 1998 to create a loss. *Indexation* is adjusting the starting price of your asset for inflation. It applies only on assets up to April 1998 when the Capital Gains Tax rules changed. In theory, you could create a loss by using inflation. For example, if you bought a share in 1990 and its price remained unaltered until April 1998, the effect of inflation would be that you would have an asset whose real value had dropped.

Shares in companies that are worthless because they've gone bust can have their uses! You have to tell the Inland Revenue the shares have a *negligible value.* Negligible may sound like a few pence – it really means nothing. So, if you paid £10,000 for shares in a company that went bust, you have £10,000 worth of losses to offset against £10,000 of gains elsewhere. Taking £10,000 out of the equation can save up to £4,000 from a future tax bill if you're a top-rate tax-payer.

Chapter 15

Saving Tax with Bricks and Mortar

. . . .

In This Chapter

▶ Buying a home, paying tax

▶ Running your buy-to-let as a business

▶ Letting rooms, or caravans, or more

▶ Moving property along – selling it and willing it

. . . .

*A*s share prices slumped and the price of an average dwelling soared in the early years of this century, a growing number of people concluded that bricks and mortar added up to a great investment idea. Many moved out of stock market-linked investments into buy-to-let properties, holiday homes, and even into buying office blocks and shopping centres. The jury is out on whether that judgement is right or wrong as an investment – only time will tell.

But it's long been a truism to say your home is the biggest single investment you will ever make. For most people, whether it's a family pile, a bachelor pad, or a typical suburban semi, the roof over your head is probably worth more than all your other assets, including pension funds, put together.

To make home ownership even better, the tax collector is generally only interested in your property when you buy it and when you die. The Inland Revenue does want to know all about any property you own outside your own home, though, and if you take in lodgers, or run a business from your home, they may also be interested in what happens under your roof.

This chapter talks about tax issues related to property, whether you're buying or selling, living or letting.

Paying Stamp Duty and Council Taxes

The UK has two specific property ownership taxes. You have to pay Stamp Duty on the purchase price of the property. And then there is Council Tax each year (most pay in monthly instalments). Council Tax varies according to where you live as each local authority sets its own rate. How much you pay also depends on the value of your property – the more it's worth, the more you pay.

Stamping on Stamp Duty

Stamp Duty, nowadays more properly known as Stamp Duty Land Tax (SDLT), is an extra cost you pay when you buy property. There is no escape. You have to pay Stamp Duty whether you want to live in the property yourself or are purchasing the property as an investment.

The tax authorities like Stamp Duty because it is almost impossible to dodge as it's all part and parcel of the conveyancing routine that you follow when you purchase property.

The amount of Stamp Duty you pay depends on the purchase price of the property. Table 15-1 shows the threshold levels and percentage of the purchase price payable in Stamp Duty.

Table 15-1	Stamp Duty Percentages
Purchase Price	*Per Cent Due as Stamp Duty*
Up to £120,000	0
£120,001 to £250,000	1
£250,001 to £500,000	3
£500,001 plus	4

Stamp Duty is calculated on the price of the property so you pay the rate for the purchase value on the whole sum, not just on the amount over each tax threshold. Buy a home for £250,000 and you pay Stamp Duty of 1 per cent, or £2,500. But go up £1 to £250,001 and the whole deal is charged at 3 per cent, giving a bill of £7,500 (plus three pennies to be exact). Wherever possible, look for properties priced just below thresholds. House-sellers tend to know there is no point in asking for £251,000, let alone £250,001.

Buying in disadvantaged areas for Stamp Duty advantages

There are comparatively few UK properties changing hands at £120,000 or under. But if you buy a house or flat in one of the UK's 2,000 most disadvantaged postcodes, there is no Stamp Duty payable on properties selling up to £150,000. This can save you up to £1,500. The Inland Revenue Stamp Duty Web site at www.inlandrevenue.gov.uk/so has a full list of these areas. Whether you are really better off or whether prices adjust to the Stamp Duty freedom is not clear.

Seeking advantages without going too far

If you're interested in a home priced a few thousand over the Stamp Duty threshold amount, look to see if there are items that can be sold separately outside the main property deal so you can bring the price of the house or flat itself below the threshold. Anything portable can fit in this separate category, including curtains, carpets, moveable furniture, washing machines, dishwashers, fridges, pot plants, and some garden sheds. But you can't include fixtures such as fitted kitchens, bedrooms and bathrooms, or, as some have tried, fuse-boxes, or blades of grass!

The Inland Revenue pays especial attention to home purchases just below thresholds to prevent arrangements between buyer and seller to hand over cash so that the purchase price on paper looks lower or to pay ludicrous sums to purchase moveable items. The taxman will be happy with prices that reflect a balance between a willing buyer and a willing seller. Pricing a nearly-new washing machine in good condition at £300 is probably fine. Putting a £3,000 tag on a clapped-out dishwasher is definitely not, even if you claim it's so old that it's a collector's item.

Contributing Council Tax

Council Tax pays part of the cost of local authority provisions such as schools, parks, libraries, and refuse collection. The rate varies widely from area to area but is based on the worth of your home. This value decides which band is used to calculate the amount you pay. In many cases, the band has little connection with the real value of the property. My own home, for instance, was last valued in 1990, although in 2005, the government announced that a new round of valuation will take place.

The system sorts out properties into the right order, treating small, low-cost properties in the lowest band and huge homes in the highest band. However, if the local authority valuation of your property appears widely inaccurate, you can appeal against this. Your local authority can explain how to do this. Note that few appeals are successful, however. You can apply for help with the bill in two ways:

- ✔ The **second adult rebate** reduces the bill by 25 per cent if you live alone or live only with children under 18 years old. It can also apply if the only other resident or residents are full-time students.

- ✔ **Council Tax Benefit** is a means-tested benefit that can pay up to 100 per cent of the Council Tax bill. If you qualify for pension credit and a number of other benefits including income support, you should be assessed for Council Tax at the same time. You can also apply to your local council for help. You cannot apply if you have more than £16,000 in savings.

Your local Citizens Advice can give you confidential, unbiased help with applying for Council Tax Benefit.

Buying to Let

Buying a property to let it out to tenants has soared in popularity as an investment tool.

The rents you take in from buying to let are technically seen as investment income and not as earnings from a trade. You can't count it for pension planning. But, on the plus side, you don't have to pay national insurance on your rental profits.

As this isn't your principal residence, you're liable for Capital Gains Tax on any profits made when you sell. You can use the Capital Gains Tax taper relief at the non-business asset level if you keep the property more than three years before you sell. Remember that buying a property in partnership with your spouse gives you two sets of Capital Gains Tax allowances if you sell at a profit.

Looking at the tax issues

Even though the term buy-to-let does not appear in tax law, that doesn't stop the Inland Revenue seeing the practice as a business. So you have to declare profits: Basically what you take in from tenants less what you pay out in various costs I list later on. Keep records of all your income from tenants and all the costs related to letting your property so that you can back up the deductions you list on the accounts that form the basis of your self assessment return. And remember to report your new landlording business to the tax authorities. A simple letter to your tax inspector will do.

Here's a list of the main items you can deduct from the rent before arriving at a profit (or loss) for the year:

- **Mortgage interest:** This is probably the biggest single item you can set against the rental income. See the next section for more details.

- **Repairs, maintenance, and insurance:** Anything from window cleaners to roofers to plumbers qualifies. As well as the buildings and contents, insurance can include contracts for the maintenance of central-heating systems or drainage.

  You cannot deduct upgrades to the property against tax so putting in a flash kitchen to replace an adequate but dull affair, or adding an extension, do not count. But you can replace old single-glazed windows with double-glazed windows. And you can deduct the interest on any loan used for upgrades.

- **Advertising costs:** You can deduct what you pay to attract potential tenants.

- **Management expenses:** Deductions from the rental income are allowed when you employ an agent to manage your property.

> ✔ **Legal fees:** These can include solicitor fees when you purchase a property, the costs of chasing tenants who do not pay, and any expenses you incur by taking tenants to court.
>
> ✔ **Council tax:** You deduct this cost only if you (and not the tenants) pay it.

Deposits charged to tenants do not count as income as long as they are refunded when the tenant leaves. If you keep all, or part, then the cash retained will be taxable in the same way as rental income.

You can deduct the expenses involved with your buy-to-let business only against the income you receive from your tenants. If lettings dry up, you can't offset your losses against Capital Gains or other income.

Claiming interest against your buy-to-let income

The biggest tax difference between buying a home for your own use and purchasing a buy-to-let is the ability to offset the mortgage interest of a buy-to-let against the rental income. This cuts back on any taxable profit figure.

You can't offset the *principal,* the amount you borrowed and need to repay over the life of the loan, however, only the interest.

One often ignored tax break is the ability to charge the interest on any personal loan you take out that is used wholly and exclusively (it does not have to be necessarily) for the purpose of the property.

Most buy-to-let mortgages are limited to 80 per cent of the property's value and if you need to borrow the balance, you may do this through a personal loan. The interest is a deductible expense, even though the interest level is usually higher than the rate charged on the main mortgage.

So if you take out a personal loan to buy replacement windows, a new heating system, white goods, or furniture, you can deduct the interest against the rental income.

Making the most of interest deduction

Here's a tip that can get you a tax-deductible loan to use in your life outside of buy-to-let. Very few people know about it as those that do are paranoid the Inland Revenue will stop it if it becomes widely publicised.

It's known to the tax cognoscenti as *Paragraph 45,700* after the number in an Inland Revenue internal manual. It enables you to re-mortgage a property for a greater sum than the original loan and use the cash released for any purpose whatsoever, not necessarily for the property. This means you can be getting tax relief on your highest personal tax rate for cash you use to buy a yacht or a car or a round-the-world cruise.

The one proviso is that the new loan cannot be greater than the market value of the property when it was first used in the letting business.

Here's how it works. Suppose you bought a house ten years ago for £100,000. It is now worth £250,000 and you decide you want to move to another town and to a better property but let out this house. The market value is £250,000, so you can borrow up to £250,000 and offset the interest against rental income. You repay the original £100,000 mortgage leaving you with £150,000 to spend where the interest is tax-deductible.

A more common scenario is where you bought a buy-to-let for £100,000 but were restricted to an 80 per cent loan. The property is now worth £125,000 so you can take out a re-mortgage for £100,000 (80 per cent of £125,000). This remains within the rules as you have not borrowed more than the value of the property when it became a buy-to-let. You now have £20,000 to spend as you wish, with the taxman picking up part of the interest payments.

A third possibility is where you buy 'off-plan' (that is purchasing before the property is built) at a discount. If the off-plan cost is £150,000 you will borrow against that. But once complete, and hence available for letting, the property is worth, say, £200,000. The Inland Revenue will allow tax-deductible interest on a loan up to £200,000.

If you buy furniture for a furnished property, avoid 0 per cent deals. The interest is built into the price but as you can't separate the cost of the goods from the cost of the financing, you can't claim interest.

You can find more information about the financial implications of buy-to-let in *Renting Out Your Property For Dummies* by Melanie Bien and Robert S. Griswold (Wiley).

Renting Rooms and Saving Tax

The reason is now lost in the mists of time, but back in 1992, the then Chancellor of the Exchequer thought it would be a good idea to encourage people to rent out spare rooms in their homes. Or perhaps he thought it was too much trouble to work out the profits and expenses to tax the hundreds of thousands of people who take in lodgers. Either way, the rent-a-room scheme was born. It lets you receive up to £4,250 (around £80 a week) a year from lodgers totally tax-free.

The rented room can be in your own home, or in one that you rent from someone else, but it must be your main residence. The accommodation has to be furnished. You can provide food or laundry services without losing the tax savings. But you can't claim any expenses against the rent.

The £4,250 limit was last increased in April 1997. Today, many lodgers are likely paying more than £80 a week. Where this happens, landlords have a choice:

- Count the first £4,250 in rent as the tax-free allowance and pay income tax on the balance.

    If this option is selected, the landlord only has to keep records of the income taken from the lodgers.

- Treat the whole rental situation as a normal business, working out a profit-and-loss account using income and expenditure.

In most cases, the first option (known as the *alternative basis*) works out more profitably unless the landlord is running a substantial business with high-paying guests.

You have up to one year after the end of the tax year when your income from lodgers went over the £4,250 mark to decide on which option to take.

Taking on holiday homes

If you have a furnished country cottage which you rent out to holidaymakers, or a city centre flat desirable for tourists, or a caravan you're willing to rent out, then you can be in the furnished holiday accommodation game and set up for tax savings.

Moving in tenants over your shop

There are special tax incentives for converting unused or storage space over shops into habitable accommodation. These *flat conversion allowances* come with rules. They are intended for tenants whose agreement runs from one to five years, the flats must not have more than four rooms (excluding hallway, kitchen, and bathroom) and the property must be accessible directly from the street and not through the downstairs business. Needless to say, you can't live there yourself.

You can set all the renovation costs against the rent you receive from tenants in the first year. But you can carry over the costs into following years so you may not have to pay any tax on the rent for some time!

And the rules cease to apply if the rental is very high. The Inland Revenue publishes weekly rent limits for London and outside London, adjusting them from time to time.

Don't worry if your property is not in the midst of a national park or does not enjoy stunning views of the Thames or Edinburgh Castle. To qualify, the property can be anywhere, not just in an area desirable to holidaymakers.

The tax inspector will see your property as a spare-time business provided you follow these 'furnished holiday lettings' rules:

- ✔ The property must be in the UK – anywhere.

- ✔ It must be furnished so it can be used immediately (but you don't necessarily have to provide sheets and towels).

- ✔ The rent charged must be commercial, with a view to profits.

- ✔ The accommodation must be available to the public for at least 140 days a year. And it must be occupied by paying customers for at least 70 days each year.

- ✔ For at least seven months each year, the property cannot be occupied by the same people for more than 31 days continuously.

  If you own more than one property, you can average the occupancy periods.

Looking at what you get from a holiday let

You can offset loan interest against the rental income. The cost of the furniture and other items such as washing machines and crockery can be set off against tax. You can also claim tax against costs such as advertising, agents' fees, insurance, and Council Tax. If you make a loss, you may be able to deduct that from your other income.

And, of course, there is no rule to prevent you enjoying a few weeks in your own property. Always assuming you want to because it's somewhere attractive!

Running a furnished holiday let is counted as a trade. It's taxable under the old Schedule D (now income tax on profits), similar to most other self-employment activities but unlike buy-to-let. This means you can save tax by buying a personal pension with part of your holiday let earnings.

If you sell your furnished holiday let at a profit, you can claim business taper relief on any Capital Gains Tax (CGT) bill. Chapter 14 deals with CGT in more detail.

Dealing with your overseas holiday home

Money you make from renting out a house or flat outside the UK is treated in much the same way as a holiday let in this country. You can offset your costs, including interest, against the rental income.

But non-UK letting activities have to be kept separate from those within the UK. And you may have to pay tax in the country where your property is situated. Such tax payments can generally be counted as credits against UK tax payments so you won't have to pay twice.

Moving into big-time property ownership

Serious property investors who are prepared for a long haul (and taking quite a bit of risk) can save tax through Enterprise Zone schemes. *Enterprise Zone schemes* involve buying new (or up to two years old) commercial buildings such as factories, office blocks, and shops in certain designated areas with a view to owning them for 25 years.

Living the lotus-eating life overseas

If you quit the UK for somewhere sunnier, you no longer have to worry about UK income tax except to settle for your final tax year.

You will, of course, have to deal with the tax authorities where you end up. Their tax rates and rules may be more or less stringent than those in the UK.

You have to move completely to avoid the UK tax system. This means you can no longer have a UK home. And you can't come back to stay with friends and family for long periods. The rules say you cannot make 'habitual and substantial visits' to the UK. Visits are habitual if they carry on for more than four years in a row. And they are substantial if they average more than 90 days in any tax year over a four-year period (unless there is an emergency such as illness).

Even then, the tax authorities can decide you should be subject to UK tax if it can be shown you intended to come back for up to 90 days a year when you left.

If you want to avoid taxes altogether, you can become a perpetual traveller. Very few countries tax you if you spend less than 90 days there in any tax year and then move on. You can stay in a hotel, short-term rented accommodation, or live in a motorhome. The same would apply if you kept sailing from country-to-country in a yacht. If you spend all your time on the high seas, only putting into port to refuel, you will never pay tax. Admittedly, it's not everyone's idea of fun! And you need a private income from somewhere as well!

You can do this on your own if you are really rich, or through specially set syndicates known as *Enterprise Zone Property Trusts*. You get full tax relief on the investment in the buildings but not on the cost of the land. And you can offset any interest payments against other income.

This type of property ownership is strictly for top-rate taxpayers who are happy to invest for up to the next 25 years.

Selling Up and Passing Along

The good news is that there are no tax ramifications of selling your own home providing it's your main residence. So if you bought a run-down place for £5,000 three decades ago and now sell it on for £500,000, the gain is totally tax-free. That's cheerful news!

Telling the tax inspector about selling your home

You have to tell the tax inspector about selling a home if it's not your main residence. You might, for instance, have a holiday home, or a flat you use during the week because it's near work, or a second home because you have complicated child custody arrangements. Alternatively, you may own two homes while one of them is on the market but not attracting a buyer.

If you use part of your property exclusively for the purpose of trade, business, or a profession, that part is taxable should you make a profit on a sale. This would apply where a garage is used as storage or a workroom or where an extension serves as an office. But it has to be 'exclusively'. So this rule doesn't count if you write your next blockbuster best-seller on a laptop on the dining-room table.

Deciding on your main residence

In most cases, it is obvious where your main home is. It is probably where the taxman sends his missives. But if there is doubt, you can always exercise your *tax-payer's right of election* and tell the Inland Revenue which property you want to have treated as your main residence.

You can declare that your main residence is a home you live in abroad. But whatever you decide, you're wise to declare the higher-valued property as your main residence. Your more expensive property is likely to create a bigger gain. You can only have one main residence so it would be daft to assign that tag to a property that will create a smaller, rather than a larger, profit on selling.

This choice is not written in stone. You can change it from time-to-time when your circumstances alter. Tell your tax inspector.

Married couples can only have one main residence between them. Unmarried couples, whether same sex or of different sexes, can have one each.

Following special rules when you're between properties

If you buy a new property before you finalise the sale of your previous one, don't worry about having two homes. The old one still counts as your main residence for the tax saving for 36 months.

And if you buy a new property but cannot move in yet, you have a 12-month window when it can count as your main home. In some circumstances, perhaps because you had to carry out building works to make it habitable, this can be stretched a further 12 months, making 24 months in all. This can also be useful if you are building your own new home. If you don't apply this rule, then the tax inspector might think you are never going to live there and start assessing you as though it was some sort of investment. It's always better to be safe and sure, not sorry and hit by an undeserved tax assessment.

People who leave their home and rent elsewhere have up to three years in which to sell free of Capital Gains Tax hassles.

Sorting out your main residence when living over the job

Vicars, lighthouse-keepers, and those in the armed forces and police force may have to live where their employers tell them. If this is true for you, know that you can buy a house as an insurance against losing your job, or as somewhere to live when you retire, and enjoy the tax advantages.

You can nominate the property you buy as your main residence. That way, you can get the tax savings on a sale even if you never set foot in the house.

Avoiding Capital Gains Tax – usually

Selling a property that you've lived in for a few years or more is the biggest profit-making opportunity most people will ever have. But no matter how long you've owned it and how much profit you make, that gain is also the biggest taxation bonanza most people will ever see in their lives. Selling your main home is totally free of Capital Gains Tax, in all but a tiny minority of circumstances.

You do have to pay Capital Gains Tax on any profit you make on selling a second home, whether in the UK or abroad. However, registering the second property in two names gives you two Capital Gains Tax annual exemptions.

If you have a large garden or a parcel of land as part of your property, you can sell off a *permitted area* of 0.5 hectares (about one acre) without selling the property itself, and not pay Capital Gains Tax on any profits.

You may also be able to sell off part of your house for converting that section into a smaller unit such as a granny flat without a tax charge. But you'll have to pay CGT if you sell off a separate building such as a cottage or outhouse in your grounds.

One dark cloud on this otherwise silver sky is that if you make a loss on selling your home you do not get any tax relief.

Being subject to Inheritance Tax

The tax authorities ignore all the main residence rules when you die. The value of your main property is bundled together with everything else you own for the calculation of Inheritance Tax.

You can sell your home to your children and then pay them a market-rate rent to live there. But your children have to pay tax on this rent and they face a Capital Gains Tax bill if they sell the house after your death. So this can be a case of paying taxes now yourself or having your children pay them later.

You sell your house for £250,000 to your children, who rent it out to you at £10,000 a year. Assuming they are top-rate 40 per cent tax-payers (and there are no complications such as costs connected to the property), they will pay £4,000 income tax a year on the rent. If you live for ten years, that's £40,000. After you die in ten years' time, they sell the property for £500,000. The Capital Gains Tax bill (including the taper relief detailed in Chapter 14) is £60,000. The Inland Revenue has taken in £100,000. But if you leave the house worth £500,000 in your

will, current Inheritance Tax rules point to a maximum bill of
£200,000 (40 per cent of the half-million which would apply if
you've used up all your other allowances and the nil rate band
on other things) and a minimum (if the house is the only asset
in the will) of £90,000 (in 2005–06).

The longer you live paying rent to your children, the more
expensive this option works out. If you survive only two or
three years, the commercial rent alternative would have cut
the tax bill. Chapter 7 has more details on Inheritance Tax.

You can leave your home to your legally married spouse without an Inheritance Tax bill. But the property then forms part
of your spouse's estate when they die unless they remarry
and hand the home on to a new spouse.

Chapter 16

Understanding Life Insurance and Tax

- -

In This Chapter

▶ Examining life insurance basics

▶ Going for protection

▶ Setting up a trust

▶ Considering endowments

▶ Taking care of tax issues

▶ Working through the mysteries of lump-sum insurance

▶ Buying insurance bonds

▶ Exploring the wide world of offshore insurance

- -

*O*nce upon a very distant time, life insurance was really easy to understand: You paid a regular premium in and if you died before you reached an agreed age, the insurance company would pay out a lump sum to your nearest and dearest. What can be simpler? For a few pennies each week, the family knew it would get some money in if the breadwinner died prematurely, even if the payout was only enough to ensure a good send-off at the funeral.

In fact, it was such a good thing that governments decided to encourage more people to buy life insurance by offering tax relief on the premiums they paid in. But well-meaning incentives often have consequences far different to those intended. While more people did insure themselves against an early death, the wily life insurers managed to subvert the rules and turn life cover into something largely unrelated to helping families with cash when someone died by coming up with investment-linked policies.

In this chapter, I talk about the ins and outs – and the tax ramifications – of various life insurance schemes.

Looking at the Basics of Insurance

Life insurance policies (I should say *assurance* but that's just for the really pernickety) have been, and still are, sold under various guises. With *term insurance,* you pay a fixed amount each month for a set period. If you die within this period, the policy pays the promised amount. *Critical illness policies* work in the same way but pay out if you are diagnosed with one of a number of serious medical conditions. Payments are made tax-free.

But here, I'm mainly concerned with various life insurance plans that are really investments dressed up as policies. These often have complicated tax conditions. You can purchase a wide range of policies including endowments, maximum investment plans, whole of life plans, with-profits bonds, friendly society plans, single premium life funds, guaranteed income bonds, flexible whole of life, and insurance savings plans.

To help you understand life insurance lingo, I explain some of the basic terms in the following list:

- **Beneficiary:** The person who gets the proceeds of the policy.
- **Endowment:** A mix of protection cover with investment.
- **Insurance-linked investment fund:** More of an investment than insurance. These funds exploit tax loopholes to offer gains to some tax-payers.
- **Insured:** The person covered under the policy.
- **Premium:** The amount you pay each month or as a lump sum into a policy.
- **Surrender (a policy):** To give up a policy in full or in part before its maturity date or the death of the insured.
- **Trust:** An often complicated legal device that can take your money out of the tax net.

Buying pure protection

Not all life insurance policies are investment-linked. Insurers still sell pure *protection plans* (also called *term assurance plans*, *critical illness*, and sometimes *mortgage protection cover*), which pay out a lump sum when the insured person dies or if he or she suffers one on a list of critical illnesses such as a heart attack or a stroke. Sums paid out under critical illness plans are not taxed.

You don't need to fret about any tax implications when you buy these or pay into them each week, month, or year. But you do need to worry over what might happen to any money paid out when you die. Although pure protection plan payouts are tax-free, the beneficiary of your policy can be hit by an Inheritance Tax bill. The next section tells you how to avoid paying on the policy's payout.

Looking at life insurance through the years

Three hundred or so years ago, groups of friends or groups of people in similar trades or professions put regular amounts into a pot so that if any of them died at a young age, their families would be well-provided for.

But then someone questioned what would happen if none, or very few, of the group died before the arrangement finished. There were two answers:

✔ One was the *tontine*, in which the fund continued to grow until only one survivor remained. He (invariably a 'he') would scoop the pot. This led to more than a few cases of someone hastening the deaths of others in the group. Tontines don't happen any more.

✔ The other solution was to give survivors some of their money back plus a share in the investment income that came along during the life of the policy. Calculating the sums involved required higher mathematics plus an understanding of how long people typically live and the factors that can shorten their lives. The with-profits model was born, taking insurance into the realms of investment. It eventually became the endowment.

From then on, life insurance and investment became increasingly and intrinsically interwoven.

(continued)

(continued)

In the 1960s and 1970s, life insurers realised there was not much money for them in covering people against death. But there was a fortune to be made by pushing the Inland Revenue rules to the limits regarding both premiums paid in and amounts paid out. The result was the creation of investment plans that picked up a big tax relief on premiums and grew faster, thanks to lower taxes, than similar investments outside insurance.

Insurers also discovered that they really didn't have to offer any meaningful life cover to fit the tax rules. Just one tiny per cent more than someone had invested would be fine. This was called the maximum investment plan or MIP – lots of investment but no real payout on death.

They subsequently worked out that it was a waste of time for the rich to pay in every week or month. So they invented the 'single premium' or lump-sum policy. This again only paid one per cent extra on the investment value on death but had valuable tax incentives for the well-off.

The only trouble with this apparent win-win scenario where the taxman helped you to investment riches was that life assurance premium relief (a tax refund on the premiums you paid in) started to be progressively withdrawn in the 1960s and disappeared completely on policies sold after 13 March 1984.

Many tax advantages still remain, however. These mostly only work for top-rate tax-payers. But that does not stop life insurance sales folk flogging them to all and sundry. Wouldn't you if you can grab 7 per cent in commission for doing so?

Writing policies in trust

Protection-style life policies are often for sums of £250,000 upwards. And that's a large payment to add to anything else you may leave when you die.

The policy payout is normally added to your estate and forms part of the amount on which Inheritance Tax is payable. Everything you leave over £275,000 (in 2005–06) is taxable at 40 per cent; so if your estate consists of an average UK house plus some modest savings and a few items of value such as a car, its value can quickly cross the Inheritance Tax threshold and cause your family to lose 40 per cent of the life insurance payout because tax has to be paid on it.

But there's an easy and painless way to avoid making your heirs pay Inheritance Tax – at least on your life insurance payout. It's called *writing in trust* and all you have to do is to sign a form that the insurance company will give you that sets up a trust for your insurance benefits. The result is that your life insurance payout goes straight to your beneficiaries rather than into your estate on your death. Beyond taking it out of the inheritance tax net, there's the extra advantage that your family will get the money more quickly than if they had to wait for your affairs to grind through the probate process.

Writing in trust is not just for new policies. You can also ask the insurer to place an existing policy into trust in just the same way.

Evaluating Endowments

Millions own *endowments,* a combination of life cover and a savings plan. If you die during the policy's set period, your family receives a guaranteed minimum amount. It can be more if the investment portion did well. And if you survive beyond the set period, you receive a sum of money that reflects how well (or how badly!) the investment portion fared over the period.

Just how much of the money you pay in is devoted to the life cover and how much to the insurance company's costs, commissions, and profit margins is rarely revealed in any form let alone made clear. But all salespeople preach perfect clarity on one item – especially when they try to sell an endowment as a way of repaying a mortgage. They all say the amount you get when the policy matures is 'paid to you tax-free'.

The sales pitch is true. If you buy an endowment and keep up the payments, you have no tax to pay at the end when the insurer sends you a cheque. That's only half the story, however. The rest of the story is something the sales folk don't mention. While the proceeds are tax-free to you, the fund itself is taxed. The life insurance company has to pay tax on the money it invests for you. All the dividend income and interest the fund earns on its investments are taxed. And when the fund makes a gain on selling an investment, there's more tax to pay.

How is this worked out? Don't ask! It's extremely complex, in a formula called the 'I-E basis', which takes in investment income and capital gains before subtracting the insurer's costs. If *Paying Less Tax For Dummies* was two or three times the length, it would still only scratch the surface of this subject. And even then, it wouldn't help too much as the detailed rules seem to be constantly changing.

Saving through an Insurance Policy

You can cut through the tax system and put regular savings into an insurance-linked investment fund through a friendly society policy.

In investing through an *insurance-linked investment fund,* you must contribute for a minimum of ten years to a special product offered by a small number of friendly societies. Your money grows free of all taxes. The big disadvantage is that you can invest only £25 a month, which means that quite a bit of each payment gets swallowed up in costs.

Many friendly society plans are sold when children are born so parents and others can pay into them until the child reaches 18 or 21 and can collect a (hopefully) worthwhile nest egg. Parents can invest in this policy without worrying about their own tax position.

Some life assurance firms have been selling tax-free insurance Individual Savings Accounts (ISAs) plans since 1999. They have a £1,000 a year limit on the amount you can invest. But only a handful of insurers ever thought it worth their while to offer them and very few customers bought into them, and they're set to be phased out in their present form. So why do I mention them? Well, they exist, you might have one, and it's good to know about as many tax-free options as possible.

Cutting Away the Complexity of Life Insurance Taxation Rules

A life insurance company's internal taxation is totally complex and the taxation has an impact on your investment savings.

So there are some broad-brush rules for investment-oriented life insurance funds. Generally, a fund is taxed on

- ✔ Income it gets from share dividends, bonds, bank deposits, and property.

- ✔ Capital gains on any profits the fund makes on selling shares, property, or other taxable assets.

Whatever the level of tax an insurance fund pays out, you can't reclaim it. Under no circumstances. Never. It does not matter if you were a non-tax-payer during part of the policy term or even throughout the entire term of the policy, you can't get anything back. The same applies if you paid tax at a maximum 10 per cent. I bet the salesperson never mentioned this!

If you're a non-tax-payer, avoid insurance-based funds like the plague. Your savings will end up being diminished by taxes you may not know exist and which you would never had paid outside the insurance plan.

Checking out whether policies qualify or not

Many tax ramifications hinge on whether a policy is *qualifying* or *non-qualifying*. Knowing technical terms helps ensure that you maximise any tax savings and minimise tax spending when you cash in your investment policy. Your knowledge will also impress the seller, making it less likely that you are mis-sold. Generally speaking, qualifying policies are better, especially for top-rate tax-payers.

Requirements for a *qualifying policy* are:

- ✔ It must be for a minimum ten years. They can be for longer, typically 20 to 30 years.

   Plans can become non-qualifying if they are surrendered before three-quarters of their expected time-span. The minimum for this is seven-and-a-half years because no policy can qualify if it is for less than ten years at the outset.

- ✔ Premiums have to be paid regularly according to the schedule. That's usually monthly and must be at least once a year. There are special rules if you miss out a few payments and need to catch up later on.

✔ The guaranteed sum payable on death must be at least 75 per cent of the total premiums paid in if the policy buyer is aged 55 or under when the plan is purchased. That percentage goes down by 2 per cent a year for the over 55s.

If a policy does not fit the above rules, it is a *non-qualifying policy.*

Jumping tax hurdles

If a qualifying policy matures or is paid out on death or because it is triggered by one of the listed medical conditions in a critical illness plan, the policyholder does not need to pay a penny in tax.

In some cases, top-rate tax-payers have to pay tax when they cash in a policy. If you cash in a lump-sum plan, such as a with-profits bond in full or in part, or fail to keep up a regular payment plan for at least seven-and-a-half years and then ask for the policy's current value back, you may owe tax.

You can realise tax benefits if you're a top-rate payer when you take out a policy but drop back to the basic tax level when you cash it in. Likewise, you're disadvantaged if you buy investment-linked insurances as a basic-rate tax-payer and cash them in when you are a top-rate payer. I explain this in 'Slicing from the top' later in this chapter.

Top-rate tax-payers may find that they pay less tax overall if they invest in insurance funds than if they use unit or investment trusts or invest directly into stocks and shares. Why? The typical rate an insurance fund is charged internally is lower than the 40 per cent top-rate tax and Capital Gains Tax.

If you surrender it before three-quarters of its stated term, a qualifying policy becomes a non-qualifying policy. Clever insurers have found a partial way around this. Instead of giving you one policy for your money, they give you a cluster of mini-policies, perhaps as many as 100. If you need some of your money before the policy term is up, you only need to cancel a few mini-policies, resulting in fewer tax hassles.

If you still pay into a life insurance policy that was bought before 13 March 1984, you get life assurance premium relief (LAPR) at 12.5 per cent of the amounts you pay in. The insurance company accounts for this automatically so there is no need to claim. If you pay in £10 a month on paper, the insurer will only take £8.75 from your bank account. You get this up to a maximum of £1,500 a year or one-sixth of your total income, which is an awful lot of insurance! And you get it whatever your personal tax rate. But if you extend or increase the policy, you don't get the LAPR on the extra.

Looking at Lump-Sum Insurance Bonds

The *lump-sum insurance bond,* sometimes called a *single-premium investment contract,* is a non-qualifying policy. It does not have a fixed life or any of the other attributes of a qualifying policy. So you have to be careful, otherwise you could find yourself on the end of an unwelcome tax bill.

The life cover is usually limited to 1 per cent more than the *underlying value* (the value of the investment less the commission and other charges deducted upfront) of the fund. And as life insurance companies start off by slicing off anything up to 7 per cent of your premiums in fees and commissions, they can easily afford to give you back 1 per cent if you die.

Handled correctly, lump-sum insurance bonds can give substantial tax savings to better-off investors. But handled incorrectly, they can be a tax nightmare as the nearby 'Cautionary tales' sidebar shows.

If you intend emigrating or returning to your country of origin, always tell the financial adviser what you are going to do and which country you intend moving to. Australia, New Zealand, and South Africa are among the nations whose very different tax systems can hit UK insurance bond holders with a double whammy. They can pay tax on the UK bond and then find they have to pay more tax in their new country.

Cautionary tales

Two former colleagues of mine were both made redundant at the same time. I'll call them Angela Green and Jane Brown to protect their anonymity. Both picked up £30,000 in redundancy payoffs. Neither had any need at the time to spend the money.

Ms Green went off to her bank where she was sold an investment-linked lump-sum insurance bond. Ms Brown went to a financial adviser who put her money into a portfolio of unit trusts. One year later, both noticed the value of their investment fund had gone up by 20 per cent. Ms Green and Ms Brown both decided they would rather spend their cash than stay in investment markets that were starting to look wobbly.

Ms Brown cashed in her unit trusts and received £34,200. This is the value of her original investment less a 5 per cent *upfront charge* (money taken off at the start to pay commission to the seller) plus the 20 per cent return her money earned. She is well within her Capital Gains Tax allowance and didn't have to pay Capital Gains Tax.

Ms Green's on-paper fortune also stood at £34,200. But she had to pay an early repayment penalty of 10 per cent of her original investment to her insurance fund. It was in the very small print so the seller glossed over it. She ended up with a cheque for £30,780. But her misery did not stop there. Because she had cashed in an insurance bond, the Inland Revenue got out its rulebook. It told her that profit over her original £30,000 had to be added to her income for the year and then subjected to a complicated formula known as top slicing.

The result was she had to pay an extra £156 in income tax so her final cash amount was £30,624, or £3,576 less than Ms Brown, even though both had taken the same investment risks and earned the same investment rewards.

Oh, by the way, the unfortunate Ms Green's financial adviser at the bank scooped £2,070 in commission. The luckier Ms Brown's financial adviser earned £900. This has nothing to do with tax but it's useful to know.

Taking a regular income

Insurance bond holders can take a regular payment from their policy to give themselves an income. They pay no personal tax on it, no matter what their own top-tax rate is. But they must follow these rules.

✔ You can withdraw no more than 5 per cent of the original investment sum each year for a period of 20 years. The Inland Revenue sees this as taking your own money back.

✔ If you miss out on a year or years, or took less than 5 per cent, you can catch up. Someone who missed the first annual withdrawal of 5 per cent can take 10 per cent in the second year. An investor who took 1 per cent in the first five years has a 20 per cent sum to carry forward to year 6. Again, the idea is that the original investment sum, not any gain, is paid back tax-free.

✔ If you breach the 5 per cent rule, or want all your money back, you enter the wonderful world of top slicing. (See the upcoming 'Slicing from the top'.)

If you take from 5 per cent upwards in a year (and you don't have unused previous years you can catch up on), or you cash in the insurance lump-sum investment completely, you have to do some arithmetic. First you have to calculate the profit, which is either the amount over the 5 per cent per year, or, if you want all your money back, the excess over what you paid for the policy in the first place.

Older tax-payers caught in the age allowance trap (see Chapter 6 for more details) can profit from the 5 per cent withdrawal rule because this does not count as income.

Here's some really good news. Because the fund pays tax internally, using an indecipherable formula or two, there is no more tax to pay if you are a basic-rate tax-payer.

But no good news comes without some bad. The profit is added to your other income to check whether the total falls into the top tax bracket.

The following examples show how the tax liability falls in various situations:

✔ Your income is £10,000 and your insurance gain is £5,000. The total £15,000 is well within the basic-tax band so there is no tax to pay.

✔ Your annual income is £30,000 making you a basic-rate tax-payer. Your insurance gain is £20,000, which puts your total income at £50,000. You have to pay tax on the amount over the basic level (£37,295 in 2005–06). You can use the top slicing method described in the next section.

✔ Your annual income is £50,000 and your insurance gain is £30,000. The entire insurance gain falls within the top-rate tax band. But the policy is treated as though 20 per cent has been paid to accommodate basic-rate payers, so you only have to find the other 20 per cent, not the whole 40 per cent.

Slicing from the top

Now for some better news, again. This section looks at *top-slicing*, which is a way of making your withdrawals from lump-sum insurance bonds less liable to a tax demand. Top slicing is not too easy. But bear with me. It gets better, the longer you leave your money in the fund. And if it applies to you, then it could save you a lot of tax payments.

Take someone earning £17,295 whose bond has produced a £40,000 gain over ten years. Adding the income to the gain gives £57,295, so £20,000 falls in the top tax rate. You would expect this person to pay tax at 40 per cent on this £20,000 profit in the highest tax band, equalling £8,000.

Wrong. The fund is tax-free at the basic income tax level as 20 per cent has already been paid internally. So you might expect to pay 20 per cent on the gain, equalling £4,000.

Wrong again. The tax collector knows it would be really nasty to take ten years' worth of growth and hit the holder for it in one year. There is, instead, a wonderful but little known process called top slicing. With top slicing, the gain is divided by the number of years the insurance bond has been in force, in this case ten.

So divide the total £40,000 gain by ten to give £4,000. Add that £4,000 to the holder's other income for the year, (in this case, £17,295) and the total is £20,145 that falls well within the basic-rate band. The result is no extra tax is payable.

Being aware (and wary) of costs and commissions

Always ask your financial adviser or bank for as much information as possible on the costs you will incur in buying an insurance-based investment compared with a similar investment outside the insurance policy wrapper. You can find these expenses outweigh any tax benefits.

Someone investing a £10,000 lump sum into a low-cost investment such as an investment trust or an exchange-traded fund with an upfront 1 per cent in costs and growing at 7 per cent after annual fees will have £20,513 after ten years, ignoring tax.

Another person investing a £10,000 lump sum into an insurance-based fund where the upfront fee is much higher at 6 per cent, but otherwise growing at the same rate, will have £19,530 at the end of ten years.

You need to sit down with the adviser to see if those higher costs are worth it in your particular situation. Remember that lump-sum insurance bonds can cost you as much as 7 per cent in upfront commission.

Now suppose the bond holder had a £35,295 income. Add the £4,000 to that making £39,245, and half (£2,000) falls into the higher rate (starting at £36,145 in 2005–06). Only that top half is hit for higher-rate tax at 20 per cent with the result that overall, the tax rate falls to 10 per cent. Apply that new rate to the £40,000 and the charge is £4,000.

If the entire sum had fallen within the top rate, the holder would have had to pay at 20 per cent, gaining nothing from top slicing.

Top slicing can also work if the bond is partially encashed beyond the 5 per cent annual tax-free withdrawal.

Top-rate tax-payers who expect their income to fall back when they retire or downshift their work can combine the 5 per cent rule with top slicing to cut down on tax bills. While they are earning high amounts, they can take the 5 per cent tax-free withdrawals to give themselves a regular income, saving on the extra tax they would have had to pay on income from other investment types. But when their earnings fall to basic-rate tax levels, they can cash in the bond, use the top slicing rules, and pay less tax (or none at all) because all or part of the gain now falls into the 20 per cent basic savings tax band.

Top slicing on cashing in a bond does not apply in calculating whether you can apply for children's tax credits or whether you qualify for the extra age allowance given to the 65 plus age group. In these cases, you add in the complete gain to your other income for that year.

Eyeing Guaranteed Bonds

Guaranteed income bonds (or GIBs) pay a fixed sum annually or monthly for a set period after which you get your initial investment back. A variation is called a guaranteed growth bond, in which the income rolls up to increase the eventual payout rather than being distributed. Either way, the rate you see quoted is tax-free for basic-rate tax-payers. Top-rate tax-payers have to pay extra (see the earlier 'Slicing from the top' section).

Gains, if any, from high-income bonds linked to stock market indexes are also treated in the same way.

Going Offshore with Your Money

You don't have to buy insurance-style investments issued in the UK. If you live abroad or are thinking of living abroad, you may want to consider a tax haven policy. These usually come from offshore offshoots of well-known UK insurers who have set up offices in places such as the Isle of Man, Jersey, Guernsey, and Luxembourg for this purpose. Investments in policies with these tax haven companies mount up without any tax charges.

Looking at the legalities

There are no restrictions on any UK tax resident moving their money offshore. You can invest where you like, what you like, and how you like.

If this were as far as it went, then no one would bother paying UK tax because we would all ship our investments offshore. But life is never that easy. You have to tell the Inland Revenue about any gains you make on offshore bonds in the same way as if the bond were onshore.

To make sure you do, the tax authorities are working to ensure that many offshore life companies (including almost all those with onshore business in the UK) send in an annual return showing who has encashed what. This is part of a European Union crackdown on cross-border tax evasion. When these regulations are finally in place (and this is expected in the next year or so), insurers will have to report gains whatever the laws on policyholder confidentiality say in the country where the insurer has its legal home. So no cheating.

Weighing up costs versus savings

Unless you wish to court illegality by tax dodging, or you want to invest in an esoteric asset not available in the UK, there may be no point in going offshore if you are a resident in the UK for tax purposes. Costs are usually higher, and you will be hit for taxes just as if you had dealt with a UK-based company.

But if you work offshore and then return, there is a big plus point. The gain is reduced proportionally by the number of years you were not resident in the UK. An offshore bond-holder who cashes in after 14 years but who spent seven of those years overseas, has the gain halved for tax computation purposes. Of course, if you never come back or cash in the policy entirely before you return to the UK, you're liable only for local taxes (if any) where you were living.

If you intend moving permanently to another country, it can be worth using an offshore bond as it will roll up without any tax. You then cash it in when you set up your new home. But always check first on the tax rules in the country you want to go to.

Chapter 17

Depending on Pensions for Your Retirement

compulsory. Bry

Pensions show the Inland Revenue's generosity at its greatest. The money you pay in qualifies for tax relief at your highest personal rate, your pension fund grows without any income tax or Capital Gains Tax worries, and you get a big tax-free lump sum when you finally retire. And these tax advantages are there whether you pay for a personal pension, have one through your employer's retirement scheme, or get a mix of the two.

It all adds up to a monster-sized package of tax freedoms. Or so it appears. Remember the saying 'there's no such thing as a free lunch'? Well, there's no such thing as free cash from the taxman either, or at least not without a whole load of strings. In return for the tax concessions, there are rules to follow.

In this chapter, I explain the rules and how you can use them to your benefit.

Looking at Pension Particulars

Pensions are a regular income in retirement. But because the state pension can be inadequate, the government offers tax carrots for pension plans.

But once you invest money into a pension plan, it's farewell, auf Wiedersehen, au revoir, and adíos to your cash. You can't have it back next year, or the year after that. You only get to put your hands on it when you reach a pensionable age (currently a minimum 50, but due to rise to 55), normally when you retire – although that doesn't mean you have to give up work altogether.

When you finally can get access to your investment, or that of your employer along with your own, you have to put most of your money toward buying a regular income. In most cases, you get just a quarter of your pension pot back in cash.

Looking to the future

Many rules are due to change in 2006 when pension simplification comes in. Pension simplification will end all the complications of annual limits on what you can contribute. Instead, there will be a lifetime fund limit of £1.5m rising to £1.8m at some undefined future date. So instead of having a ceiling on what you can put in, there will be a limit on how big your fund gets. But tax relief will remain.

You'll be able to put a wider range of assets into your pension if you have a self invested personal pension (SIPP).

These assets may include anything from buy-to-let properties to stamp collections as well as more traditional investments. The wisdom of including any of these less-usual investments is uncertain, and beyond a book on paying less tax. But the Inland Revenue is not going to let you buy a holiday home, put it in your SIPP, take the tax relief, and then stay in it each summer. If you do, you'll have to pay a commercial rent to your own pension fund. And you could be taxed on the benefit as well.

25% lump sum
50 yrs

When you start taking your personal pension, you can get 25 per cent of the fund you've built up in most plans in a tax-free lump sum (which I talk about in the 'Living it up with the tax-free lump sum' section later on). The balance goes into an *annuity,* an insurance company-backed plan that guarantees you an income for the rest of your life (and sometimes that of a partner or dependant child) in return for taking your remaining pension money into its coffers.

Annuity payments are taxed as income. Even the basic State Pension is taxable. This is where the Inland Revenue gets its revenge.

Saving for a Pension at Work

Many firms offer *occupational pensions,* in which the employer pays in money to help build your pension. Employers can knock off their contributions against their own tax. Most employers demand that their employees pay something towards their own pension – usually around 6 per cent of pre-tax pay.

A minority of employers do not require employee contributions. These are known as *non-contributory* pension plans.

There are two basic forms of occupations pensions, each with its own tax advantages:

- ✓ **Defined benefits plans,** also known as *final salary plans,* are those that use a formula based on your years in the scheme and how much you were earning just before your retirement in order to work out how much pension money you get.

  The maximum pension you can earn from a defined benefit scheme is two-thirds of your final salary, according to Inland Revenue rules. But only a tiny minority get that much. Most employees end up with far less because they swapped jobs during their working life or missed out on past contributions. Both swapping and missing payments reduce your final pension.

Don't worry. There are top-up options, which I explain in the 'Looking at topping up and matching payments' section.

✔ **Defined contributions plans,** also known as *money purchase plans*, are plans in which the pension you get is based on how the money that you paid in grows in a pension fund. This is similar to a personal pension.

What sort of scheme you are in and how much you pay into it helps determine how you can get the best out of tax relief.

Calculating how much you can pay in

If you contribute to your pension, the money you pay in is offset against your taxable income using the PAYE system or via your self-assessment. This relief is at your highest tax rate, and the pension payment comes off your salary before anything else other than national insurance. A basic-rate tax-payer gets £1 worth of pension value for each 78p paid in real money. For the top-rate tax-payer, the deal is even better. They only have to pay 60p to get a full pound's worth of contributions.

The only proviso is that you can't count earnings over the pensions cap – £105,600 for 2005–06 – towards tax relief on pension contributions. But, hey, if you earn that much, you can probably subsist without help from the tax authorities!

Looking at topping up and matching payments

Additional voluntary contributions (AVC) is a workplace scheme through which you can put more than the required monthly amount into your firm's pension plan. But there are limits.

To work out the maximum you can put in, calculate 15 per cent of your salary. Then deduct the amount you already contribute to your company pension plan, ignoring any employer payments. What's left is what you can put into an AVC. If your employer doesn't require you to contribute to your pension, you can invest up to 15 per cent of earnings; if your scheme asks for the typical 6 per cent contribution from you, then you can invest up to 9 per cent of your salary into an AVC.

You are not obliged to put anything in or, if you do, contribute the maximum amount that you're allowed to add.

Tax relief on AVC money works the same way as a contribution to your employer's main fund.

You decide on whether you want to pay into your firm's AVC on a tax-year by tax-year basis. Those with big ups and downs in their salary should stay out of AVC contributions in poor earning years and hit the AVC big time when their salary shoots up. But you can't go backwards and make up for low-earning years!

An employee who can put up to 10 per cent of earnings into an AVC, because the compulsory contribution is 5 per cent, makes £15,000 one year, giving a maximum £1,500 and realises tax relief of £330 (£1,500 times the basic 22 per cent tax rate). But the following year, this person knows there's going to be a mega-bonus plus loads of overtime and the salary shoots up to £50,000. Putting the same £1,500 into the AVC that year brings top-rate tax relief at 40 per cent, which works out to £600 in tax relief, almost twice as much as the previous year. And you could probably afford more, saving further tax. High earners who are downshifting should aim at a maximum AVC contribution while they earn at the 40 per cent tax level, and then cut the AVC when their salary drops.

You won't get a tax-free lump sum based on your AVC pension (although that changes in 2006). Why? No one knows. It's one of those inexplicable pension rules someone thought made sense when it was invented in 1987.

Many employers boost your AVC with matching contributions. For each £1 you pay in (before tax relief), they contract to add a pre-agreed sum such as £1 or 50p. You don't get tax relief on this but the boss can count the contribution against the firm's tax bill, and the extra amount increases your pension, so you gain in the end.

Discovering the Benefits of a Stakeholder Plan

If you're in the vast majority of workers who earn less than £30,000 and you aren't a company director, you can boost your pension potential with a stakeholder pension plan. Non-working spouses, students, and even babes-in-arms can have a plan.

You can skip this section if you earn more than £30,000 a year or if you are a controlling director of a company, no matter how much you earn. Under present rules, you can't join a stakeholder plan.

The £30,000 limit does not count job perks such as a company car or company private medical insurance. You may want to consider a stakeholder pension plan if one is offered through a flexible employee option package.

Stakeholder pension plans are low cost, flexible schemes from life insurance companies in which you can start and stop payments without penalties.

You can invest up to £3,600 a year into a stakeholder plan irrespective of how much you have already paid into your employer's main scheme or an AVC plan. You get automatic tax relief at 22 per cent on your contributions, so each £1 invested only costs 78p. Non-tax-payers and those who pay at the 10 per cent rate also collect the 22 per cent deal. Top-rate tax-payers go one further in paying less tax because they can bring the figure to 40 per cent.

If your salary goes past £30,000 in the future you can still pay up to £3,600 not counting basic-rate tax relief (£2,808 in real money) into a stakeholder pension for up to five years. And you can also pay this same maximum for up to five years if you stop work – useful if you downshift or take time off for family responsibilities. New rules that take effect in 2006 will simplify the whole affair.

If you have an income from a second job or you do freelance work, you can contribute to a plan based on these earnings.

Buying a pension for your baby

Better-off parents and others can give a newly-born child up to $2,808 net (that's real money) a year for a stakeholder pension. With the tax collector's generosity, that becomes $3,600 going into the fund. And then they can repeat that every year. The money grows tax-free and there's a tax-free lump sum at the end when the child draws her or his pension.

Under present rules, the child cannot touch the money until she or he reaches 50! And under proposed changes, which are almost sure to happen before one of today's newborns even reaches kindergarten, the minimum pension age is going up to 55. So don't expect to be around to see the child spend their pension money.

Regular payments into a stakeholder pension for a child can help reduce the size of your estate for Inheritance Tax purposes on your death.

Getting life cover

You can buy life insurance with the extra benefit of tax relief by using up to 10 per cent of your personal or stakeholder pension contribution to pay for this cover.

Here's how it works: If you put $3,600 a year into a stakeholder pension plan, you get $360 a year (or $30 a month) available to buy life cover if you want. What this buys depends on your age, sex, and health (and, of course, the insurance company's own rates, which vary immensely) but, for example, $30 a month should probably buy around $200,000 worth of cover for a woman in good health in her mid-twenties. Thanks to the tax relief, a basic-rate tax-payer would pay $23.40 in cash for the $30 of cover; someone on the top-tax rate would only need to pay $18.

Building up a Pension When You Work for Yourself

Around half the working population either works for themselves or has an employer that does not provide an occupational scheme. But they can still save up for a pension – with lots of help from the taxman.

Personal pensions are plans into which you make your own contributions. Anyone who is not in an occupational scheme and who is under 75 can pay in. But until new rules come into force in 2006, there are annual limits on what you can pay in based on percentages of net relevant earnings, which go up as you get older. These are based on your age at the start of the tax year. *Net relevant earnings* is the amount of your salary before deductions if you are employed or your profits after all allowable expenses if you are self-employed. You cannot count earnings above £105,600 in 2005–06.

Table 17-1 shows the percentage of your net relevant earning you can contribute to a personal pension plan.

Table 17-1	Personal Pension Limits
Age	*Percentage of Net Relevant Earnings*
Up to 36	17.5
36–45	20
46–50	25
51–55	30
56–60	35
61–74	40

There are special rules on how much you can contribute for some very old pension policies called Retirement Annuity Contracts, which were first issued before April 1988. Your pension provider can give you this information.

Carrying back your tax savings if you're self-employed

You usually get tax relief in the year when you pay in to your pensions plan. But if you are self-employed, you can have substantial ups and downs in your earnings. There can be circumstances when you want to backdate a payment to the previous tax year because it produces a greater tax saving as you earned more that year.

Suppose you earn £50,000 in one year, and only £5,000 in the next one but your cash for a pension is only available in the second year. Using something called *carry back* you can choose to have the payment count against your higher-earning year. The result is you get tax relief at 40 per cent instead of 22 per cent. Carry back applications can be made on the self assessment form or on form PP43 and work for one year.

Carry back can be complicated, so check out your eligibility with a pensions adviser first.

Basic-rate tax-payers get tax relief automatically as contributions to personal pensions are worked out net of income tax. So each 78p you pay in buys £1 worth of pension payments as the Inland Revenue pays in the other 22p. You get this even if your highest rate is 10 per cent or you don't earn enough to pay tax.

Top-rate tax-payers can claim extra tax relief over and above the basic rate. They need to apply either on their self assessment form or by sending form PP120 to their tax inspector. This brings the cost of each £1 of pension payments paid into a plan down to 60p.

Earning Less But Saving More

There are schemes where you can opt to take a salary cut but pay more into your pension plan. That sounds a bit upside down but it can gain extra tax relief for you and a better deal for your employer.

If you own your own company, or if you are a director or senior manager of a larger firm, you can be in a position to improve your pension while taking a pay cut or, at least, not taking pay rises. This trick is called 'salary sacrifice'. Its main purpose is to enable someone who has paid in insufficient amounts in the past to accelerate payments into a company pension fund.

The way it works is that the employer reduces the salary of the person concerned and sends a formal letter to the employee to confirm this. The money saved goes from the employer to boost that person's fund.

Someone earning £50,000 a year from their job would normally be able to pay in 15 per cent (£7,500 in this case) as a maximum pension contribution. Now if that person agrees to reduce their salary to £46,000 a year, their maximum contribution according to the 15 per cent rule goes down to £6,900. However, the employer now has £4,000 extra to put into the fund for the individual. The result is the employee is effectively receiving £10,900 in pension contributions.

The salary foregone or sacrificed falls out of the tax net for both employee and employer. And this arrangement avoids national insurance as well, so the employee saves 1 per cent (£40 in this example) in national insurance but the employer's bill is cut by a very useful 12.8 per cent (£512).

Salary sacrifice works best for those who negotiate individual employment contracts. But there are disadvantages:

- ✔ The reduction affects your salary amount for other purposes such as borrowing money for home purchase.

- ✔ The money is tied up in a pension fund so it cannot be spent.

- ✔ Your final salary can be lower, which can have a knock-on effect on your occupational pension as this cannot be more than two-thirds of your final earnings level.

Realising What Happens When You Retire

At the moment, you can collect a pension at age 50, even if you are still working. Certain occupations such as professional footballers and catwalk models can collect pensions at

35, according to Inland Revenue rules. By 2010, the pension collection age for all professions is planned to rise to 55.

At the other end of the scale, the current maximum age to turn a pension plan into a regular pension payment is 75. This will remain.

 You can retire from your main job but still contribute to a pension plan if you take on another job or go self-employed. You can also continue to pay into a stakeholder plan to a further five years.

When you retire, your pension money provides a tax-free lump sum – usually about 25 per cent of the pension amount. The rest of the money has to be converted into an income for life known as an annuity. The following sections talk about the lump sum and annuities.

Living it up with the tax-free lump sum

When you decide to take your pension, you will be offered a choice between a higher pension and a smaller amount plus a lump sum. This is a no-brainer. Always opt for the lump sum even though it cuts your pension.

The lump sum is totally tax-free. Those in personal and stakeholder funds can claim 25 per cent of their pension pot. The calculation for those in final salary schemes and some very old self-employment plans is more complicated but it works out roughly at a quarter of the fund as well.

The tax-free lump sum is yours to do as you want. You can leave it in your will or give it to your family. But you can also use it to get a better tax deal should you want to give your retirement income a further boost. Read on to find out how.

Entering the world of annuities

After deducting the lump sum, the balance of your personal pension fund, or what is left in a money purchase plan, buys an annuity. How final salary pensions are financed is down to your former employer's pension fund arrangements.

An *annuity* is a life insurance policy in reverse. You pay in a lump sum which you will never see again and in return receive a regular income until the day you die.

There are two types of annuity:

- **Compulsory purchase annuity:** What's left of your pension pot after the tax-free lump sum has to be used to buy an annuity before you reach 75. This is called, unsurprisingly, a compulsory purchase annuity. The regular payments from this are taxed as income just like any other money coming in (although there is no national insurance to pay).

- **Purchased life annuity:** You can buy an annuity with other money you might have including the tax-free lump sum. But the tax treatment of these annuities is more generous than for the compulsory variety. Here, the tax authorities realise that part of each payment you get is a return of your original capital. The balance comes from the way the money is invested by the company providing the annuity.

The amount set aside for return of the capital depends on your age when the annuity is purchased. The older you are, the greater the amount that comes out of capital and is tax-free. Because every one is different, it's impossible to be exact but, as a general rule of thumb, you can be talking about losing 8 to 15 per cent of your purchased life annuity payment in tax compared to 22 per cent for a basic-rate tax-payer in a compulsory product.

Paying in today, collecting tomorrow

There's a really good deal called immediate vesting you can use provided you can invest in a personal or stakeholder pension. And it can give your retirement income a big tax benefit boost.

Immediate vesting is a plan in which you buy a personal or stakeholder pension today, and start to draw on it literally tomorrow. Thanks to a mix of tax relief on the contribution and the tax-free lump sum, you can fund your retirement income at about half price.

Take Sheeba, for example, who is aged 65 with a £50,000 a year salary and with no workplace scheme. Referring to the information in Table 17-1, she can put up to 40 per cent of her earnings into a personal pension, or £20,000 in this example. She invests this £20,000 in a secure deposit fund with a pensions provider. This contribution produces a tax rebate at the 40 per cent rate because she is a top-rate tax-payer. This gives Sheeba £8,000 back, so her real expenditure is £12,000.

But then she decides to turn her pension fund into a paying pension the next day, or as soon as conveniently possible. Sheeba can do this even if she carries on working.

This encashment or pensions vesting allows Sheeba to take a 25 per cent tax-free lump sum, based on the £20,000 and not on the real £12,000 cost. So she gets £5,000 in cash. This brings the actual cost down to £7,000. But the pension fund is still worth £15,000 (£20,000 less the tax-free lump sum).

This £15,000 has to be used to buy an annuity, which means that the cash is lost. But getting £15,000 worth of annuity for a real cost of £7,000 is great value.

At current rates, a basic annuity of £15,000 will give Sheeba an annual income for life of around £1,200 a year. As a percentage of the £7,000 actual expenditure, that's around 17.3 per cent a year – a great return in anyone's book.

Part V
Self Assessment and Getting Help

"Good heavens – this tax investigation must be really serious – You're the third tax inspector to visit my little taxidermist business this month."

In this part . . .

*H*ere I show you some invaluable tips on how to deal with the Inland Revenue itself. You can't ignore the Inland Revenue because avoiding them is illegal. So it's best to approach them in a friendly manner, knowing what they can, and can't, do to you.

This part explains the self assessment form and whether you need to pay for outside help. My advice is don't pay for help – unless you really have to, or you have plenty of money and can afford for someone else to do the work for you.

And I explain the powers the Inland Revenue has to stop cheating. But that's not a one-way process. This part also shows how you can ask the tax authorities for compensation if you have been treated unfairly. Tax offices do make mistakes, and nowadays, they often own up to them!

Chapter 18

Filling In and Filing Your Self Assessment Form

. . . .

In This Chapter

▶ Looking at the form

▶ Completing the basic return

▶ Calculating the right amounts

▶ Sending in the paperwork

▶ Paying what you owe

. . . .

*F*illing in your self assessment form (or, officially, your *tax return*) is an annual chore. And it could be followed by having to send a substantial cheque to the Inland Revenue. Painful.

But if you have followed all the advice in the preceding chapters of *Paying Less Tax For Dummies,* then actually coming up with the numbers shouldn't be too difficult.

This chapter doesn't give you hints on how to reduce your tax bill. Nor does it show you how to answer all the questions, most of which are self-explanatory anyway. Instead, it points out common errors that could derail your tax return, involve you in fines, interest and penalties, and possibly an investigation. (If you face an investigation, turn to Chapter 20.)

Managing the Mechanics of the Form

In these sections, I look at who gets the self assessment form, (or forms for some), what they have to do with the form, and what happens if they don't fill it in.

Getting the forms

Around one in three tax-payers is sent a form automatically each year at, or just after, the start of the tax year on 6 April. These are people that the Inland Revenue believes should get a form because they:

- ✓ Have earnings from self-employment or are in partnerships.
- ✓ Are top-rate tax-payers or are approaching the cut-off point for basic-level tax.
- ✓ Are company directors.
- ✓ Have more than one source of income.
- ✓ Have earnings from overseas.
- ✓ Are pensioners with a complex income mix.
- ✓ Own substantial land or property.
- ✓ Regularly have capital gains or losses from investments.

This is not an exhaustive list. And you may find the reason that you were sent a form no longer applies – perhaps you moved from self-employment to employment or spent all your savings. You do not have to send in a completed form if you do not owe tax.

The Inland Revenue is trying to cut down on the number of tax-payers who receive forms each year. It is experimenting with simple forms for those who only have the odd item to declare and taking around one million people out of the tax net altogether as it is more efficient to use PAYE to collect any extra tax an individual might owe.

Discovering the basics of self assessment

Self assessment is still under ten years old. And the Inland Revenue admits it is not perfect. It is testing a simplified form for those who only need a few lines of the existing return.

Self assessment replaced a complicated system which had grown up over the previous 200 or so years. This involved dealing with one tax office for the assessment, possibly a second if you had income or capital gains from another source, and yet another for the payment. Then there were countless appeals, appeals against appeals, and appeals against appeals against appeals, on matters which are now completed in just one box on the form.

However, if you wish to, or have to, communicate with the taxman, you can always ask for a form or download one from the Inland Revenue Web site at www.inlandrevenue.gov.uk.

If you go for the traditional paper-based method when you submit your tax forms, you are likely to receive three documents from the Inland Revenue. These are:

- ✔ **Tax return:** Everyone has to complete this as it provides the basic information for your self assessment (around ten pages).
- ✔ **Tax Return Guide:** This booklet offers substantial detail on how to fill in the return (around 36 pages).
- ✔ **Tax Calculation Guide:** This helpful guide enables you to work out the amount you owe (or are owed as a rebate) with no more technology than a pocket calculator (around 16 pages).

  The Inland Revenue does not send out the Tax Calculation Guide to everyone. You may not receive one if you have previously filed over the Internet or sent in forms based on a recognised computer program.

There are also supplementary pages that cover such areas as employment, share option schemes, self-employment, partnerships, owning land or property, receiving foreign income, receiving income from trusts or estates, capital gains and losses, and being not resident in the UK for tax purposes. The Inland Revenue normally sends supplementary pages you used previously. In many cases, these pages are bound together with your basic form. (The upcoming 'Seeing about supplementary pages' section talks about these pages in more detail.)

These supplementary pages are designed to cover some 99.9 per cent of needs. But if you're in doubt, or have a source of income that should be taxed that doesn't seem to fit any of the supplementary pages, you can make use of the additional information section on the form. You can always write a letter, as well, if you need to communicate with the Inland Revenue for any reason.

It is your legal duty to fill in a form if you have to. It is not an excuse to say you did not receive one. Or that you left it all up to your employer to sort out. Or that you thought an accountant would do it all for you. If you are in any doubt, apply for a form by telephoning the Inland Revenue Order Line on 0845 9000 404. You can also fax your request to 0845 9000 604 or download the form from the Internet at www.inlandrevenue.gov.uk/sa. And don't forget to send it in. If you have not received a tax return and have further tax to pay, you must tell the Inland Revenue by the 5 October following the end of the tax year.

Your local tax office can provide you with the form and other material in Braille, large print, and audio format. You can also communicate with the Inland Revenue in Welsh. There is a Welsh language helpline on 0845 302 1489.

The standard forms are also available to print or use on screen in the many tax return computer program packages on sale.

Discovering you don't have to fill in a form

If your total earnings are from one employer under PAYE, you only have to fill in a form if you are a top-rate tax-payer. If you have an ordinary job and no extraordinary income, you pay tax through the PAYE system on a regular basis. So you don't have to fill in a self assessment form or pay anything extra at tax time.

If your total income, including investment income and savings interest and the value of any workplace perks such as a company car or company health scheme, leaves you firmly in the basic-rate tax zone (or lower), you do not have to fill in a form. The only exception is where you have other sources of taxable income from which tax was not deducted at source.

If you believe that your only need to contact the Inland Revenue is to ask for a rebate of previously paid tax, you can either fill in a self assessment form or, more simply, ask for form R40, which is a claim for repayment. R40 is also available as a download from www.inlandrevenue.gov.uk/forms/r40.pdf.

Keeping records

Self assessment works on a file now, check later procedure. This means you file your self assessment return, then the Inland Revenue checks it. So saving the records of your finances is really vital. You have to keep paperwork for one year after the final filing date (31 January) after the end of the tax year (ending the previous 5 April). This one year is extended to five years if you are self-employed. Chapter 3 has complete details of what you have to save and for how long.

Filling In the Return

If you're like most tax-payers, you can ignore around four-fifths of the form. If you do not tick the 'yes' box to any section, you can move on. You do not have to write in 'not applicable'. The Inland Revenue's gadgetry is trained to recognise blank pages.

Avoiding the most common self assessment errors

The great majority of self assessment errors have nothing to do with confusing foreign income credits or Capital Gains Tax losses. They're far more basic – the sort of thing you probably learned at primary school. Here's the top list of errors:

- ✔ Failing to sign the form – it's your responsibility.

- ✔ Failing to tick all the mandatory boxes.

- ✔ Failing to provide complete information about any repayment due to you.

- ✔ Failing to tick your choice of repayment. You can opt to have repayments sent by cheque or repaid through PAYE (if you're an employee). And if you're feeling generous, you can have a refund sent directly to a charity.

- ✔ Failing to tell the Inland Revenue where any repayment should go. You have to remember to put in details such as bank account numbers.

- ✔ Failing to tell the Inland Revenue to whom any repayment is to go.

- ✔ Failing to complete the correct supplementary pages (see the 'Seeing about supplementary pages' section) or to attach all the supplementary pages.

- ✔ Entering weekly or monthly amounts in an annual box – this applies especially to pension payments.

- ✔ Recording the capital in your savings account as well as the interest in the interest box on the form.

The Tax Return Guide is not the easiest document to use. Although not a legal document, it is written like one in many parts and is full of Inland Revenue jargon. But you can call the Inland Revenue's helpline and get someone to translate it (and more) into everyday language. The telephone number is 0845 9000 444.With patience, you can make the Tax Return Guide, combined with the Tax Calculation Guide, work for you. You may still need a pocket calculator (or a good ability with long multiplication and division).

Listing income and credits

The basic tax return is designed to gather information about certain income including interest you earn from National Savings, bank, and building society accounts. You also need to provide information about interest from unit trusts and dividend income from trusts and investments.

If you draw a pension or receive Social Security benefits, the Inland Revenue wants to know about them. Remember state pensions and contribution-based jobseeker's allowance are taxable.

You also need to report any miscellaneous income, which can include small amounts of casual earnings, royalties, and commission you might get from selling for mail-order companies. In many cases, it's easier to record details by filling in a supplementary section. The basic form lists all the supplementary sections, which range from employment and self-employment to Lloyd's insurance names and foreign investment income.

The form also has space for you to list items you can claim against your overall tax bill. These include:

- Personal and stakeholder pension contributions. Don't record these contributions if your only pension payments are through your employer as relief should occur automatically through PAYE. (See Chapter 17.)

- Venture capital trusts. (See Chapter 14.)

- Tax-deductible contributions to trade union and friendly society sickness and funeral plans. You cannot claim for standard trade union membership fees.

- Gifts to charities. (See Chapter 21.)

- The Blind Person's allowance.

- The Married Person's Allowance, which applies only if at least one partner was born before 6 April 1935.

You should not put pence into any box when you fill in the form. You can round down income and gains (items you owe tax on) to the nearest pound. Equally you can round up credits and deductions (items that the Inland Revenue owes you) to the nearest pound. This can sometimes lead to slight differences between boxes on the form. And it can save a few pounds!

Going into savings and investments

You should get an annual return for each UK savings account you have. This report shows the amount of interest, the amount taken off for taxation at source, and what you are left with. Investments such as shares, unit trusts, and investment trusts include similar information with each dividend payment. But if your investment does not pay dividends, you don't receive any such information.

Less than obvious areas to note include:

✔ **Purchased life annuities:** The annuity provider give you a certificate to show what proportion of each payment is tax-free.

✔ **Relevant discounted securities:** Items under this heading can include retail price index-linked UK government stocks, zero-dividend split capital investment trust shares, and some stock market index-tracking bonds which offer a minimum guaranteed return irrespective of the performance of the shares in the index.

✔ **Scrip dividends:** A scrip dividend is an offer of shares in place of cash. You should show the cash equivalent in the correct box. *Dividend reinvestment schemes,* in which you choose to have any dividends automatically go to buying new shares instead of getting cash, do not count as a scrip.

Don't forget to count investment trust shares under the 'dividends from companies' heading, but not dividend distributions from UK authorised unit trusts and UK authorised open-ended investment companies (OEICs).

Realising a surprise bonus

This could make you feel better about something that no one considers fun – you could find a bonus in completing your tax return. As you have to list all your savings and investments to comply with the Inland Revenue rules, you have a once-a-year opportunity – one you cannot put off with excuses – to look at your portfolio.

So, instead of congratulating yourself that you have only had to pay £10 tax on your savings bank interest, seize the opportunity to see if you could have paid £20 tax by finding an account that paid twice as much interest. Or discover if you could have avoided tax altogether with an alternative such as an Individual Savings Account.

Making friends with the blank page

You can use the blank box at the end of the form to tell the tax inspector about items you are not sure about. By showing your doubts at this stage, you can probably head off trouble later on.

You can also use this space to confess to any items you have estimated because, for one reason or another, you do not have the paperwork to hand.

Always over-estimate tax due if there is any doubt. You cannot be penalised if you overpay your tax and then receive a refund. Underpayment is a different matter entirely.

Seeing about supplementary pages

The basic form, with details such as your name and address and your national insurance number, is only the starting point. Most people have to fill in extra pages known as *supplementary pages*. These cover what makes you different as a taxpayer – you're employed or you're self-employed or you have overseas investments, for example. In fact, in many cases, the supplementary pages are the most important! They are part and parcel of the self assessment form so you can't avoid them.

The supplementary pages, in order of the Inland Revenue reference numbers, are:

 ✔ **Employment (SA101):** Fill this in if you have to file a self assessment return and were employed under PAYE on a full-time, part-time, or casual basis. This category also includes agency work and 'IR35' work where you provide your labour through a company. Ask the Inland Revenue for special pages if you are a paid minister of religion.

 ✔ **Share schemes (SA102):** On this page, you record the options granted and options exercised under a number of employee incentive schemes. You do not need to fill this in if you were in an Inland Revenue approved scheme such as Save As You Earn and have met all the conditions.

✔ **Self Employment (SA103):** In addition to those who get some or all of their income from self-employment, you will need to fill this section in if you are a buy-to-let landlord or provide furnished accommodation in your home where you also offer meals, such as in a bed-and-breakfast. You need to complete a separate SA103 for each business you have. So if you work for yourself as a builder but also rent out properties, you have to complete two forms. If you invested your money into a Lloyd's of London insurance underwriting syndicate, there are special extra pages.

✔ **Partnership (SA104):** There are two versions of this form. The short version covers the standard situation in which you earn money from a partnership whose trading income is the only or main source of money coming in. The full version covers more complicated situations. Most partners can use the short version but if you are not sure, ask for the full version. All partners are jointly responsible for completing the partnership's returns.

✔ **Land and Property (SA105):** This section covers income from land and property in the UK, including furnished holiday lettings, but excluding buy-to-lets.

✔ **Foreign income (SA106):** This is a catch-all section for all sorts of income produced from sources outside the UK. It includes offshore bank accounts, investments, and insurance policies. It does not matter if the income has already been taxed at source by the overseas tax authority, you still have to fill in this section. There are a number of tax treaties between the UK and other countries that sort out what you pay in the source country and in the UK. Filling in this section enables the Inland Revenue to know whether you have more to pay or whether you qualify for a rebate.

✔ **Trusts (SA107):** If you are a beneficiary of trusts or settlements (but not the bare trusts used often by grandparents and others to give money to those under 18 who (or whose parents) have to account for any tax due themselves), you need to complete this page. You should also use this page to record regular income from a deceased person's estate, but not for one-off payments from a legacy (these are not taxed). If you receive an income from an income-producing asset such as shares you inherited, include the income in the standard return along with any other investment income.

✔ **Capital gains (SA108):** If you disposed of assets liable to Capital Gains Tax worth at least four times the Capital Gains Tax annual allowance, you have to fill this part in even if you don't have to pay any tax. In 2005–06, the allowance is £8,500 so the reporting level is £34,000. You also fill in these pages if you have a loss.

✔ **Non-residence (SA109):** This part is for people who earn income in the UK but are not regarded as UK 'tax citizens' (the proper phrases are 'not resident', 'not ordinarily resident', or 'not domiciled'). It can also apply if you are resident in the UK for tax purposes but also a tax resident of another country with which the UK has a 'double taxation' agreement.

Looking at the employment pages

You have to fill these in if you are a top-rate tax-payer or a director (even if you own the majority of the company's shares).

You do not necessarily have to enter any more than the name of your employer and the amount of pay you received (noted on your P60).

Considering the self-employment pages

You will need a separate set of forms for each form of self-employment. For instance, if you drive a cab as a self-employed driver by day, but earn a living as a freelance entertainer by night, you have two totally different forms of self-employment.

You also fill in these pages if you provided accommodation with a service attached such as regular meals or nursing. Buy-to-let is included under 'investments'.

You have to fill in the capital allowances section, where applicable, no matter what your turnover. This is where you can claim *depreciation* (the declining value of cars, plant and machinery, and some buildings) against your profits.

In general, you can write off 40 per cent of the value of most items in the first year, followed by 25 per cent of the balance in each successive year.

You need only show turnover (sales), expenses against turnover and the resulting profit or loss if your turnover is under £15,000. You still have to keep records and accounts, however, to show the Inland Revenue if your return is subject to additional checking. The £15,000 level has remained unchanged for many years. If your turnover exceeds £15,000 you have to show a more detailed breakdown of costs and tax adjustments as listed on the form.

If you received small or one-off earnings and you have no expenses to set against the sum, you might put these under 'other income' in the main pages. This might include a single payment for writing an article for a magazine or for selling a patented idea to a firm.

Counting the Ways of Doing the Sums

Even if you get professional help with your self assessment form, you still have to assemble all the paperwork needed. But you can find assistance at no cost. The following sections tell you how to figure out your bottom line as far as tax liability goes.

Finding out that the early form-filler works less

Filing a paper tax return before 30 September gives you the option of asking the Inland Revenue to calculate your tax. The calculations, of course, depend on you filling in the return correctly. You're told how much to pay or whether there is a repayment coming your way by the following 31 January. You can, if you disagree with the Inland Revenue's figures, rework them yourself or hire an accountant. But the reality is that this 30 September option is generally only used by those with relatively simple tax affairs.

If, for some reason, your tax form was sent to you late, the window for asking the Inland Revenue to do the sums extends to two months after the return was sent to you.

Using purpose-built software

You can put all your details into a number of computer programs. These then lead you into the right additional sections and work out what you owe (or are owed).

The Inland Revenue Web site at http://www.inlandrevenue. gov.uk/individuals/index.shtml has a list of software providers with kits that work. There are packages such as Quicken and Microsoft Money that include tax form software amongst other financial applications. Expect to pay around £10 for the most basic downloadable software.

Some programs don't support all the supplementary pages, although most do. So check the 'Seeing about supplementary pages' section earlier in this chapter for the reference number of the pages you need before buying.

Filing Your Form

Self assessment depends on a strict annual timetable with deadlines reinforced by fines, interest, and penalties. These dates can be stretched by a day or so year-by-year to avoid bank holidays and weekends.

The four basic dates in each tax year are:

- ✔ **6 April:** New forms available.

- ✔ **30 September:** The final date to submit your form if you want the Inland Revenue to calculate your tax.

- ✔ **30 December:** The final date for Internet filing if you owe less than £2,000 and want the payments taken out of your regular salary through PAYE.

- ✔ **31 January:** The deadline for returns to avoid automatic penalties and interest.

Paying a £100 penalty for filing a day late can easily undo all the tax-saving work you have done over the past year. Get your payments in on time!

Posting in your form

Around 90 per cent of self assessment tax-payers use some form of paper-based return. You can send it in through the post – you have to pay the postage – or you can hand deliver the forms to your local tax office (even if it isn't the office that handles your affairs.) If you post it, ask for proof of posting. If you hand it in, ask for a receipt. Many tax offices stay open from 8.30 a.m. to 8 p.m. on deadline day.

Submitting your form online

You can file electronically, and more and more people do so each year. The Inland Revenue is a big online filing enthusiast. Large companies and accountancy firms already do much of their communications online. The system is much better after a sticky start a few years ago when the process was hit by criticism and crashes. The Inland Revenue's reputation was damaged some years ago when it offered a £10 rebate for online filing (good) and then made it so difficult that even downloading the basics took hours (bad).

There is no longer a £10 rebate. And it still takes seven days between registering and receiving, by post, an ID number and a separate unique activation PIN number. This expires if you forget to activate it within 28 days of receipt, so you have to start all over again if you forget.

But the service is improving. You get automatic calculation without having to buy a software package that only lasts for one year. The system guides you through the questions and automatically steers you away from parts of the form that are not relevant to you.

Repayments are faster than with paper-based filing. And you have until 30 December (rather than 30 September) to file if you want any tax you have to pay to be collected through PAYE.

The disadvantage is when you are cut off by your Internet service provider in the middle of filling up a section! – don't forget it can still take some time to fill in the form. You can, however, take your time over the filing and go back to it in a new online session. You do not have to get it done in one go.

Print out a hard copy anyway, just to be sure. If you have some idea of your potential tax bill first, then you will see if you have done anything silly such as turning a £5,000 spare-time earning into £500,000 or £5!

Paying on Account

The self assessment tax system works with two formal payment dates a year. On 31 January you have to pay anything still outstanding from the tax year which ended on the previous 5 April, plus half your likely tax bill for the year which will end on the forthcoming 5 April. So on or before 31 January 2006 you should have paid any outstanding balances for 2004–05 plus half of what you are likely to owe in 2005–06.

The final payment date for the other half of the period 2005–06 is 31 July 2006. If it turns out that these two payments are not enough – a situation that may happen if your earnings are rising – you make a third and final payment on the following 31 January.

 You do not have to make payments on account if 80 per cent or more of your income tax bill (but not Capital Gains Tax) is covered by tax deducted at source – PAYE and automatic deductions from savings interest are common deductions. It's up to you to work this out. It is best to ignore this concession if you are a 'borderline' 80 per cent case.

There is no interest benefit if your payment arrives early (but at least you know you've done it and won't get penalised!).

Asking for a reduction in payments

If your tax liability for this year is likely to be significantly lower than the previous year, you can ask for a reduction in your payments on account. Otherwise, you could end up paying more than you need until it is corrected in the following year's tax return.

You can claim a reduction on your payments on account on a tax return, or by writing to the Inland Revenue. You must give valid reasons to back your claim. The Inland Revenue adds interest to your repayment, but the rate is far lower than the interest they charge you if you owe them money.

Adding up the potential penalties

You face an automatic £100 penalty if you fail to get your return in by 31 January. And there is a further £100 if you have still not filed by the following 31 July. In addition, there is a 5 per cent surcharge on tax unpaid on 28 February, and a further 5 per cent if it is still unpaid (plus interest on the first surcharge). This is a painful sum!

Penalties cannot be greater than the tax owed. If you discover you owe nothing or are due a rebate, the 31 January deadline does not apply.

Some people who cannot fill in their form properly make an estimate and then pay over more tax than needed. If you pay more than you owe, you cannot be fined. You can claim any excess back later.

Chapter 19

Paying for Outside Help with Your Tax Affairs

. . . .

In This Chapter

▶ Checking various services

▶ Evaluating form checkers

▶ Looking at accountants

▶ Discovering what a financial adviser can do for you

▶ Insuring yourself against an Inland Revenue investigation

▶ Cutting costs with the Inland Revenue's own services

. . . .

*P*rovided you're happy with the first 18 chapters of this book, you should be well on your way to paying less tax, and avoiding all the fines, interest, and penalty payments the Inland Revenue uses as the stick part of its approach to taxpayers. You may not need to read this chapter at all.

And if you read this chapter only to conclude that you don't need any of the information in it, then great. You can easily have saved yourself £100 or more (or much more!) by discovering you really didn't need costly professional help with your tax affairs.

But if you're curious about what tax agents do and how much they cost, I do my best to satisfy that curiosity here.

Surveying the Services

According to figures from the Inland Revenue (and it should know) around half of all those who fill in self assessment forms employ a professional tax person at some or all the stages of making the annual tax return. Most of these are company directors or have substantial self-employment earnings.

The type of professional they hire is another question. There is a bewildering variety of services. These include:

- ✔ **Chartered accountant:** A person who claims chartered status must be a member of a recognised professional organisation such as the Institute of Chartered Accountants in England and Wales or the Institute of Chartered Accountants in Scotland. These professionals are generally regarded as the top of the accountancy tree. They cover the widest field from auditing huge companies to providing tax advice to individuals. Details of members, services, and complaints processes can be found on www.icaew.co.uk or write to the Institute at PO Box 433, Chartered Accountants Hall, Moorgate Place, London EC2P 2BJ. The Scottish organisation's Web site is www.icas.org.uk.

- ✔ **Certified accountant:** This person is a member of the Association of Chartered Certified Accountants. A certified accountant often offers practical, hands-on advice to small businesses and individuals. You can find further details of members, services, standards, and complaints mechanisms on www.accaglobal.com or write to the Association at 29 Lincoln's Inn Fields, London WC2A 3EE.

- ✔ **Tax technician:** Members of the Association of Taxation Technicians tend to carry out complicated but specialist tasks.

- ✔ **Form checker:** A person who does basic work around self assessment. I talk about form checking services in the upcoming 'Trying a Tax Form Checker' section.

- ✔ **Rebate firm:** A company that tries to get a refund for non-tax-payers of any tax deducted at source. They often appeal to people who are only in the UK for a short time. They usually charge around 30 to 40 per cent of the amount recovered.

✔ **Banks and building societies:** These institutions may have specialist tax departments or outsource this work to other companies. Expect to pay for this, especially if all the bank or building society does is to point you to an outside provider.

Whether they are chartered accountants from one of the biggest international accountancy firms charging £500 or more an hour, or low-level bank workers checking figures on your tax return for less than a tenner an hour, the Inland Revenue calls all hired professional help *tax agents*.

Deducting the cost of advice

The self-employed can deduct the cost of accountancy services for their business against their profits. This could mean that up to 40 per cent of the costs of dealing with the Inland Revenue are picked up by the taxman if the payer is on the top rate. A £1,000 bill offset against tax is a £600 outlay. Basic-rate tax-payers end up with 22 per cent of the accountant's bill paid for by the Inland Revenue. Limited companies can also count the cost of accountancy and auditing against their profits. All accountants charge VAT on their fees. Businesses that are VAT-registered can reclaim the VAT charged on the accountancy costs.

You cannot set off the cost of accountancy for your personal tax affairs against tax.

The self-employed often have two accountancy bills, one for business affairs and a second for other tax including investment dividends, personal pensions, and savings interest. The first bill will generally be larger than the second.

Assigning responsibility

Tax agents work for you – but you sign the forms. Whatever the status of any professional you employ, you are ultimately responsible for the contents of the form you submit. It is no excuse to say 'my accountant did this' or 'the form filler didn't bring this to my attention'. The Inland Revenue has heard every excuse in the book, and blaming your tax agent is a complete non-starter.

If a tax professional is negligent, making an error that is not your fault, you may be able to seek compensation for negligence from the tax professional. They should have 'professional indemnity' insurance cover. So check they have this before signing up.

Trying a Tax Form Checker

Tax form checkers endeavour to ensure you have filled in your self assessment form correctly. This type of firm is often staffed by retired Inland Revenue personnel.

They sell their services on the grounds that the form is very complex, that you will put off completing it if left to your own devices, and that you will worry about whether it is correct. They also promise to check previous Inland Revenue calculations and your PAYE tax code to see if there are errors.

Tax form checkers can only work with what you give them such as annual returns from savings accounts or dividend statements. They are unlikely to know whether anything is missing as they do not have the full details of your taxable affairs.

Affording the fees

Form checkers usually set fees for their basic services at around £100, the same as the lowest level penalty for not getting the form filled in on time.

This £100-style service completes the form for you based on figures and paperwork you supply. The checker will enter amounts such as earnings from employment or pensions, employee benefits, investments, interest, and overseas earnings. Most will also calculate any Capital Gains Tax you have to pay.

Always ask for details of what you will get in writing before you sign up for a service. Some firms use the 'from £90' formula which turns into £190 or £290 by the time you are finished! And always ask if VAT is included in the fees.

For the basic price, you probably won't get help with other parts of the form such as profits from self-employment or buy-to-let investments that you may have.

Most checking firms will, however, fill in the self-employment sections (or file your buy-to-let figures) using paperwork you supply for around £175 to £250 on top of the basic fee.

Most increase fees in line with your turnover. Typically, the fees go up to around £400 a year once your sales top £40,000, and to around £750 if your sales top the £100,000 mark.

Landlord packages for buy-to-let investors start at about £250 for three or fewer properties. Expect to pay more for bigger property portfolios.

Some firms charge monthly instead of annually to enable you to budget.

If you are VAT-registered for your self-employment, you can reclaim the VAT charged on any tax form filling for your business.

Helping to recover overpaid taxes

A number of tax checking firms also offer to go back up to six years (the maximum allowed) to see if you are owed rebates. These firms, and others who aim at non-UK workers who should not pay tax, usually work on a no-win, no-fee basis. Typically, they take 30–40 per cent of any amounts they recover for you.

Working Out the Value of Accountancy Services

There is no clear blue water between form checkers and accountants – a description that has no legal basis as anyone can call themselves an accountant although they can't use the terms 'chartered' or 'certified'.

Looking at a unique tax help charity

TaxAid (`www.taxaid.org.uk`) is a registered UK charity that gives free tax advice to people who cannot afford to pay for professional accountancy advice.

It will help anyone on a low income whether employed, self-employed, on benefits, or retired who needs advice on Inland Revenue-related affairs. Often the sums involved for its clients are small but the anguish caused to them as individual taxpayers is great.

It helps those with worries because they are the subject of an Inland Revenue enquiry; it works for those facing legal proceedings for non-payment of taxes; and it aids those who think they are due a tax refund.

The service, which is staffed by qualified tax professionals and largely financed by donations from accountancy firms, also helps people who work for advice agencies with queries their own clients bring to them.

But chartered and certified accountants will usually charge you more than form checkers. You can easily pay £1,000 plus VAT at a top accountancy firm for a basic return even if your affairs are no more complicated than earnings from employment and some investments. Smaller firms tend to start their fees at about £250. What do you get for your extra outlay compared with a form checker? Sometimes nothing! But you should get a personal service with hints on how to arrange your tax affairs better in the future and help with more complicated affairs.

A registered accountant will also take the disorganised contents of a box of financial bits and pieces and sort them out, provided you pay for this at a pre-agreed per hour rate. So your messiness can be expensive!

Trying Out a Financial Adviser

Independent financial advisers can sometimes offer tax advice. This is usually limited to help with specialised tax investments such as Individual Savings Accounts, venture capital trusts, Enterprise Investment Schemes, and onshore and offshore trusts. They can also provide advice on Inheritance Tax and how to minimise it.

Financial advisors are not qualified or set up to fill in the self assessment form itself. However, some are linked to accountancy firms that offer form-filling help.

Different regulatory controls apply to each part of these organisations. The financial advisers operate under the auspices of the Financial Services Authority, and you will be able to complain to the Financial Ombudsman Service if necessary. The accountants are controlled by whatever body they belong to. Your complaint route will start with that body if it cannot be solved by negotiation with the accountant.

Taking Cover against Inland Revenue Action

Inland Revenue investigations can be costly for you even if nothing is found or if the tax inspector's victory is for a relatively small sum – it's easy to run up a £5,000 bill or more.

The Inland Revenue does a number of random investigations each year. If you're the subject of an investigation, the tax inspector does not give you a reason, and there may not be one other than that your name came up.

And there will be more investigation and actions. The small print of the 2004 budget reveals that the Inland Revenue intended spending £66m more to bring in a further £1.6 billion in tax revenue.

But you can insure against the costs of a probe. You can get a policy that covers professional fees and other costs up to £50,000 to £100,000.

The policy does not pay any additional tax, fines, interest, or penalties you're liable for. It won't compensate you for mental anguish, either.

Considering the costs

Many accountants market plans to individuals. Accountants often buy bulk schemes from specialist insurance firms and then sell them to clients.

Some small business lobbying groups and trade associations also offer cover to their members as part of their annual package. These policies generally include business taxes such as corporation tax and Value Added Tax.

There is a wide difference in annual insurance fees – anything from as little as £50 to £500 or more – often without much difference between the cheap end and the expensive policies. Policies are often sold for whatever the provider thinks their particular market will bear!

Avoiding voiding your policy

Insurance policies only help when the insurer is happy you have not brought the problem on yourself. So don't expect help if you:

- ✔ Deliberately set out to defraud the Inland Revenue.

- ✔ Failed to comply with the legal requirements for keeping records and sending in tax returns.

- ✔ Ignored the time limits both for self-assessment returns and other taxes.

- ✔ Did not register for VAT when you should have done so.

Saving Fees with Inland Revenue Helplines

Believe it or not, the Inland Revenue is like Goldilocks. It wants everything 'just right' so that the Three Bears family – and your family – pay the correct amount, not too much and not too little.

And the Inland Revenue is willing to help you get it right. It offers a number of facilities to tax-payers small and large, which, with a few exceptions, are free-of-charge. So using what the tax authorities offer can save you a bucket load of cash – money that you might otherwise pay at a rate of £250 an hour to an accountant.

Getting practical advice

You can write to, or phone, your own tax office with queries. Both the address and the number should be shown on your self assessment tax return. Your employer or pension provider also has details of the tax office you should deal with.

If you have a specific query, writing is best. For instance, if you have sold £20,000 worth of shares quoted on the London Stock Exchange and £20,000 worth of shares listed on the Alternative Investment Market the tax office can help you sort out the Capital Gains Tax treatment for each (they can be different). And writing tells them you are willing to report your gains.

Many items can, however, be dealt with over the phone with a call to your tax office. The person there can tell you if your query requires something in writing.

Alternatively, you can call the self assessment helpline on 0845 9000 444 – the hours are longer than the offices as this is open from 8 a.m. to 8 p.m. every day of the week, including weekends and bank holidays (oh well, not including Christmas Day).

If the helpline can't help, it will know another helpline that may be able to come to your rescue. The appendix to this book has a list.

Always give your national insurance number whether writing or calling.

Keeping your expectations realistic

Whether you contact the Inland Revenue in writing or over the phone, you will not get individual advice on how to best arrange your personal tax affairs.

You can get generic help such as a definition of what savings you can hold tax-free and which you need to pay tax upon. But figuring out which savings plan is right for you is a personal decision only you can make – helped perhaps by an accountant or financial adviser.

And if you are worth a few tens of millions and your tax lawyers think they have found a loophole, your advisers can now run the idea across the tax inspector to see if it will work or not. But if you are rich enough to afford tax help like this, you probably won't need to be saving tax by phoning up helplines!

The Inland Revenue won't help you dodge tax. And anything you say on the phone or put in writing can be retained.

Chapter 20

Dealing with an Investigation

● ●

In This Chapter

▶ Examining reasons for investigations

▶ Undergoing an enquiry

▶ Finding out where to go to complain

● ●

*Y*ou've done everything that's applicable to you as explained in *Paying Less Tax For Dummies.* You've kept records just like the Inland Revenue says you should. And you've followed all the self assessment form instructions.

So why have you received a letter from the tax inspector which, while not accusing you of anything, suggests everyone at the Inland Revenue would be happy to have a further look at your tax affairs and returns?

Don't panic, unless you have deliberately defrauded the Inland Revenue. There are several reasons why questions could be raised about your tax return, one of them being that you've been chosen at random to see if the self assessment system is working properly. I explore the various reasons and the entire investigation process in this chapter.

This chapter is not designed to reduce your tax bill. But the information should help save you fines, penalties, interest payments, and legal and accountancy fees. And all that could easily add up to a big saving. Oh, and you'll also avoid a whole load of sleepless nights and personal misery.

Explaining the Basics of Investigations

Around ten million people dealt with the Inland Revenue each year when it was just involved with tax. Now its scope has widened to take in additional areas such as child tax credit and national insurance, its customer base is far larger.

So the chances of getting it wrong either by accident or deliberate action increase. This chapter is mainly concerned with looking at what can happen if you try to cheat or dissemble. But I first look at the situations that can arise when you make a mistake inadvertently. Don't forget that the taxman is not an idiot. The folks at the Inland Revenue have heard it all before so they have a good idea of what happens because you make an innocent error compared with trying to pull a fast one.

Keeping proper and complete records aids everyone concerned and keep down costs if you use an accountant.

Misleading the taxman inadvertently

The tax authorities realise they make mistakes. But tax-payers sometimes do things wrong as well. The Inland Revenue corrects many of your minor errors such as putting various investments in the wrong place on your tax return; failing to add up properly; or missing out whole pages because you turned over two by mistake. It knows these errors are not deliberate and they rarely have much impact. In fact, around half of arithmetical errors the Inland Revenue discovers would have resulted in the tax-payer handing over more! You do, however, have to pay if you make an innocent error which results in under-estimating the amount of tax due.

Here are the most common errors:

- ✓ Failing to sign the form.
- ✓ Failing to tick all the boxes you should.

✔ Failing to complete all the repayment instructions on the form. These tell the taxman where and how to send any money you are due back as a refund.

✔ Ignoring supplementary pages. Don't forget many people have more pages to fill in on the self assessment form than the basic pages.

✔ Confusing the capital with interest or the investment amount with the dividend amount.

✔ Mixing up investments such as unit trusts with interest-bearing bank accounts.

✔ Entering weekly or monthly sums when they should be annual amounts.

The Inland Revenue usually rectifies these simple mistakes, including obvious arithmetical errors such as getting a decimal point or a percentage sum wrong. This is called *repairing*.

Rectifying your tax errors

You can amend your self assessment form if you discover an error or change your mind about accounting for something. To do so, write to your tax inspector. In general, you can change your form within one year of the filing period at the end of a tax year. For example, you can amend your 2005–06 return, due in by 31 January 2007, up to 31 January 2008. You have to pay interest on any amounts owing, but you don't face anything more serious. If you miss this deadline, it is still worth owning up rather than facing a potential enquiry.

If you amend your form, the Inland Revenue's 12-month limit for most non-fraud enquiries starts on the date the tax office receives the amended version.

Setting off warning bells

A number of triggers cause the taxman to be suspicious of your form. Generally the Inland Revenue looks for anything unusual, for example:

✔ **Your self assessment form is unusual in some way:**

• It's largely incomplete or substantially late – or both late and incomplete year after year.

- It is wildly different from previous years.

- It includes many provisional figures instead of real amounts.

- It isn't on file because you didn't send it in.

✔ **You lived overseas but have returned.** You may be suspected of keeping assets hidden in tax havens.

✔ **You live a lavish lifestyle but it's unclear how you maintain it.** This one is fairly obvious. You're seen around at flash parties but you say your income is poverty level. Or you drive a Rolls Royce on a minimum wage.

Ringing alarm bells when you're self-employed

If you're self-employed or run a small business, the Inland Revenue may have reason to look at your forms more closely if any of the following circumstances apply to you:

✔ **Information from another source does not tally with the form.** Inland Revenue computerisation is increasingly linking your returns with other information such as VAT forms and this throws up discrepancies.

Other sources of discrepancies may be a letting agent if you have a buy-to-let business, a major customer if you supply sub-contract labour to a firm, or an anonymous source such as a former employee or a neighbour. The Inland Revenue does not normally act on anonymous sources unless the source backs up information it already has.

✔ **You are in a high-risk occupational group.** Although it has no official policy on this, the Inland Revenue targets certain groups it believes are prone to strong temptation or deliberate fraud.

The list of such occupations includes those that involve handling large amounts of cash such as small shopkeepers; industries where the cash or black economy is suspected such as construction; and professions in which the Inland Revenue believes lifestyle issues tend towards being economical with the truth (show business is a special target in this category).

✔ **Your income or expenses are out of line with the norm.**
Your profits are substantially lower than other similar
businesses or your expenses are far higher than most
similar businesses.

The Inland Revenue has a number of manuals which give
an idea of costs and profits in a wide variety of business
areas. If your numbers are over or under expectations,
you may be suspected of having undeclared income or
profits.

Placing time limits on the Inland Revenue

In general, any enquiry the Inland Revenue starts must begin
within 12 months of the final filing date for the tax year. So, a
form due in by 31 January 2006 and filed on time cannot usually be questioned after 31 January 2007.

However, there are no time limits for suspected fraud cases.
Some such cases take ten or even 20 years to come to trial or
a settlement.

The key word is *discovery*. If the Inland Revenue discovers
something very wrong with your current tax return, they can
start to trawl backwards through past years to see if you have
concealed anything.

But this discovery-assessment process can only look at items
and matters that cannot reasonably have been deduced from
the self assessment form.

Being the Subject of Investigation

Most enquiries, other than those of the random test variety,
are aimed at people who run their own business or who have
very complicated investments including money held offshore.
The former are likely to get a *full enquiry*, during which their
whole return is questioned. An *aspect enquiry* concentrates
on just one area of a tax return – a property transaction or a
Capital Gains Tax computation, for example.

Insuring against the costs of a probe

An Inland Revenue probe can be expensive to deal with. Besides possible accountancy fees (never cheap!), there are costs involved with finding and reproducing documentation such as bank statements and business accounts. A number of accountants sell insurance plans that pay these costs should you be investigated.

The cost of such policies varies from £100 to £500 or more, but the more expensive ones do not necessarily offer more. They are often priced on a 'what will the customer put up with' basis, where the price is higher for those who the accountant thinks will be able to afford more.

But these policies do not pay out if you are suspected of fraud or other malpractice. Nor will they pay fines, penalties or interest. You have to take one out before there is any Inland Revenue action against you. Once you have received a notice of an enquiry, it is too late.

If you're the subject of a full enquiry, you are not told whether the enquiry is random or targeted.

Getting a Dear Tax-payer letter

An investigation starts with a letter that usually asks you to provide further information to back up the details on your form.

A letter of a formal notice names the documents – such as invoices and bank accounts – that you're required to produce. It warns you of penalties if you do not comply but also contains general information on your rights, including your right to appeal.

You are given 30 days to produce the required documents. You can ask for an extension if you're ill or the paperwork will take longer to assemble, but you have to tell the tax inspector you need the extra time.

At this stage, you can phone a named Inland Revenue person, or you can contact an accountant (start with *Yellow Pages* if you have no personal recommendations) or, if the problem is basic, obtain free help from the Citizens Advice Bureau (now called Citizens Advice – try the local phone book for details).

Exchanging information

You can carry out all communications in writing if you wish to avoid face-to-face meetings with an inspector. If you attend a meeting, you may take your accountant or other adviser with you. The Inland Revenue makes notes at such meetings and is required to give copies of these to you or your representative.

Not co-operating is a very bad idea. If you fail to respond to questions either in writing or in person, you will be sent a formal notice requiring the information needed. This will give you a set time (normally 30 days) in which to comply.

If you fail to respond to formal notices, you can be charged penalties of up to £150 a day.

Don't freeze just because you have an enquiry outstanding. Continue to file returns and pay tax on due dates.

Behaving well during an investigation

You do not lose your legal rights just because the Inland Revenue is investigating your tax returns. But investigations are easiest for both sides when there is as little confrontation as possible.

The tax inspector is generally quite business-like. He or she would far rather sort the matter out quickly with payment of back taxes, interest, and perhaps a penalty than go through the whole range of legal methods available. Many probes are settled in this way.

Coming under suspicion of fraud

Things can get heavy where deliberate fraud or evasion rather than carelessness or a lack of knowledge are concerned. You will know you are in this deep abyss if you're asked some or all of the following questions:

✔ Have any transactions been omitted from, or incorrectly recorded, in the books of any business in which you are or have been concerned whether as a director, partner, or sole proprietor?

✔ Are the accounts sent to the Inland Revenue correct and complete to your best knowledge and belief?

✔ Are all the tax returns of each and every business correct and complete to the best of your knowledge and belief?

✔ Are all your personal tax returns correct and complete to the best of your knowledge and belief?

✔ Will you allow an examination of all business books, business and private bank statements, business and private records so the Inland Revenue may be satisfied that your answers to these questions are correct?

This is heavy duty stuff. And false statements could result in a criminal prosecution. If you are in this deep, get a good lawyer and accountant!

Ending the investigation

Normally investigations end in mutual agreement. In most cases, the Inland Revenue comes to a settlement with the subjects of its enquiries, so you never read about them in the newspapers!

You can breathe a sigh of relief when you receive an 'Enquiry Closure Notice' which details how much, if any, you have to pay in extra tax, interest, and penalties.

Just a tiny minority of offenders end up in a criminal court. Only 60 people a year go to prison, and many of them have other criminal charges outstanding.

Coming away clean and clear

Sometimes, the Inland Revenue accepts your explanation for the discrepancy it noticed, and you walk away just a little the worse for wear. (See 'Asking for compensation' later in this chapter if you want to pursue getting reimbursed.)

Sometimes, the initial issue is resolved, but during the examination of your records, the tax inspector finds something else is wrong. In the second case, expect the investigation to continue, but with a different tack.

Negotiating penalty payments

If errors are found in your tax return then you have to pay the difference between what you reported and what you should have reported – as well as any interest and penalties!

You can help prevent your eventual bill running away with penalties and interest by making a payment on account during the investigation. This is not seen as an admission of guilt, and can be reclaimed if the enquiry proves your innocence.

And, if you have to pay extra, do so as soon as possible. Otherwise interest and penalties could mount.

The Inland Revenue can reduce penalties by taking into account the amount of information you volunteered during the investigation on your income or gains that you omitted or understated.

Interest rates on late payments tend to vary in line with Bank of England base rates. They are greater than you can get by depositing the money in a bank. And these rates are usually between 3.5 and 4.5 per cent higher than the Inland Revenue gives you on rebates when it overcharges.

An alternative to a closure is the *contract settlement,* in which you agree to pay an agreed sum to cover all outstanding amounts. This can sometimes save money compared with calculating tax owed, national insurance, interest, and penalties separately. It is legally binding on both sides.

Dealing with the Aftermath or Continuing the Process

In this section, I tell you how to pursue legitimate complaints about advice from your accountant or the actions of the Inland Revenue.

Putting your accountant on notice

Blaming your accountant isn't something you can generally do if you get an adverse judgement, at least as far as the Inland Revenue is concerned. You have to sign your tax returns, which means taking ultimate responsibility for what they report. From the Inland Revenue's perspective, it's a waste of time trying to switch the spotlight onto your accountant.

However, if you were deliberately misled by your adviser, it is worth complaining to the accountant and then to the accountant's professional body (the Institute of Chartered Accountants in England and Wales on 020 7920 8100 or the Institute of Chartered Accounts in Scotland on 0131 347 0100). A few accountants have led gullible clients into trouble by offering to 'reduce' their tax in return for higher fees.

Climbing the Inland Revenue's complaints ladder

If you still feel aggrieved at the result of an investigation, the closure notice tells you how to appeal and gives details of the Independent Appeal Commissioners. Any challenge must be in writing but there is a form that can be used for this.

There is a clear route for complaining about the Inland Revenue's actions. Complaints can include allegations of poor service, unreasonable decisions, and heavy-handedness. Follow these steps:

1. **Complain in the first instance to the Officer-in-Charge of your local tax district.**

Just write to that title at your nearest tax office or the one you deal with normally.

2. **Next, approach the director or controller with overall responsibility for that office.**

   Details are in leaflet IR120, which is available from all Inland Revenue offices or on the Inland Revenue Web site at www.inlandrevenue.gov.uk.

3. **If you still feel aggrieved, go to the Revenue Adjudicator's Office.**

   Contact information is 3rd floor, Haymarket House, 28 Haymarket, London SW1Y 4SP – phone 020 7930 2292.

   The adjudicator publishes leaflets on its work and an annual report with more details of what it achieves.

4. **If all this fails, complain to your local Member of Parliament.**

   Your MP can refer the case to the independent Parliamentary Commissioner for Administration (also known as the Parliamentary Ombudsman).

Asking for compensation

If you have to undergo an enquiry but you are either innocent of the specific points raised or you were chosen at random and there is nothing wrong with your form, you can claim compensation.

You can ask for reasonable costs such as postage, phone calls, travelling expenses, accountancy and other professional fees, and financial charges such as interest and bank charges where you wrongly handed over extra tax.

You can also claim payment for worry and distress, although the usual range from £25 to £500 is not intended to put a value on your hurt. Some payments for more extreme cases have hit the £2,500 mark but these have required considerable evidence of breach of confidentiality, misleading advice, inappropriate handling of vulnerable tax-payers such as the elderly and those who are physically or mentally ill.

The bonus is that such compensation payments are not taxable!

Part VI
The Part of Tens

"... and when you get into power, you'll end income tax inspectors? Tell me more about your party."

In this part . . .

This part contains two vital chapters. I start with the ten most important tax-saving tips. The top one is not dealt with elsewhere. It shows how you can give more to charity and good causes with some help from your friendly tax inspector. The others are all dealt with more fully elsewhere in this book but I find having the topmost ten all in one place a great help.

Then I continue with a final chapter that is a quick resume of the ten most essential factors to bear in mind when dealing with a tax inspector. Remember you are dealing with an organisation holding immense powers but is staffed by human beings. They have their bad hair days, just like you.

If you keep all the contents of both chapters in this part in your memory bank, then you will pay less tax and do so with less hassle. What more could you want?

Chapter 21

Ten Top Tax-Saving Tips

*T*ax-paying is tedious. Tax calculations and decisions are tough. So take a break, and give a break to someone else. This chapter's ten tax-saving tips kicks off with a way you can help those less fortunate than yourself, and get the Inland Revenue to help you on the way.

The first tip is about giving money to charity and then claiming tax relief. So, why did you have to wait until Chapter 21 to learn about it? Well, it didn't fit too well anywhere else. And everyone reads a chapter headed Ten Top Tax-Saving Tips. Now you have no excuse not to give – especially as each £1 you donate can be worth as much as £1.66 in the hands of the good cause recipient of your generosity.

A final free bonus tax-saving tip I'll give you right here and now is to reread the sections of this book that apply to you and put my advice to work!

Helping Your Favourite Charity

Putting a £2 coin into a collector's tin may make you feel that you have done something to support the cause. You have. But if you give that £2 in other ways, the Inland Revenue adds back the income tax (or occasionally Capital Gains Tax) it has taken away from you once the money is with the charity and gives at least some of it directly to the cause you're supporting.

The effect of this is your £2 can be worth £3.33 for the good cause if you're a top-rate tax-payer or £2.56 if you're a basic-rate payer. The extra cash comes because as far as you are concerned, your gift comes out of your after-tax income in the same way as any other spending. But charities, and a number of other good causes including universities, museums, and non-professional sports clubs, can reclaim the tax that you paid. You're happy because you saved on tax and your gift is worth more. And, more importantly, the charity or other cause is happy because it gets more.

Some ways you can do this are

- Check if your employer has a **payroll giving scheme** – the best known is Give As You Earn from the Charities Aid Foundation (an umbrella charity which sends on money in a tax-saving way to other charities). Under payroll giving, the employer regularly takes an agreed sum from your pay packet. It treats this as the first deduction from your gross salary so you automatically get tax relief at your highest rate. Your employer may only offer a limited range of charities but if the Charities Aid Foundation is offered, you decide where the money should go.

- Use **Gift Aid**, a government scheme to encourage tax-payers to support charities, to make lump-sum donations. Provided you sign a form to declare you have sufficient taxable income, the charity can claim the tax. So, you donate £78 and the cause can claim the £22 basic tax deducted and have £100 for its aims. Top-rate tax-payers can then reclaim the other £18 (the 40 per cent top rate less the 22 per cent basic rate) in each £100. You can donate this £18 to further charitable work – or you can keep it.

  If you have already given to a charity via a cheque or credit-card donation but forgot to claim Gift Aid, you can ask for proof later on so the charity can reclaim the tax.

  Ensure that any cash or cheque is given in an envelope with a signed Gift Aid declaration form. This applies to the sterling equivalent of any foreign currency you donate.

- **Give your tax refund to charity.** The self assessment tax form allows you to nominate a charity to receive any tax refund rather than yourself. These donations qualify for Gift Aid.

✔ **Give assets subject to Capital Gains Tax** on their sale to a charity which will not have to pay the tax. This can equal a double tax-saving as you can give the shares or other assets and claim their value against your income under the Gift Aid rules.

✔ **Leave assets to charities in your will** to avoid your estate paying Inheritance Tax on their value.

If your estate is not large enough to pay inheritance tax, give to charity while you are still alive, if you can. That way, you qualify for income tax relief on the donation under Gift Aid. Income tax relief dies when you die.

Non-tax-payers cannot claim tax relief on their donations.

Paying Attention to the End of Tax Year

The tax year ends on 5 April each year. You may not want to buy shares (or shares-based investments such as unit trusts or investment trusts) on risk grounds. If you don't, you should make sure you use the mini-cash versions of Individual Savings Accounts to shelter savings from £1 to £3,000 a year from income tax. It's a use-it-or-lose-it tax saving. I offer tax and savings advice in Chapter 13.

Making Gifts When You Can

Don't forget that you have an annual £3,000 exemption from future Inheritance Tax bills if you give this sum away in any tax year. You can catch up on the previous year if you failed to give up to this amount. For more information on inheritance issues, turn to Chapter 7.

Using Capital Gains Tax Exemptions

Your annual Capital Gains Tax exemption is a use-it-or-lose-it relief from the tax levied on profits you may make on shares and a number of other investment transactions. Consider selling parcels of shares each year to take advantage of this. It can be worth up to £3,400 in cash terms (2005–06) for you and the same for your spouse. You can't buy the same shares back again without a 30-day break. But there's rarely anything wrong in turning paper profits into cash in the bank. Chapter 14 talks about capital gains.

Checking Pension Possibilities

Paying into a pension can be the best way of getting help from the taxman with saving for your future. Whether you pay tax or not, you can invest up to £2,808 a year into a stakeholder pension plan and then have the Inland Revenue make it up to £3,600 in your fund thanks to basic-rate tax relief. Turn to Chapter 17 for more on pensions.

Driving a Company Car

Company cars are not always a great bargain because you're taxed on them. It can all depend on the vehicle itself, how many miles you drive for business and for private use, and the proportion of each. Many personnel departments, specialist benefits firms, and a number of car dealers can help select the best deal. So check whether you should have a company car, if you are offered one, with all the tax baggage that comes with it, or whether you might be better off with a higher salary instead, which will enable you to finance your own car.

Claiming Family Friendly Credits

You have to stake your claim to child tax credits. They are not given automatically. You can only backdate your application by three months, so when your household income changes, always check how the change affects your child tax credit status.

Don't forget you can apply for help with childcare costs as well. Chapter 5 explains child-related taxes and credits.

Double-Checking Your National Insurance Contributions

With the 1 per cent national insurance surcharge on higher incomes, there is no limit on how much national insurance you can pay. But there is a ceiling on the total amount you can pay in Class 1 (for employees), Class 2 (for the self-employed), and Class 4 (also for the self-employed). This can affect those who have more than one job or a mix of employment and self-employment.

Repayment of excess national insurance is not automatic, so you have to claim.

Ensuring You're Not Caught in the Age-Allowance Trap

If you are over 65 and have earnings approaching £19,500 (in 2005–06), check to see if you can avoid the age-allowance trap – a really nasty increase in the tax take which hits a number of older people – by re-arranging your investments. But don't fall from the frying pan into the fire by making a new investment purely on tax grounds. You can find more age-related information in Chapter 6.

Claiming Tax Back on Savings

Don't forget to claim tax deductions on savings accounts if you're a non-tax-payer or if your child is a non-tax-payer (which most are!). The Inland Revenue doesn't give you money unless you claim, although they do now send out reminder letters to those who might be able to benefit.

Chapter 22

Ten Top Tips for Dealing with the Tax Inspector

*M*any people have no idea who their tax inspector is. Their affairs are simple so they never have to fill in a self assessment form. Others are aware of their tax office's existence. But their dealings are amicable. They pay what they should, when they should.

It's best to keep it that way. Remember that *Paying Less Tax* also means Paying No Penalties and avoiding hassles. So in this chapter, I offer some painless and basic ways of keeping on the right side of the increasingly powerful Inland Revenue.

Getting Yourself Organised

This sounds really obvious so it's worth repeating. Tax returns depend on many pieces of paperwork, in some cases over 100. The number depends on complexity and not your actual wealth. A person on a middling income owning many individual shares could have much more paperwork than a millionaire with just one source of income.

No matter how clever any computer program might be, there is no substitute for the paperwork. Acquire a basic filing system. You shouldn't need to spend more than £5 for each tax year. And then look at the headings in a self assessment form so that you can file your bits and pieces away as soon as you get them. That way, you can devote more time to tax planning and less to tearing your hair out trying to find that vital piece of paper. Hopefully, you have something better to do with your life than search through old boxes filled with paper!

And tax inspectors will accord someone who's organised more respect than someone who drops an old shoebox-full of paper on their desk.

Researching before Form-Filling

No one has ever pretended our tax system is easy or logical. So it's essential to read as much as you can before sending in any return.

Go through the material that the Inland Revenue sends you and check through their Internet site. On the Web site you can read Inland Revenue press releases, and while you cannot phone the press office (unless you are a journalist), you can contact one of the many helplines for clarification. The telephone numbers are listed in the appendix at the end of the book.

Don't forget search engines. You'll be pleasantly surprised at how many sites offer free advice from tax experts who normally charge very high fees. Not all of what you see will apply and some will be wrong in your circumstances. But in general, you can gain from Googling. And don't forget to make sure you're looking at a UK site. Many other countries have taxes with the same names but different rules!

Remembering that Rules May Not Last Forever

The government publishes a Finance Act every year. So what was right for one tax year may not be correct for the next. Few taxes are ever completely re-written in one year but the rules can and do change.

In particular, this affects long-term taxes such as Capital Gains Tax and Inheritance Tax, where what you do now could affect tax bills in five, ten, or even 20 years to come. Loopholes are closed; tax-free levels change; and rates can alter.

Equally, there is no guarantee that present rules on tax freedom for pension contributions will last forever.

You will need to keep up-to-date with any changes. But one good news item is that tax rules rarely change other than at the start of each tax year on 6 April unless there is a real risk of major tax dodging.

Taking All Taxes into Account

The Inland Revenue is now responsible for just about every item of tax gathering including national insurance and Value Added Tax as well as income tax, Capital Gains Tax and Inheritance Tax.

At the moment, this overall control is more managerial than day-to-day. There is no one-stop shop for paying tax and you still deal with different places to pay national insurance and VAT.

But the systems and computers are increasingly joined up. Even without electronic link-ups, however, there is nothing to stop the exchange of information between various departments. You can no longer get away with different sets of figures for different tax-gathering organisations.

So assume that one person is going to look at all aspects of your affairs from trusts to national insurance. And remember that what you do in relation to one tax can have knock-on effects on another.

Ensuring You Keep to the Timetable

If you have followed all the advice in this book, you will be on time with your tax returns. You pay a £100 penalty if you are late with your self assessment form. Yes, it's unfair that the same amount applies to someone who would find it hard to get £100 as to someone for whom £100 is less than they pay for a bottle of wine. But it's called administrative convenience. It's clear. And don't forget that *Procrastination For Dummies* hasn't been published and nor will it be!

Going Back to Previous Years

Don't throw away all your precious paperwork after you file your forms for this year. Besides the 12 months past the final filing date (five years for self-employment) that the Inland Revenue has to challenge or check your figures, you might find you have something such as a charity payment or pension contribution you can claim for. In any case, keeping past records is a good help towards planning your financial future.

Steering Well Clear of Illegal Tax Dodges

Avoidance is legal. Evasion is illegal. The tips and advice in this book are designed to help you get the best out of the tax system by avoiding paying unnecessary amounts.

If you keep your money offshore and don't declare it, or if you are part of the cash-only black economy, you will have the book thrown at you if you are found out.

And for those who are still not convinced, what about some risk assessment? Ask yourself what you might gain from evasion and compare that with what you could lose, including your liberty in the worst case scenario.

Realising They've Heard it all Before

There can't be many stories the tax authorities have not heard already. And the same applies to excuses you come up with. So don't blame a lack of paperwork on your pet hamster eating it or the dry-cleaner zapping it with chemicals because you left documents in your pocket. It won't wash to say that someone down the pub (or even golf club) told you to do it.

You have a personal responsibility. If you do something wrong, it's best to come clean as soon as possible. You know whether you have made an honest mistake or tried evasion.

Taking Professional Advice

When matters get complicated, don't dig yourself in deeper. Get some professional advice from an accountant. Speak to several before giving any single one your business.

Try and find out what they specialise in and watch how they react to your problem. Some accountants are street-fighters, others timid and often unable to handle anything tougher than a standard return. Expect tax inspectors to accord more respect to someone with a tough reputation than a pushover person. Remember, tax inspectors are only human.

Be Sure before Signing

Once you sign your self assessment form, that's it. You're committed to whatever you have put down. Yes, the tax inspector will repair obvious errors such as a slip of decimal points or listing unit trust dividends in the wrong column. But earning £1,000 from self-employment and claiming for a £15,000 van could raise eyebrows.

If you have doubts or know you have missing information, own up to it on the blank pages in the self assessment form. Wherever possible, work out approximately what the missing information would mean in extra tax paid. Add 10 to 20 per cent to this and pay it. You can always ask for a rebate later on. Overpaying avoids a range of penalties, fines, and interest.

Finally, remember you are responsible for figures produced by any accountant or other tax agent you employ. You can't blame them if they get it wrong. And suing them for negligence could be pricey, and tough.

The declaration that 'the information I have given in this tax return is correct and complete to the best of my knowledge and belief' means what it says. Really.

Appendix

Inland Revenue Helplines

● ●

*T*his appendix lists various helplines that the Inland Revenue offers. You can call all of them during normal nine to five weekday hours. And don't forget that you can gather a lot of information from the Inland Revenue's Web site at www.inland revenue.gov.uk.

Benefits Anti-Fraud (0800 854 440): A confidential line to report a suspicion that someone is defrauding the benefits system.

Business Anti-Fraud (0800 788 887): A confidential line to use if you suspect an employer (including your own) of either not deducting income tax and national insurance properly or deducting it but not handing it over to the Inland Revenue.

Centre for non-residents (national insurance) (0845 915 4811 or 0044 191 225 4811 from overseas): Answers queries on the state pension and health-care provisions for people under retirement age who live or work abroad.

Centre for non-residents (tax) (0845 070 0040) (0044 151 210 2222 from overseas): Answers income tax and Capital Gains Tax queries from UK citizens who work abroad.

Charities Helpline (0845 202 0203): Deals with the various tax reliefs on charitable donations as well as providing help for charity administrators.

Child Benefit (0845 302 1444) (0845 603 2000 for Northern Ireland): Provides help on child benefit claims.

Customs and Excise National Advice Service (0845 010 9000): Gives general advice on customs duties and rules.

Debit Card Payment Line (0845 305 1000): Takes payments for tax by debit card (there is no credit card facility).

Deficiency helpline (0845 915 5996): Deals with people who have been told they have missing amounts in their national insurance contribution records.

Individual Savings Accounts (ISAs) helpline (0845 604 1701): Answers general queries about ISAs that aren't covered in printed material.

Inheritance Tax and probate helpline (0845 302 0900): Provides information on tax issues and procedures to follow when someone dies.

Interest Helpline (0845 980 0645): Helps arrange to have bank and building society interest paid without having tax deducted at source.

IR35 Contract Advice Line (0845 303 3535): Provides advice on IR35 rulings that apply to personal service companies which only provide the labour of the director(s).

IR Online Services new tax credits (0845 300 3938): Explains tax credits to new applicants.

IR Online Services Helpdesk (0845 605 5999): Offers information on corporation tax and electronic filing.

National insurance registration Helpline (0845 915 7006): Provides advice to those approaching 16, and to adults (including recent immigrants) who do not have a national insurance number.

National Minimum Wage Helpline (0845 600 0678): Advises both employers and employees on minimum wage rules. It also deals with complaints from employees who are being paid below the threshold. These complaints are treated confidentially.

Self assessment Helpline (0845 900 0444) (44 870 1555 445 from overseas): Gives general advice plus help on filing your return and the associated supplementary pages.

Self-employed contact centre (0845 915 4655) (0845 915 4515 for the newly self-employed): Handles enquiries relating to tax payments and national insurance contributions, and issues forms for those making their first steps into self-employment.

Stamp Office Helpline (0845 603 0135): Deals with all forms of Stamp Duty queries.

Tax and Benefits Confidential (0845 608 6000): Offers confidential help and information to those working in the 'black' or 'hidden' economy who want to get their tax affairs back on a legal footing. You can talk to someone without declaring your name and address. The Inland Revenue says it does not try to track down phone numbers used in calling but if you are really paranoid, use a public call box or an untraceable pay-as-you-go mobile.

Tax Credits Line (0845 300 3900) (0845 300 3900 in Northern Ireland): Provides information on tax credits and working tax credits.

Ten per cent helpline (0845 307 5555): Gives advice and assistance for those whose highest tax rate is 10 per cent.

Welsh language helpline (0845 302 1489): Provides information for those who prefer to discuss problems and ask queries in Welsh. Many leaflets are also available in Welsh.

Index

FOR

DUMMIES®

The easy way to get more done and have more fun

PROPERTY

UK editions

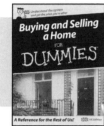

Buying and Selling a Home

0-7645-7027-7

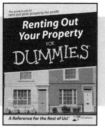

Renting Out Your Property

0-7645-7016-1

Buying a Home on a Budget

0-7645-7035-8

PERSONAL FINANCE

Investing

0-7645-7023-4

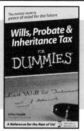

Wills, Probate & Inheritance Tax

0-7645-7055-2

Sorting Out Your Finances

0-7645-7039-0

BUSINESS

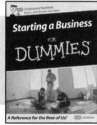

Starting a Business

0-7645-7018-8

Understanding Business Accounting

0-7645-7025-0

Business Plans

0-7645-7026-9

Other UK editions now available:

British History For Dummies
(0-7645-7021-8)

Cleaning and Stain
Removal For Dummies
(0-7645-7029-3)

CVs For Dummies
(0-7645-7017-X)

Diabetes For Dummies
(0-7645-7019-6)

Divorce For Dummies
(0-7645-7030-7)

Formula One Racing For
Dummies
(0-7645-7015-3)

Neuro-Linguistic
Programming For Dummies
(0-7645-7028-5)

Pregnancy For Dummies
(0-7645-7042-0)

Rugby Union For Dummies
(0-7645-7020-X)

FOR DUMMIES®

The easy way to get more done and have more fun

LANGUAGES

0-7645-5194-9

0-7645-5193-0

0-7645-5196-5

Also available:

French Phrases For Dummies
(0-7645-7202-4)

German For Dummies
(0-7645-5195-7)

Italian Phrases For Dummies
(0-7645-7203-2)

Japanese For Dummies
(0-7645-5429-8)

Latin For Dummies
(0-7645-5431-X)

Spanish Phrases For Dummies
(0-7645-7204-0)

Hebrew For Dummies
(0-7645-5489-1)

MUSIC AND FILM

0-7645-5106-X

0-7645-2476-3

0-7645-5105-1

Also available:

Bass Guitar For Dummies
(0-7645-2487-9)

Blues For Dummies
(0-7645-5080-2)

Classical Music For Dummies
(0-7645-5009-8)

Drums For Dummies
(0-7645-5357-7)

Jazz For Dummies
(0-7645-5081-0)

Opera For Dummies
(0-7645-5010-1)

Rock Guitar For Dummies
(0-7645-5356-9)

Screenwriting For Dummies
(0-7645-5486-7)

Songwriting For Dummies
(0-7645-5404-2)

Singing For Dummies
(0-7645-2475-5)

HEALTH, SPORTS & FITNESS

0-7645-5167-1

0-7645-5146-9

0-7645-4233-8

Also available:

Controlling Cholesterol
For Dummies
(0-7645-5440-9)

Dieting For Dummies
(0-7645-4149-8)

High Blood Pressure
For Dummies
(0-7645-5424-7)

Martial Arts For Dummies
(0-7645-5358-5)

Menopause For Dummies
(0-7645-5458-1)

Nutrition For Dummies
(0-7645-4082-3)

Power Yoga For Dummies
(0-7645-5342-9)

Thyroid For Dummies
(0-7645-5385-2)

Weight Training For Dummies
(0-7645-5168-X)

Yoga For Dummies
(0-7645-5117-5)

FOR DUMMIES®

A world of resources to help you grow

HOBBIES

0-7645-5232-5

0-7645-6847-7

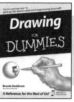
0-7645-5476-X

Also available:

Art For Dummies
(0-7645-5104-3)

Aromatherapy For Dummies
(0-7645-5171-X)

Bridge For Dummies
(0-7645-5015-2)

Card Games For Dummies
(0-7645-5050-0)

Chess For Dummies
(0-7645-5003-9)

Crocheting For Dummies
(0-7645-4151-X)

Improving Your Memory For Dummies
(0-7645-5435-2)

Massage For Dummies
(0-7645-5172-8)

Meditation For Dummies
(0-7645-5116-7)

Photography For Dummies
(0-7645-4116-1)

Quilting For Dummies
(0-7645-5118-3)

Woodworking For Dummies
(0-7645-3977-9)

EDUCATION

0-7645-7206-7

0-7645-7837-5

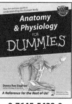
0-7645-5422-0

Also available:

Algebra For Dummies
(0-7645-5325-9)

Astronomy For Dummies
(0-7645-5155-8)

Buddhism For Dummies
(0-7645-5359-3)

Calculus For Dummies
(0-7645-2498-4)

Christianity For Dummies
(0-7645-4482-9)

Forensics For Dummies
(0-7645-5580-4)

Islam For Dummies
(0-7645-5503-0)

Einstein For Dummies
(0-7645-8348-4)

Philosophy For Dummies
(0-7645-5153-1)

Religion For Dummies
(0-7645-5264-3)

Trigonometry For Dummies
(0-7645-6903-1)

PETS

0-7645-5255-4

0-7645-5286-4

0-7645-5275-9

Also available:

Labrador Retrievers For Dummies
(0-7645-5281-3)

Aquariums For Dummies
(0-7645-5156-6)

Birds For Dummies
(0-7645-5139-6)

Dogs For Dummies
(0-7645-5274-0)

Ferrets For Dummies
(0-7645-5259-7)

German Shepherds For Dummies
(0-7645-5280-5)

Golden Retrievers For Dummies
(0-7645-5267-8)

Horses For Dummies
(0-7645-5138-8)

Jack Russell Terriers For Dummies
(0-7645-5268-6)

Puppies Raising & Training Diary For Dummies
(0-7645-0876-8)

Available wherever books are sold. For more information or to order direct go to www.wiley.com or call 0800 243407 (Non UK call +44 1243 843296)